The Basecamp Manifesto

*How A Secure Base Can Save Your Life
and Leadership In A Scrambled World*

by
TERENCE C. YOUNG, PHD

 FriesenPress

One Printers Way
Altona, MB R0G 0B0
Canada

www.friesenpress.com

Copyright © 2024 by Terence C. Young, PhD
First Edition — 2024

All rights reserved.

No part of this publication may be reproduced in any form, or by any means, electronic or mechanical, including photocopying, recording, or any information browsing, storage, or retrieval system, without permission in writing from FriesenPress.

ISBN
978-1-03-831174-0 (Hardcover)
978-1-03-831173-3 (Paperback)
978-1-03-831175-7 (eBook)

1. BUSINESS & ECONOMICS, PERSONAL SUCCESS

Distributed to the trade by The Ingram Book Company

Dedication

To the Marvelous Marmot!

Table of Contents

Foreword	vii
Author's Muse	ix
Bearings	xi
SETTING UP BASECAMP	**1**
Chapter One — Welcome to the Scramble	3
Chapter Two — The Myth of the Solo Climber	19
Chapter Three — Leader, Where Art Thou?	29
Chapter Four — The Basecamp Backstory	45
THE BASECAMP ADVANTAGES	**65**
Chapter Five — Sharpening Our Clarity	67
Chapter Six — Improving Our Agility	91
Chapter Seven — The Deep Threat to Agility	107
Chapter Eight — Strengthening Our Durability	133
Chapter Nine — Heightening Our Generativity	161
Basecamp Excursus	179
GETTING TO BASECAMP	**181**
Chapter Ten — From Hesitation to Embrace	183
Chapter Eleven — Bring on the Scramble	201
References	205

Foreword

Our best insights are often in retrospect. "Hindsight is 20/20," we say. We all can recall decisions made that did not turn out well. Time and experience revealed missing information that, had we known, we would have chosen differently. We call these insights "wisdom."

It takes time and experience to discover and distill wisdom. No wonder the Bible equates wisdom with white hair - you don't get this depth quickly or in the early years of life. This is why it is always a good idea to listen as our elders reflect over their life.

I heartily recommend Dr. Young to you, white hair and all. We have worked together for over fifteen years in the Crest Leadership Program. He is the Dean of our Master in Christian Leadership credential. Together we have helped scores of leaders in the second half of life reflect deeply and make the shifts necessary to flourish in life and leadership.

Here are the reflections of a seasoned leader who has lived a fruitful and faithful life. I know him well, and he's the real deal. Dr. Young is gifted with a brilliant mind. He's read practically all the best books on leadership and distilled the essential learning. I never get tired of listening to him.

Here's a key insight into gaining wisdom: you can't do this alone. It is important to have times of deep solitude and reflection, but then one must come back to a trusted small group of friends and transparently debrief life. Without this second aspect one can end up in weird spaces far from reality. This is why some older folks end up grouchy and irrelevant.

Dr. Young has been reading and reflecting on this matter for many years. He earned a Doctorate in this field. Save yourself years of study by reading this distillation of decades of research.

This is a book leaders need to pick up and digest - it could be the difference between coping and flourishing. It might even save your life.

Better than just reading it, put the key principles into action. You will be forever grateful.

Dr. Dan Reinhardt
Founder, CREST Leadership Center
www.CrestLeadership.Academy

Author's Muse

After forty years of leadership, it is time for me to come clean about my life and leadership journey. The road I have traveled for forty years has brought a mix of delights and discouragements, ups and downs, a lot of joys and some sorrows. The journey has also contained struggle. For years, I externalized the struggles of leadership, thinking everything in my external world was why leadership was hard, confusing, and wearying. My quest for success, effectiveness, and impact would be realized if I could just manage, manipulate, or mitigate the barriers and challenges of the mountain I was striving to climb. I fell into the common trap of blaming the mountain, something Sir Edmund Hillary, the first man to conquer Everest, said we must stop doing. The mountain is not our greatest challenge.

In the final days of writing this book, I stumbled across a book entitled *The Mountain Is You*. In these four words there is a world of wisdom. Our mountain or quest in life is one thing, but if honest, we would all admit our greatest challenge has been our own self. I am coming clean through these pages about the extent to which my greatest challenge has been the mountain called "me." As someone in the third-third of life, I am writing to and for younger leaders and leaders in mid-life, to do better than I did at forming yourself to face and tackle your most challenging mountain—yourself. Wise leadership begins with self-leadership. This is not selfish obsession; it is taking in hand your own mind, heart, body, and soul and tending these with diligence and care for your own sake and for the sake of the world. I regret I did not tend more diligently to my own care, development, and most importantly, the shaping of a vital connection to a band of trusted and trusting friends.

The Basecamp Manifesto

My father grew up in the era wherein talking publicly about personal doubts or regrets was discouraged. Yet, everything in life can be instructive. Even regret can be powerful if it prompts learning for oneself or others. So, I have a few regrets to share, with the hope that you can learn on my dime. First, I regret not finding the insight and counsel I needed in my earliest days about what directed and drove me to isolation and autonomy in my life and calling. I kept so much to myself. I had the sense that I needed to figure things out and make things happen. I lived with a "life sentence" that I needed to be a fix-it-all, a know-it-all, and everywhere-for-all in my leadership presence. No wonder I burned out after thirteen years of climbing my mountain. I did not tend well to myself as the climber.

My second regret is not finding, and shaping, a circle of trust and support that was consistent over time. At times, I had a kind of basecamp, but we gathered irregularly, and a covenant of bringing caring and daring to one another was not in the room. What I experienced was a hint of the potential gifts in a cadre of peers who gathered to support one another, but the full provision of a robust secure base never grew. I am thankful, looking back, for those times I could talk of "my people" and name my band of brothers. I imagine I could have called them in for reserves, resources, and reminders about what was truly important, but I'm not sure the call would have been answered. At other times, "my people" were hard to find. Life changed, locations changed, and proximity was difficult. The regret of not tending well to myself as the mountain climber was made worse by climbing most days alone. Looking back, the basecamp or secure base of which I write in these pages was what I wish I had found and nurtured from the beginning. I want for you much better than I gave to myself.

These regrets have planted in my life a desire to encourage leaders of all stripes to tend much better to two dimensions of care. Pay diligent attention to your self-care and your peer care. It is peer care, or what we frame as a secure base, that becomes a force multiplier for the care you take for yourself. The mountain is you, and we need support and strengthening for all that is within us if we are ever going to take on what is before us.

The Basecamp Manifesto is written as a call for leaders to find, shape, and nurture their secure base as if their life depends on it, because we believe it does.

Bearings

The Basecamp Manifesto centers around two questions:
What is our quest?
Where is our basecamp?

What Is a Quest?

A *quest* is seeking something of importance and value, and it always involves a journey; it is a long search for something that is difficult yet important to find. In medieval romance, *the quest* was the daring and difficult journey undertaken by an individual to procure or achieve a particular object or end.

What Is a Basecamp?

A *basecamp* is an encampment that provides reconnaissance, support, resources, and preparation for persons engaged in or anticipating an exploration or adventure. The basecamp is the place from which a quest proceeds and hopefully succeeds.

If our quest is small and easy, we will not likely need a basecamp.

If our quest is demanding, difficult, and of importance to the world, we will need a robust basecamp to ultimately succeed.
No basecamp; no summit.

The Basecamp Manifesto

Our Challenge

In the kind of world, we now inhabit,
we must find, shape, and nurture our own basecamps.
We must find our people, our secure base of relationships, our circle of trust,
our happy and committed few, who will regularly gather with us to find clarity,
agility, durability, and greater generativity.

SETTING UP BASECAMP

CHAPTER ONE

Welcome to the Scramble

In 2018, I was curious about the daily real-world experience of leaders. I decided to engage in an informal research project dubbed, "A Week in The Life Of…" My curiosity focused on the goings-on in the typical week of a leader in a non-profit organization. Time-tracking and journaling was part of the process, with a follow-up interview designed to get at deeper issues of what was engaged in with joy or endured with dread. The "life" for most was a kind of blur with intermittent periods of clarity. These leaders knew how to focus but were inundated with the unexpected, unplanned, and often unwanted—most spoke of their contexts being increasingly fraught with complexity, ambiguity, and at times volatility.

The conditions echoed those framed by the US Army in the 1960s and more recently by Bob Johansen in his work *The New Leadership Literacies*. The depiction then to now is of a VUCA world (Martin, 2018). VUCA is shorthand for an environment of volatility, uncertainty, complexity, and ambiguity. In more recent days, Johansen and others have warned that we haven't seen anything yet and the future will get even more complex over the next decade. There appears to be no let-up on the horizon for ominous conditions that challenge leaders of all stripes and situations. This alone should raise the need for all leaders to find a better, stronger, and more consistent base of support and challenge.

Back to VUCA for a moment. The encouraging twist in the writing of Johansen is his proposition for a positive VUCA. There can be some hope that a negative VUCA can turn toward an positive reality. Volatility can in turn yield to vision; uncertainty can yield to understanding; complexity can yield to clarity; and ambiguity can yield to agility. Yet, how is this positive reality to be shaped and nurtured? How does one get to vision, understanding, clarity, and agility (Johansen, 2020)? This is the developmental challenge that lies at the heart of the Basecamp Manifesto. There is a way to mitigate the negative realities in a VUCA world and to master a healthier, stronger, and more resilient way.

The shift noted above does not happen by chance or drop into our lives like some magical special effect. Perspective, skills, and the vital dimension of a relational constellation must be nurtured if we are ever to live well in "a week in the life of" our own journey. This is exactly our hope with the Basecamp Manifesto: providing a practical yet robust way towards a positive VUCA.

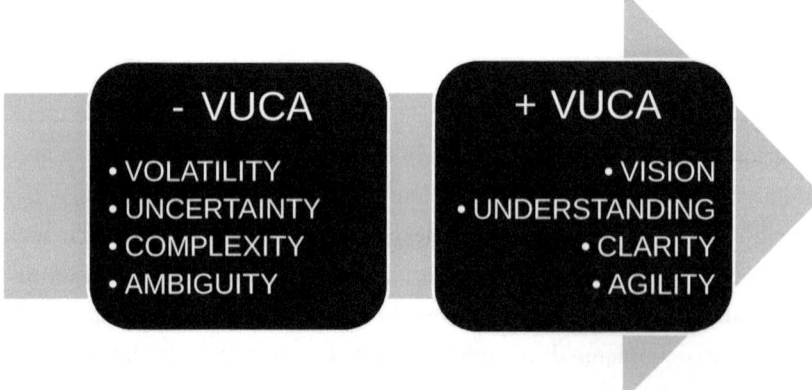

More recently, Bob Johansen has framed our challenge environment as "the scramble" (Johansen, 2020). The VUCA characteristics are helpful, but they are descriptive bullet points. They describe the conditions but don't fully portray the feelings and experience of it all. The scramble is a more visceral framing of current reality. We are in a maelstrom of misinformation, disinformation, and truth decay; our greatest hunger is for some circle of trust where the confusion can be mitigated by perspective-taking with others (Johansen, 2020, p. 7). We can all picture a person scrambling. A person running back and forth, doing this then doing that, deafened by ambient din, and caught up in the rush of ambient momentum, scrambling to find some measure of clarity and stability through it all.

Chapter One   Welcome to the Scramble

As I hearken back to my interviews with leaders in "A Week in The Life Of…" project, the time tracking provided the proof of the scramble. Most leaders were navigating each day with a kind of serpentine back and forth. Hoping their day would unfold according to some pre-ordained plan, it often unraveled into a moment-by-moment "sense and respond" narrative. As much as they thought their life was a plan-and-implement exercise, the reality was quite different. They were scrambling. We are scrambling. This scramble condition requires new leadership literacies, particularly the literacy of creating and sustaining energy through intentional relationships.

At the core of the scramble is the intensifying confusion and conundrum of finding trustworthy direction. The scramble is our reality in the present world of more and more misinformation, disinformation, and distrust (Johansen, 2020). These conditions raise the challenge of finding trustworthy and reliable bearings in a scrambled world. Ambient momentum or velocity is wrapped in ambient din or noise, and wisely finding our way through becomes essential for wiser life and leadership navigation.

THE SCRAMBLE

*If you don't have some fear about
the future, you're not paying attention.*
Bob Johansen (2017, p. 39)

Added to the information dangers and deficits are the new twisting paths toward distributed everything. What are we to do with the speed, frequency, scope, and scale of disruption? Johansen, writing in 2017, prior to the launch of ChatGPT, anticipated explosive technology way beyond that year's connective technologies as the drivers of distributed everything. Welcome to asymmetric upheaval wherein there would be few patterns to the disruption so that even the disruption would be disruptively incomprehensible. In all of this, we must learn to look long, to use foresight to provoke wise insight and purposeful action. His prediction and proposal in the end focused on the currency of distributed organizations. The currency would need to be reciprocity and mutual benefit partnering (Johansen, 2020, p. 91).

The burning questions in all of this are: Where can one find a circle of trust in the scramble? Where can a leader find a still point in such a churning world? For many, the small circle of self is the primary locus for insight and control. We'll figure it out. We are leaders, and it is our job to lead others through the turbulence. If we get through the fuss, it will be up to us. For Johansen, the wise futurist will pursue his ten literacies, but then he notes, "They will need new ways to partner in guilds or communities, so they don't have to go it alone" (Johansen, 2020, p. 39). Hearkening back to a former era in which most trades emerged out of the guild is a model he proposes for our scrambled modern and disruptive technological era. It is time for the return of guilds, people in a community of practice honing their skills and craft in concert with others. This is the precise focus of the Basecamp Manifesto. A basecamp can serve as a guild for scrambled times. It can be the secret haven for us to navigate well and wisely in an increasingly scrambled world.

Proof of the scramble is now more accessible than ever. Looking in on the world of business leaders, educators, clergy, and social workers provides the living proof that we are surrounded by such a world. If Bob Johansen's 2017 observation, we haven't seen anything yet, is now updated, he would likely say we have only just begun to feel the turbulence and tumbles of a scrambled world.

One qualification is in order. The scramble is nothing new. A VUCA world is nothing new. On our watch we tend to describe with hand wringing angst our time as the worst of times. Nothing could be further from the truth. On our watch we do have pressures and problems that come with an ever-expanding technological age. However, we must remember, every generation is the same in its own unique way. We are people navigating the terrain of life and fear, mistrust, uncertainty, complexity, and ambiguity can fill the air. Yet, my great-great-grandfather, fighting with a Wisconsin regiment in the Civil War must have wondered if a good tomorrow would ever appear. Leaders throughout human history have wandered through mist and fog and felt the gathering clouds of some impending doom. The details in their scramble were unique to them but the human challenge was the same. How do we wisely navigate through our time in history to find our way, flourish for the sake of our children, and hopefully leave a good legacy? The scramble may feel like a new phenomenon, but it is as old as human history. However, it is still important to clearly see the scramble of this moment up close and personal, and to that we turn in the pages that follow.

Business Scramble

For those on the front line of business, the press is chock full of wondering and warning about increasing complexity and disruption on every front. John Kay and Mervyn King spend almost 400 pages outlining the challenge of *Radical Uncertainty*. These authors note that as much as we think and hope our problems are tame or can be tamed, we find ourselves facing more and more wicked problems. In today's world, "real households, real businesses and real governments do not optimize; they cope." (Kay & King, 2020, p. 41). In the face of such coping, Keith Ferrazzi calls for a newfound radical adaptability in the face of a new world of work: "In 2020, the entire world was struck with a level of disruption that few had ever imagined. The need for a new level of adaptability in the workplace became a dire necessity, not just a competency of the truly best" (Ferrazzi, 2022, p. 3).

Jeffrey Pfeffer, professor of organizational behavior at Stanford, notes the peril of modern business where more and more people are, as the title of his book says, "dying for a paycheck" (Pfeffer, 2018). He notes the confused and contorted value system in such behemoths as Wal-Mart, the largest employer in the US with over one million employees. Wal-Mart boasts of three grand sustainability goals that cover energy, waste, and products (Pfeffer, 2018, p. 41). What is missing is a focused promotion of human sustainability. The bottom line and environmental markers are clearly in view while human due diligence receives lesser care or concern. These authors and many more echo in various ways the scrambled conditions now upon us.

> *Most leaders today feel like a stray dog at a whistler's convention.*

The field of business leadership is full of development and training dedicated to getting the job done, making products and services better, and mastering the success side of the enterprise. What is needed is a deeper dive into stronger forms of support that weave together both care and challenge for those who inhabit our businesses and organizations. In a scrambled world, how can we best take on the clarity, agility, durability, and generativity challenges of leadership? The Basecamp Manifesto, in its store front version, is a strong call for business leaders to find, shape, and nurture a cluster of caring and daring. In the face of ever-increasing complexity and uncertainty in our communities, men and women on the front line of business leadership must find a robust secure base to survive and thrive for the journey ahead.

Education Scramble

For leaders in educational settings, the news and research paint a picture of administrators and teachers feeling the intensifying pressure of a world on fire. Whether at the early grade-school levels or the highest levels of graduate and post-graduate studies, the challenges of the scramble seem to be escalating exponentially. In the earliest days of my doctoral process, enrolled at the time in an EdD (educational doctorate), I was introduced to the extent to which educators could be viewed as canaries in the coal mine. One educator's way of capturing the ominous turns in the field of education was via the title, *When the Canary Stops Singing* (Barrentine, 1995). Administrators, teachers, or specialists on the front line of childhood education or at the mentoring table of graduate students absorb the strain marks of the wider world, entering a student's life, showing up in the room, and then entering the core of an educator's heart and soul. Educational leaders at the helm or teachers in the classroom absorb trauma in ways not consciously known, like a canary in the coal mine blithely breathing the air. In time the song leaves, and like that canary in deteriorating mine conditions, educators can act as precursors of dangerous conditions that must be noted and responded to, or many more lives will be in jeopardy.

In 2018 I collaborated with Dr. John Picard and Dr. Sherry Martens, Dean of Education at Ambrose University in Calgary, in shaping a Graduate Level LQS (Leadership Quality Standard) for the certification process for Principals in the Province of Alberta. The process was entrusted to schools of education to frame, in keeping with Province competency guidelines, certification for those who would apply for a school principal position within Alberta. Our purpose was to design a learning journey for prospective principals that would give them a clear sense of the competencies required but to do so through the lens of every person's unique leadership signature. We framed *The GET Model*, Growth in Educational Transformation, as two 39-hour courses covering five aspects of transformational leadership (Marten, Picard, and Young, 2020). All five were designed to guide a potential head of school in how to best navigate in the scramble of school leadership. The GET's are detailed below:

> GET REAL – How does your story and your core beliefs inform who you are as a leader? How will these inform your work as a leader and shape the vision of a school?
>
> GET FOCUSED – How will you know what to pay attention to? What is most Important to you in shaping a flourishing school?
>
> GET ALONG – How will you build trusting, collegial relationships to wisely navigate change and conflict? How will you best engage all members of the learning community to create an optimal learning environment?
>
> GET INFORMED – How will you best utilize educational research and real world observation to understand your context? What principles will guide decisions around allocating and managing resources
>
> GET GOING – How will you develop an ongoing personal leadership plan?

In the context of the scramble and the never-ending challenge of school leaders, participants were guided to connect their own professional and academic learning experiences to the course content, culminating in a personal leadership growth plan and portfolio that demonstrated their consideration of the five question sets in The GET Model. Our goal was to provide educators with some solid bearings for leadership in the turbulent waters of school leadership. If you are going to be in a scramble it is best to have your wits about you, but to also have some navigational markers for setting and then recalibrating your journey.

For my own learning, the process of working with John and Sherry, both career educators, was my plunge into the deep end of educational complexity.

I had always viewed the schoolhouse from a distance, understood some of the leadership challenges, but this project brought the work of a principal into a whole new light. Every day begins with the known and the unknown. Every school is a unique ecosystem of potential. Every educational team is its own wonder, mystery, and possible six act drama. Every year is an additive process from powers on high in terms of guidelines, initiatives, policies, and reforms. Every year the students who walk the halls bring a distinct presence of joy and sorrow, hope and hurt, fun and frustration. To this a principal is seen by all as the bringer of strength, stability, success, and hope in an increasingly scrambled world. The principal that has a secure base of peers is on much better ground in such a world.

The domain of educational leadership is one of society's important realms for shaping and nurturing every emerging generation. In the setting of every school there must never be a teacher, administrator, specialist, or support staff in a state of isolation or aloneness. What is needed is a dedicated insistence on robust support that weaves together both care and challenge for those who inhabit these places of learning and life development. The Basecamp Manifesto, in its schoolhouse version, is a strong call for educational leaders to find, shape, and nurture a cluster of caring and daring peers who can discern together how to stay alive and well, regardless of the wider conditions in the mine that is our society. In the face of ever-increasing complexity and uncertainty, men and women on the front line of educational leadership must find a robust secure base to survive and thrive for the journey ahead.

Religious Scramble

For those in the realm of religious leadership, the news is not good in terms of what it means to be a sustainable and faithful pastor or priest. The increasing scramble of the wider culture seeps into the pores of every religious calling and context and makes the roles and responsibilities of clergy a morass of confusion and complexity.

In 2013, Mendoza School of Business at Notre Dame University, released their *Flourishing in Ministry* Project, noting the revealing analysis on the work of clergy in the United Methodist Church. A thorough study looked to address these questions: What is the real front-line work of a local church pastor and what does this real picture tell us about flourishing and non-flourishing in pastoral work? My sense is that this analysis can be extended across many religious denominations and groups due to the common nature of parish work.

The findings portray leaders navigating a complex and nearly impossible array of roles and responsibilities. As the study met the eyes of a seasoned official from the US Department of Labor, he stated, "I have never seen a more complex job" (Flourishing in Ministry Project, 2013, p. 41). With thirteen major areas of focus, each major area including four to six sub-dimensions of work, the weekly plate of clergy work was noted as beyond heroic to humanly accomplish.

Clergy work is a tangle of changing role definitions, complexifying role challenges, confusing role expectations, and an ever-changing ministry landscape. In the middle of this, a clergy member must seek to be healthy, vibrant, and at their best, while also having a life, a family, a friendship circle, and a retirement plan. In my earlier days of pastoral ministry, I was drawn to the book *It Only Hurts on Monday*. The authors had been reading my mail and summarized the conditions well. Clergy leaders, pastors, and priests feel they are always on duty, often in crisis mode, and ever navigating with uneven and unpredictable expectations (McIntosh, 1998, p. 122). At the time, it gave words to what I was personally experiencing, but I sadly missed the closing call of these authors. These realities call for a circle of trusted others acting as life savers, not only for the Monday morning blahs, but for the longer-term sustainability in one's calling.

In early 2022, the Barna Research Group, released a study on the state of church leaders across the USA. In their survey, 43 percent of pastors had seriously considered resigning from their ministry roles in the past year. The three top reasons: 1) the immense stress of the work; 2) the constant atmosphere of political/partisan division; and 3) isolation and loneliness. The last reason deserves a serious pause. How can pastors who are immersed in relational work be lonely? How can isolation be present in the work of parish life? The answer is complex, but a few points of diagnosis are deserving of attention (Barna Research, 2022).

The Basecamp Manifesto

*Leading these days can feel like
a house of mirrors and a mad house,
a three-ring circus
combined with an animal farm
and a firefight.*
Dan Allender (2006)

As we process the Barna survey points, we should not be surprised at the first two reasons for discouragement, but the third reason is somewhat puzzling. Wanting to abandon a pastoral quest due to isolation and loneliness seems incongruent with clergy leaders surrounded by people. How can those who have the mission of weaving spiritual community be lacking community themselves. Reasons one and two above can't be changed, but reason three can be addressed but it remains stubbornly in place. The Basecamp Manifesto is a call to change this dynamic for clergy leaders and others so that loneliness and isolation can be banished from their lives.

Sadly, these assessments and recent honest admissions from spiritual care givers are not a new phenomenon. H. B. London in two studies in the late 1990s and early 2000s discovered that 70 percent of pastors admitted having no one they processed the pressure of ministry with. This relational deficit has translated into a lifestyle of isolation, loneliness, inadequacy, and insecurity (London & Wiseman, 2003). Dr. Henry Cloud found that 80 percent of nonprofit leaders he anecdotally surveyed had little to no stable and longstanding relationships to draw upon. What is going on here? The scramble is very real for religious leaders, but the complexity appears to be handled alone, absent any consistent circle of trusted others.

The field of clergy leadership needs fresh, ongoing forms of support, care, and challenge. The Basecamp Manifesto, in its stain-glassed version, would be a strong call for pastors and priests to find, shape, and nurture a cluster of care and challenge. In the face of ever-increasing complexity and volatility in our communities, shepherds and servants on the front line must find a robust secure base to survive and thrive on the road ahead.

Chapter One   Welcome to the Scramble

Social Work Scramble

If the field of social work is in view, the scramble is manifested in the attempt to navigate the complexity of caring well for others while also caring well for oneself. William Kahn, in *Holding Fast*, notes the four dimensions that collide for anyone in the intensive world of social work (Kahn, 2005, pp. 22–35). First, social workers engage the work itself or technique—the daily client and co-worker interactions plus the record keeping and file management. Second, there is absorption. This component involves navigating all that is encountered in the mental and emotional field of the work. Third, there is relational strain. This is representative of the sheer volume of complex relational fields. Supervisors, peers, and clients can be enriching or exhausting. Finally, there is contextual strain. No practice or clinic avoids wider-world realities and their bearing upon the inner work of the setting of care. These are aptly framed as the PEST factors: political, environmental, social, and technological influencers. These factors can be benign and peaceful or brutal and conflicted. These realities impact caregivers as well as every client being served. The ripple effects go in all directions and make the world of front-line social work a potentially maddening scramble.

In my ongoing work with CREST Leadership, we have had the privilege of working with leaders and team members in the non-profit world of agencies providing front line care to people in need. Every encounter with such leaders opens the window on the challenges of staying spiritually authentic, mentally fresh, personally vital and healthy, relationally connected, and organizationally focused. Encountering and then absorbing the trauma of those who walk through their doors is heavy work, but add to it all the other factors, vigilance about self-care and team care cannot be treated as optional. The scramble has always been present in the social work sectors of society, but on our watch, it appears to be gaining in speed, intensity, and complexity.

The Basecamp Manifesto, in its non-profit social work version, is a strong call for those at the people intensive front lines of our world, to find, shape, and nurture a cluster of caring and daring. In the face of ever-increasing complexity and uncertainty in our communities, men and women on the front line of such endeavors must find a robust secure base to survive and thrive for the journey ahead. In the words of Pope Gregory in the fifth century, those who care for souls must wear two sandals. One sandal is care for others, the other is care for oneself. Obsess over our care for others, but neglect our care for self, we end up not able to care for those who need our care. As we will see, how we hold others is directly tied to how we are held by others.

Where Are We?

The business leader, clergy worker, social worker, and educator daily inhabit a theater of operation or a field of play. Pick a metaphor. If life strikes us as a battle, a theater of operation is most fitting. In military terms, the theater is where our battle doctrine meets the real world. This model makes clear the essential nature of thinking and planning, with the full acknowledgement that every battle plan meets the enemy, and from there, adaptation must unfold. For soldiers, the theater is daunting and overwhelming absent comrades who can "muster" or gather when needed to make sense of things and then take the next move. John Bowlby references the "secure base" for soldiers as the game changer in battle. With a secure base, soldiers advance and fight. Without such a base, soldiers question the advance and feign the fight (Bowlby, 1988, p. 11).

If we feel a bit more playful, then the field of play may be the metaphor of choice. Todd Herman portrays the field of play as the turf or pitch where the game unfolds in our visible world (Herman, 2019, p. 50). Beneath our field of play are the layers of attitude, belief, core drivers, and then our core self. This is not a battle doctrine but a game doctrine. As a player on the field, we are either shaping a heroic self or living with a trapped self. The question is: How does one move from a trapped self towards a heroic self? The trapped self is often alone, absent the gift of others. The heroic self is made in community by the gift of others.

> *I wonder what kind of tale*
> *we have fallen into.*
> Sam Gamgee to Frodo, Lord of the Rings

Most leaders jump into the field of play or into the fray of battle with unexamined actions and unchallenged beliefs. Our days begin with our engagement predetermined by default settings. If we live with an isolated self or trapped self, the day unfolds accordingly. If we struggle to prove who we are, we pose and

Chapter One   Welcome to the Scramble

pretend we have a better self. The blinders are on in this scenario, and it often takes someone else to point out the irony. Our view of self is perfectly designed to achieve the results we are realizing in our field of play. The warrior self or the heroic self, require honest examination and ongoing formation, and it is virtually impossible to do this alone.

Every so often there is an advertisement that captures where we are in very personal terms. A few years back *Lending Tree* sought to draw people to their lending site by portraying the reality of many North Americans. Stanley Johnson with a smile on his face introduces himself and then tells his story. "I have a great family. I have a four-bedroom house in a great community. Like my car? It's new. I even belong to the local golf club. How do I do it? I'm in debt up to my eyeballs. I can barely pay my finance charges. Somebody, help me!" We can relate. Financial overload is widespread, but how does it happen? In the words of Ernest Hemingway, the same way we go bankrupt; gradually then suddenly. These days life overload is endemic. The scramble calls and calls and the world of more and more creates pathways of consumption demanding pathways of production and we end up on a treadmill titled downward. We end many of our days quietly whispering, Somebody, please help us!

Scrambling Well

In the scramble, what is our best resource to be healthier, happier, and more effective in whatever world we inhabit? Like Stanley Johnson, where is good help to be found? In our theater of operation or field of play, there is one denominator that leads to a good life. George Valliant, the longtime study director for the Harvard Study of Adult Development and the Glueck Study, along with his successor, Robert Waldinger, have dedicated their lives to exploring what makes up a good life (Vaillant, 2002, p. 52). Their finding is simple. Stable and long-term relationships are the single-most important trait of people who are both happy and well. The TED Talk by Waldinger, *What Makes a Good Life*, viewed over 40 million times, captures the lessons from the longest studies on happiness in the world (Waldinger, 2015). Both Vaillant and Waldinger agree on two pillars to happiness. One is love. The other is finding a way of coping with life that does not push love away. Waldinger adds, "The lessons aren't about wealth or fame or working harder and harder. The clearest message that we get from these (studies) is this: Good relationships keep us healthier and happier. Period. The people who were the most satisfied in their relationships at age fifty were the healthiest at age eighty" (Brooks, 2022, p. 114).

So, the scramble is on. Whether business leader, clergy, social worker, or educator, we need some circle of trust, some guild, some community of practice that can provide a vital ecosystem whereby we can navigate reality and hopefully maintain momentum. We are not pursuing efficiency of motion in our basecamp circle. We are pursuing adaptability at the most profound level. Otherwise, we are taking on our purpose with little caring and daring for our quest in life.

> *Efficiency, once the sole icon on the hill*
> *must make room for adaptability,*
> *in structures, processes, and mindsets*
> *that is often uncomfortable.*
> Stanley McChrystal (2015)

The Basecamp Manifesto is not a recipe of ingredients or a clearly marked trail. It is a compass whereby we can get our bearings to navigate with others through an increasingly turbulent and uncertain world. It is also a way of establishing a rich picture for how to think about our quest in life and how our relational base becomes the vital link between our current reality and preferred future. We hope the concepts and principles to follow provide a fresh perspective for both leadership support and leadership challenge. Both dimensions are at the core of a basecamp setting and will be recurring themes throughout the pages that follow.

In the next two chapters, we explore both the scarcity and the strange alternatives to the secure base concept and experience. In Chapter 2, we take time to honestly address **The Myth of the Solo Climber.** The research is sobering on the extent to which many still take on life as solo travelers. Yet, history tells a different story when it comes to those who have climbed the highest mountains of endeavor. The names of those we know and celebrate have a backstory that confronts the common myths surrounding the lone hero, lone climber, or lone achiever.

In Chapter 3, we encourage you to take stock through one question: **Leader, Where Art Thou?** As we will see, most leaders admit to a scarcity of richness in their relational constellations while acknowledging an abundance of connections that are wide but not deep. Life is littered with strange relational connections or base conditions we describe as barren, shallow, pseudo, or contested. These bases of relationship are often lacking in richness or robust help in the scramble. This is where we explore our need to move from the most populated base conditions to the one that is essential for strengthening our life and optimizing our quest, a secure base.

Insight into **The Basecamp Backstory** is the focus of Chapter 4. The basecamp metaphor is much more than some newly minted idea. There is a robust history behind the basecamp concept and environment. This chapter will be the most theory-laden segment, but it is necessary to give a sense that we are on rigorous scientific and research-based footing. When we pitch our tent in a basecamp environment, we are inhabiting a place and space backed by robust research and theory, plus real-world practice sprinkled throughout the ages.

In Chapters 5 through 9, we discover the full benefits of taking on our life quest from a secure base of relationships. These chapters portray **The Basecamp Advantages.** In Chapter 5, we explore sharing our balcony and the advantage of sharpening clarity. In Chapter 6, we detail the wonder of lightening our load and the gift of increasing agility. Agility is also in view in Chapter 7 as we examine the deeper threat to agility. Chapter 8 unfolds our need for greater resilience and the gift of strengthening durability. Then, Chapter 9 will explore taking on our quest and the gift of heightening our generativity.

In Chapter 10, we provide an honest exploration of our hesitation to pursue and shape a basecamp setting. How can we best move **From Hesitation to Embrace?** We will take time to confront the barriers and then lay down practical steps toward the embrace of a secure base environment.

In the final chapter, **Bring on the Scramble,** we return to the two inquiries at the center of this Basecamp Manifesto: What is our quest and where is our basecamp? Considering the scrambled world we now encounter, our clear answer to our two questions makes the difference between flourishing and floundering. A halting or uncertain answer calls for a serious pause and hopefully an awakening to reset our life around these two questions. In the final pages, we make a modest proposal centered around the hope of secure base creation and the impact this can have on our personal futures and the future of leadership development.

CHAPTER TWO

The Myth of the Solo Climber

You don't just climb Everest!
Jim Hayhurst – The Right Mountain (1996)

In 2010, a blockbuster movie captured the attention of many wilderness explorers and climbers. It was the story of Aron Ralston, a canyoneer, barely surviving his 2003 climb in Utah's Bluejohn Canyon. The movie's title, *127 Hours*, captured the time frame for the imperiled climb and his miraculous return to where his journey began. The scene of Ralston, his right arm trapped in a crevice with no possible way of extricating himself, provides the cringe point in the story. The excruciating choice to sever his own arm with a small knife to escape and see the next day takes the viewer to places they never want to witness again. Here it is, the lone climber against his world, and it nearly cost him his life.

A few years back, I heard someone claim that if you watched *127 Hours* backwards, it tells the heartwarming tale of an armless man who finds an arm in a desert canyon. In all seriousness, the movie and the real-life story provide a cautionary tale. We can climb alone if we so choose. We can venture out on a quest with no one at our side or even aware of our expedition. Just be honest, the risk can be extreme and the consequences lifelong.

We have a strong attraction in our culture to feature and then repeat the stories of the lone victor. We seem particularly drawn to stand alone heroes. We embrace the maxim, "If it is going to be, it's up to me." *Fortune* magazine has fifty-plus covers featuring the most well-known leaders of global business enterprise. It reveals a great deal about our current culture that only one Fortune cover featured the faces of two people. Tim Cook and Steve Jobs warranted a shared cover, but the remaining *Fortune* covers had room for only one person, one leader, one shining exemplar of success. These cover dwellers were boldly standing or confidently sitting, the message clear; great men and great women are what move business ahead and make the world go round. Yet when we dig deeper, we always discover a consistent backstory. None of these people did what they did without others.

Lone heroes make for great cinema,
but in death zone environments
they become frozen corpses.
(Warner, 2009, p. 112)

The premise of the Basecamp Manifesto is simple. Every person on a meaningful quest needs a vibrant basecamp. Without it, our best quests become improbable, and if our quest is a major summit, we enter the zone of the impossible. The basis for this declaration is that every quest requires clarity, agility, durability, and generativity. We require help and support to gain clarity on what we face, why we are doing this, and how we can best pursue our quest. We need agility or lightness of being to engage our quest optimally. Unnecessary baggage or load makes the journey much harder and the realization of the quest improbable. We must also shape greater durability or resilience if we are to get through the inevitable adversity, suffering, or even trauma we will encounter in any honorable quest. We, finally, must steward well our quest and stretch for generative effort; our work itself must be raised to a higher level. For these quest requirements, we need the power of others. We need a basecamp, a secure base,

Chapter Two The Myth of the Solo Climber

a holding environment of trusted and trusting others who bring these essential gifts to life through consistent interaction and inspiration.

Right now, we are all based in some way to either flounder or flourish. The basecamp, as framed in these pages, is, we believe, an optimum way to flourish. We trust this Basecamp Manifesto is far more than an appeal for us to think deeply about our relational constellations. Our hope is that it will be a serious and "right now" call to action. A call to find, shape, and then nurture what, for us, can become the basecamp essential for our adventure.

Take a few moments to ask two questions. First, what is our quest? Second, where is our basecamp? The first question provides a prompt to think deeply about the why of our life. What is our Everest? What is the mountain we sense we must climb to live out our purpose and reason for being? Dream big. The bigger the dream, the more serious becomes our tackling of the next question. Locating our basecamp will be for most of us a frustrating inquiry because the answer will not come quickly or easily. If it does, this Basecamp Manifesto will be prime material for shaping our current ecosystem for even greater potential. If the answer does not come easily or at all, then the Basecamp Manifesto can be a prompt, an encouragement, and a much-needed guide for finding, shaping, and then nurturing our basecamp commensurate with the size of our quest. Remember, no one ever just climbs Everest. It is wise to never do it alone.

When we explore the lives of those who are now referred to as GOATs, or the greatest of all time, a consistent backstory emerges. People of great quests have ever been people with a crew, a team, a basecamp for support and challenge. Take some time to bask in the stories of Albert Einstein, Thomas Edison, William Wilberforce, Florence Nightingale, Leonardo da Vinci, J.R.R. Tolkien, Vincent Van Gogh, Eric Liddell, Roger Bannister, and Eric Weihenmayer and we discover a wonderful reality. They were never alone. All pursued quests that changed history, but none of them were solo climbers, creators, or curve benders (Nour, 2021, p. 93). If asked the questions, what was your quest, and where was your basecamp, they would all have needed a definition of the term basecamp, but once framed, they would be able to answer in short order. Their quests were monumental, and for that reason, they instinctively knew that the gift of others had to be embraced every step along the way. At some point they made the ask of others to journey with them to realize greater possibilities.

Albert Einstein, as a brilliant scientist, is remembered by many as the consummate genius, ever pictured alone. Few people know about his group, the Olympia Academy. This academy was his small cadre of friends and fellow thinkers: Maurice Solovine, Michele Besso, Conrad Habicht, and his wife Mileva. With these few, he shaped an ironclad covenant to talk, discuss, argue, and hash out the most tangled problems in the world of science. Their regular gatherings were not to be missed. On one occasion, a member of the academy, Maurice Solovine, decided to attend a music recital instead of meeting with the Academy. In protest, the remaining members, including Einstein, pulled a college dorm response to his offense. They entered his apartment, turned the place upside down, piled the furniture and books on top of his bed, and then ate all his food. Einstein lit up a pipe while Habicht lit up a cigar until the place smelled like the inside of a chimney. Solovine needed the reminder; never again should you choose a mindless bourgeoise pleasure over the mindful engagement with our Olympia Academy (Cabane & Pollack, 2017, p. 81). This group was made up of diverse fields of expertise, but it was their conversations that helped Einstein break open what and how he thought, so that he could then break open the universe.

If Einstein traveled in the company of a dedicated and thoughtful few, what can be said of Thomas Edison? One summer, during my undergrad season of education, I visited my parents in Fort Myers, Florida. A memorable day was our trek to the Thomas Edison home and museum. Edison's inventions cannot be understood without capturing the environment he created. His first principal invention was a *collaboratory*. If this isn't a word, we just invented it. It was the environment he shaped that explains the backstory of his genius. His laboratory was a collaboration space where he and others took on numerous inventive quests. If Edison had been asked, what is your quest, he would have listed numerous trails of inquiry. Yet, the light bulb is what marks the most famous of his experimental adventures.

What is intriguing about his most famous "invention," the light bulb, is the little-known fact of its actual invention in 1841 in England. Edison's breakthrough was the "long-lasting and commercially viable light bulb," forty years after a light bulb of sorts had been invented. This "first" viable bulb would not have been possible without the connectional intelligence of Edison and Francis Robbins Upton (Cabane & Pollack, 2017, p. 96). Upton, a Princeton graduate,

Chapter Two   The Myth of the Solo Climber

was recommended to Edison by German scientist Hermann von Helmholtz. Upton brought to Edison's *collaboratory* a tool for the light bulb's further development, the constraint box. It was this conceptual tool that Upton used with Edison to identify the four major constraints for inventing a long-lasting, viable bulb. This proved to be the filter through which all possible filament materials were passed until eventually they hit up carbonized bamboo, and the 1,200-hour filament was discovered. If asked, where is your basecamp or the relational space from which you learned, did reconnaissance, found support and preparation for the venture down your inventive trail, Edison would no doubt have pointed to his lab colleagues and said, "Here they are." His inventions were never solo creations. They were all put out into the world with many minds and hands, Edison acting as a kind of conductor. The light bulb went on in concert, no pun intended.

One qualifier is in order. Edison did spend time alone, thinking, musing, and wondering. His residence, lab, and present-day museum is located along a river in Fort Myers, Florida. A private dock on the property was a favorite spot for Edison. A much-loved story is of Edison, alone at the end of the dock, with a fishing pole in hand. He did this because of the fishing rule; never bother a man who is fishing. Edison's ruse, however, was to fish with an un-baited hook. He wasn't there to catch fish; he was there to catch the ideas and thoughts swirling in the eddies of his mind. One day he was bothered, not by a person but by a fish that took a dangerous interest in his bare hook. You can't remove every distraction, but you can try.

William Wilberforce stands as a pioneer in the fight against slavery and is remembered for his decades-long parliamentary battle in England to end the slave trade. His mission took place in the early 1800s, well before the American Civil War of the 1860s. His speeches on the floor of the British Parliament marked him as passionate campaigner for freedom and moral society. Those who witnessed his presence noted that, as he made his way to the podium, he looked like a bent and twisted dwarf in a fairy tale, but after he had spoken, he looked like the giant in the very same tale.

We cannot understand the life course of Wilberforce the emancipator without seeing Wilberforce the connector. He was hardly alone in his quest to end Britain's dealings across the world in the destructive and deadly slave trade. The lifelines for Wilberforce were William Pitt, Thomas Clarkson, Charles Middleton, Hanna More, plus his wife. In the early days of the struggle, this circle around Wilberforce brought him the infusions of courage and perseverance needed at the times when the cause appeared lost. Once again, the story confronts the myth of the solo hero taking on the impossible task. Behind the change agent is a change community. For Wilberforce, he would ever be in debt to those who stood with him through the thick and thin of a social change of monumental proportions.

Florence Nightingale, known for intervention in medical care that saved countless lives, did what she did with a network of nurses and researchers. The story of "the lady with the lamp" doing her nighttime rounds during the Crimean War was the fruit of connectional intelligence, according to Erica Dhawan and Saj-Nicole Joni in *Get Big Things Done* (2015, p. 17). Florence, the heroine of safer medical care, did what she did in connection with a team of volunteer nurses, three dozen in all, that she trained and then took to Balaklava in Crimea. Her care and data collection, in concert with a team of nurses, pointed to new ways of decreasing mortality rates among soldiers. In the camp hospitals, one out of two soldiers died until her work on mitigating unsanitary conditions was applied. A letter-writing campaign linked with presentations to doctors and government officials eventually led to the commission and building of Renkoi Hospital, one of the world's first prefab hospitals. It was at Renkoi where the mortality rate for wounded servicemen dropped more than 90 percent.

> *Despite the evidence to the contrary, we still tend to think of achievement in terms of the Great Man or Great Woman, instead of the Great Group.*
> Warren Bennis & Patricia Biederman (1997, p. 2)

Florence Nightingale was smart. She is credited with creating the first polar area diagram and was a pioneer in the use of graphics to display statistical data, plus the first woman inducted into the Royal Statistical Society (Dhawan & Joni, 2015, pp. 18–19). She would establish the first secular training institute for nurses at St. Thomas' Hospital in London in 1860. Yet, this story is not one of a solo nurse against the world of unsanitary hospitals during wartime. Florence, the founder of modern nursing, nursed in concert with dozens of caring and data-collecting nurses. It was their connectional intelligence that made the difference and saved countless lives. A great quest supported and fueled by a robust base camp of caring and daring nurses in the mid- to late 1800s.

The greatest artists throughout history are most often portrayed as the epitome of solitary genius. Da Vinci, Van Gogh, and Tolkien are household names and heroic figures, but their true stories punch holes in the myth of the solo hero. Leonardo da Vinci, famous for frescos, sculptures, amazing contraptions, and numerous ideational efforts, is singled out as one of the greatest minds ever to live. Yet, the backstory of his life is one of a basecamp environment, of work done in concert with others. He may even be deemed the godfather of connectional intelligence (Dhawan & Joni, 2015, p. 27). From humble and frankly negative beginnings, the artist sought out education and exposure wherever he could find it. These connections were what led him to the mapping of human anatomy, plate tectonics, and a multitude of inventions.

Vincent Van Gogh for many is assumed to have been a recluse. A sad, lonely, half-crazed genius with brush in hand whose fame came long after his last breath. Yet his quest to paint in a novel way was fueled by a circle of support and challenge. The solo artist was connected and tethered to a cadre of other artists, with the primary base for his life being found in his brother, Theo Van Gogh. Art historians agree: if there had not been a Theo Van Gogh, there never would have been a Vincent Van Gogh. Joshua Shenk notes in *The Power of Two*, "Though his brother Theo never picked up a brush, it's fair to identify him—as Vincent did—as the co-creator of the drawings and paintings that are among the most significant in history. The Van Gogh brothers were like aspen trees—entwined at the roots. They had supremely distinct roles, styles, even identities. But from their separate domains, each contributed to a joint project of honest, daring art" (Shenk, 2014, p. 70).

> *Every real friendship is a sort of secession, even a rebellion.*
> C.S. Lewis (1960)

J. R. R. Tolkien's *The Lord of the Rings* stands out as one of the most epic tales ever written. However, the backstory is about one man ever indebted to a circle of friends. The Inklings, the small cadre of friends and writers around Tolkien through the years, represents a classic basecamp story. The Inklings were a basecamp. A group of peers living out a form of mutual benefit partnering to learn, do reconnaissance, provide support and resources, and then journey both individually and collaboratively towards their quest to write for the sake of the world. For Diana Glyer, who spent twenty-three years researching the Inkling's letters and drafts, there was a mysterious reality in their gathering. For the seventeen years they gathered, she wanted to know the answer to two simple questions. First, what did they do when together? Second, in what way did it practically help them with their individual writing? She came across something she describes as "wholly unexpected, something bigger. I wasn't prepared for how important this group was, how essential it had become to the work of these writers … and I began to wonder if there were larger lessons here, ones that could make a difference in the projects I was working on, in the breakthroughs I was seeking" (Glyer, 2016, p. 8).

Tolkien's quest was daunting and at times, to him, impossible. His own admission was that sheer encouragement is what saw him through to carry on, get through, and finally complete the epic tale we now experience as *The Lord of the Rings*. Tolkien stated in 1954, when the first reviews began to be printed, "Only by his (C. S. Lewis') support and friendship did I ever struggle to the end of the labor." Ten years later, he added, "The unpayable debt that I owe to him was… sheer encouragement. He was for long my only audience. Only from him did I ever get the idea that my 'stuff' could be more than a private hobby. But for his interest and unceasing eagerness for more I should have brought *The L. of the R.* to a conclusion" (Shenk, 2014, p. 32).

In the cinematic portrayal of Tolkien's work, *The Fellowship of The Ring*, there is a pivotal moment when a circle of deep concern must determine what to do with the ring. Gandolf, the Elves, Aragon, and Mordimo are wrestling with the monumental task of stewarding the ring to the place of necessary demise. In the most unlikely of happenings, Frodo steps forward and then Sam and two other friends. The final friend to join speaks of their willingness to join "the quest, or the thing." Gandolf then declares those wonderful words, "This is to be the fellowship of the ring" (*Lord of the Rings*, 2001). Four unlikely and obviously ill-equipped shire dwellers carry the future in their hands and on their hearts. Earlier, Sam Gamgee had declared to Frodo as they left the shire and soon

Chapter Two The Myth of the Solo Climber

found themselves encountering places they had never been to or seen before, "I wonder what kind of tale we have fallen into?" These words were about to intensify exponentially. The fellowship was their basecamp, and their quest demanded of them a loyalty, courage, and bond to see it through to the end. The tale they had fallen into would be an epic journey, and the four would discover and display a bond worthy of all fellowships to follow.

Shifting from artists and writers to the hyper-individualized world of track and field, most of us can name track stars who stood on championship podiums. Eric Liddell of *Chariots of Fire* fame and Roger Bannister, the first man to break the four-minute mile, come to mind. Nothing seems more private, personal, and individual than the track star. Yet, these two men did what they did through myth-busting connectivity. Their podium presence was an expression of everything but the myth of the solo record-breaker.

In 1924, Eric Liddell won a 100-meter race in the time of 10.6 seconds, a feat immortalized in the movie *Chariots of Fire.* His gold medal performance at the Olympics of 1924 stands out in sports lore as one man defying the odds, standing on principle, and claiming the ultimate victory in the sport of running. Yet, few of us know the name Sam Mussabini. Sam was the professional coach employed by Liddell. At the time, his presence and work as a coach was viewed by many as tantamount to cheating. In fact, Mussabini was prohibited from being in the stadium during the race and only knew Eric was victorious when he heard the British national anthem being played. Liddell won that race, but he did not do so alone. The connectional skills and intelligence of Liddell the runner and Mussabini the coach provide yet another backstory of a quest pursued in community.

Another legendary runner, Roger Bannister, represents for many the consummate solo achiever. He took on the seemingly impossible task of running one mile in under four minutes. On May 6, 1964, Bannister put on his personally designed, lightweight track shoes and ran a one-mile circuit at six in the evening in under four minutes, 3:59.4 to be exact. The problem with this story is that it is not true. Roger Bannister always told the story by including two others—Chris Brasher and Chris Chataway—who made the Roger Bannister story possible. These two friends were his pacers-in-training beginning in 1953 and up to that May evening in 1954. They trained with Roger for many hours, days, and months, helping with the pacing that would eventually help a solo runner break the barrier of the four-minute mile.

Roger was also indebted to Eustice Thomas, his spike-sharpening and shoe-weight expert. "The first four minutes" story was a collaborative and resourcefully creative journey on the part of a rich, relational ecosystem. "His achievement arose out of the ground of friendship" (Whitaker, 2016, p. 127).

Amy Whitaker, in her telling of this amazing quest, frames the Roger Bannister story as a classic example of a "lighthouse question" being asked and answered. Bannister dared to ask the question, "How can we break the mysterious four-minute mile barrier?" Such a question and quest held the space of belief absent proof. It was this question that determined the story structure of their lives in the early 1950s. The answer was, "Together, through training, support, and determination" (Whitaker, 2016, p. 111). Bannister had a basecamp that made his and their quest a reality. Whitaker's application point is fitting for any basecamp group. Could it be that our lives are an answer to a question we hadn't meant to ask?

Finally, a tale of one who conquered Everest itself, against unimaginable odds. For those who follow Everest adventures, the name Erik Weihenmayer marks one of the amazing firsts in the Himalayan Mountains. He was the first blind person to summit Everest. As Maria Coffey tells his story in *Where the Mountain Casts Its Shadow*, "It is on his forehead that the laurel of honor is placed" (Coffey, 2003, p. 76). The reality, which Erik is generous in the telling, requires credit to the twelve-person crew who made each step possible and the ultimate summiting an amazing accomplishment. Yet, we know none of the names of the twelve. We can reach the summits of life, but we must ever remember, we don't reach our personal Everest on our own.

Stories don't lie. These stories make a compelling case for the power of connectional artistry, intelligence, and encouragement in the face of the impossible. We take on quests, achieve great things, and bring light to the world in concert with others. The myth of the solo quester may appear to exist but do some digging and you always discover a crew, a team, a community of practice. There is a basecamp, an intentional encampment that provides support, resources, reconnaissance, and preparation for a great exploration and adventure. One wonders how much "work" and "stuff" remains locked away or is tossed aside for lack of sheer encouragement. How many quests are lost for lack of the power of others. John Bowlby, the champion of the secure base idea and experience was right, "Life is best organized as a series of daring ventures from a secure base" (Bowlby, 1988).

CHAPTER THREE

Leader, Where Art Thou?

One must always remember, there is more than one way to be in a place.

Teresa of Avila

In spring of 1995, I found myself engaged with a significant quest without a basecamp. In the deepest sense, I was climbing my mountain but was lost and not sure how I would find my way back home. After a decade plus of work in the nonprofit world of congregational leadership, I was tired, disillusioned, and looking for some way to survive and wondering what could possibly be next. My wife, Deb, called this "the time of the deep sigh." My common expression through many days was to audibly sigh as if I was trying to capture some kind of relief or exhale some form of angst that I could not articulate in words. This season led me into a season of liminality, that strange place betwixt and between current reality and some future day. I chose a kind of self-imposed sabbatical as my only option for the foggy path ahead.

The word transition begins with the word "transit" so I knew I would have to move in some other direction if I was to find my way out and through my state of lostness. I was living in a fog but also in a world on fire, a personal and professional environment that was confusing but intense. I personified the adage that when we fail to tend well and daily to our own soul development, we either become shallow or we drown in the deep end of burnout or flameout. A counselor friend, firmly but graciously, confirmed a diagnosis of depression and fast-approaching burnout, and then had the audacity to say that I would require three years to recover. I thought at the time he was crazy. Three years was too long to heal anything. It turned out that he was right, as three years later I stepped back into a position of full-time leadership. Thankfully, I was wiser and healthier.

With no support system or life raft that I could see in the environment I had served for thirteen years, I did what I knew to do. I resigned from a good church and got to work painting houses, doing gig work, stepping in from time to time to do some presenting work on a topic of someone else's choosing, and then, of all things, pursuing a doctorate. It was the doctorate quest that was most surprising because it involved a mid-life risk with no known landing place on the other side. The words of Dante, in *The Divine Comedy*, resonated deeply, "In the middle of the road of my life, I awoke in a dark wood, where the true way was wholly lost" (Alighieri, 2001). I was scrambling, but Deb's support and encouragement kept my feet moving through the fog and gradually away from a burnout or, worse, a flameout.

When I walked on to the campus of Gonzaga University in the spring of 1995, I wasn't sure why I was there or ultimately what I was going to do. I only knew that I was hungry to learn and at some level unpack my tangled mess of life and leadership confusion. At the time I thought an EdD (doctorate in education) would be a good resource plus a great escape from a world that I had inhabited since 1982. My first encounter was with Dr. Nancy Isaacson. This academic relationship became a life changer. I was welcomed, affirmed, but also challenged to explore much more than I had ever been challenged to explore. In fact, I found some words of empathy that were strangely missing in the previous contexts I had inhabited. Here I was, being affirmed in gifts and abilities by someone outside of my "church world" in ways that were strangely absent inside my "church world." I began a journey of discovery that would unveil one of my missing dimensions, the presence of a secure base or holding environment that could help me navigate life and the confusing terrain of front-line leadership.

Chapter Three Leader, Where Art Thou?

As I sat in the Gonzaga University library in the summer of 1996, I came to a turning point in my life while reading *Leadership Without Easy Answers* by Ronald Heifetz (1994). The final pages recalled the final months of Martin Luther King's journey and his acknowledgement of weariness of body, spirit, and mind. He needed a respite of some kind, but the cause he was serving and the insistence of those around him to carry on without abatement, kept him pressing forward though exhausted at all levels. Three months later he was assassinated while fully engaged on the front line of the civil rights movement.

In rehearsing this saga, Ron Heifetz notes a strange non-negotiable in the modern world of leadership. This non-negotiable principle is that leaders are wholly expected to hold the environment they lead. This is what MLK Jr. was doing in 1968. This is what we expect all good to great leaders to do … to the end. MLK Jr. will ever be remembered for bravely holding the environment of the civil rights movement. Yet, Heifetz raises the tragedy of such a leadership expectation by stating, "The question, however, that no one seems to ask is this, 'Who is holding the leader?'" (Heifetz, 1994, p. 250). It seems that we have a serious holding dilemma in our current leadership environments. We are missing a vital dimension that permits the primary holding work to be supported and fueled by a deeper and more hidden holding work that we give little time or consideration.

I will never forget the place and time when these words struck my heart and then slowly wound their way into my thinking about the future. It put in words what my life to date had involved. A lot of holding. A series of excursions into environments in need of holding. A journey of responsible caregiving, leadership providing, and cause inspiring but a dearth of holding of my life by others. In such conditions, Heifetz adds, we run the risk of moral regret where our ethic of responsibility goes awry. I had fallen for, what Heifetz later describes as, the myth of the lone warrior: the solitary individual whose heroism and brilliance enable him to lead the way. This is the notion that reinforces isolation (Heifetz, 1994, p. 250).

This was the point in my journey when the holding environment concept was planted in my mind, and since then I have been wrestling with the why, what, and how of this concept and application for all who seek to lead. Since then, I have listened to the stories of businesspeople, educators, pastors, and others in positions of leadership and I have noted how many witnessed to the burden of holding their environments yet hesitated and stammered when asked, "Who is holding you?" It has turned out, MLK Jr. was not unique.

The holding environment can be framed several ways, but for the purpose of this work, I have chosen the metaphor of the *secure base*. Before diving in, I wouldn't be surprised if some of you are objecting to the absence of holding by others. We all have friends, work colleagues, family, and networks that touch us and help us and support us. This is true, but a holding environment and a secure base is of a different quality and depth.

Every day we are all held in some way, but seldom do we look closer at the nature of these relationships. The fact is, right now, everyone of us is based; that is, we have a base condition that is directly affecting our lives for good or ill. Our journey is hopefully to the land of the secure base or a basecamp that supports and fuels our life quest. The conviction of the Basecamp Manifesto is simple: a secure base is where we discover a holding that dramatically changes the way we hold the rest of life and leadership. Our question in this chapter is, leader, where art thou? We are taking time in the pages that follow for some honest and likely sobering assessment of how and where many of us are "based" for our life journey.

Assessing Our Base Conditions

Truth be told, none of us go through life without a base. The question is, "What kind of base are we standing on and in?" "Base-less living" is not possible because at some level our very lives are grounded in some relational place or condition that shapes how we take on life. We are never not connected to some "other," and in today's so-called ever-connected world, we are influenced, swayed, prodded, and cajoled to say, think, wear, or believe any number of things. What we seldom ask is, how are my connections truly helping me to flourish and succeed at living? The present state of our base conditions and quality requires brutal honesty. Our assessment will either lead us to honest reflection and next steps or keep us in the fog of denial that we are just fine the way we are.

It is the premise of this work that secure bases and circles of trust are rare and becoming rarer in an age of alternative bases. The most common base conditions can be captured through a series of adjectives—barren, shallow, pseudo,

Chapter Three   Leader, Where Art Thou?

or contested. Based upon the following rich descriptions we ask the question, might one of these be our quality of base right now?

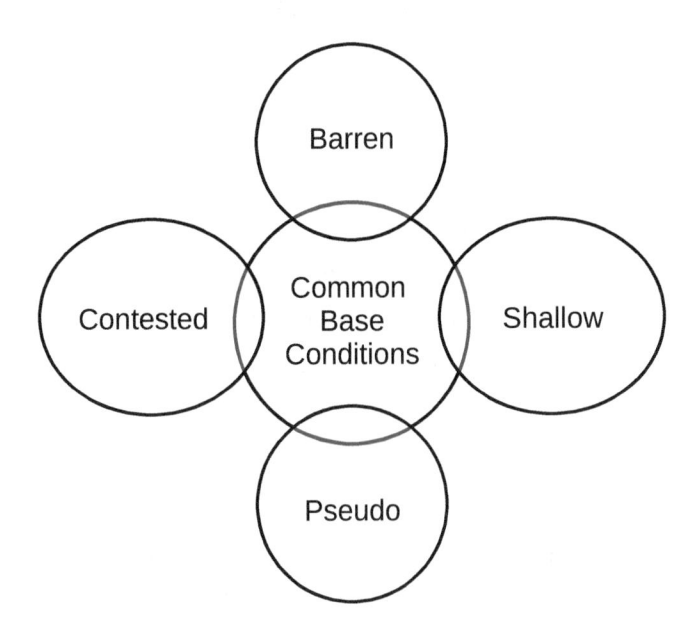

```
         Barren
Contested  Common Base Conditions  Shallow
         Pseudo
```

The Barren Base

The barren base condition is found in more lives than we could ever imagine. The barren base is quite simply us against the world. It is founded upon much of what we learn from our earliest days that standing on our own two feet is what makes the strong person. In much of our education and socialization, the value of individualism convinces us that at the start and end of the day, it is our own circle of self that will see us through. In thinking about these environments, imagine for a moment "the coins of the realm." In the barren condition, there are few to no coins of value being circulated in our relational marketplace. There is little to no currency of relationship being given, exchanged, or even borrowed.

The barren base is a state of deprivation where true belonging is missing. This deprivation leads to a whole host of issues and problems and affects health, well-being, and advancement. This base has been growing in recent years as more and more attest to loneliness and lost connections. Recent research on the state of youth in North America revealed that 24 percent claim they have zero friends.

The generation of Facebook, Instagram, and TikTok has become an atomized generation. People are surrounded by contacts but missing in true connections. Johann Hari posits in *Lost Connections* that this barrenness now permeates our lives, and we are suffering on every front from the wilderness conditions we have created, chosen, or been guided into by a world of individualism and autonomy (Hari, 2018).

> *Commanders who isolate themselves in the "loneliness of command," keeping their own counsel and not having the strength of a leadership team to draw on, are less effective.*
> Gordon Sullivan and Michael Harper (1996)

The isolation and loneliness of leaders is the symptom of a wider problem in our current culture. In 2023, the US Surgeon General released his report on the loneliness epidemic sweeping the country (Office of the Surgeon General (OSG, 2023). Compared to 2003 data, the number of hours of social isolation per month has increased by twenty-four hours. Social engagement with friends has decreased twenty hours per month. Simple companionship or shared leisure has decreased fourteen hours per month (OSG, 2023, p. 14). These increasing relational deficits bear directly upon health: biology, psychology, and behavior with negative outcomes in heart disease, stroke, and diabetes. This growing isolation can lead to an individual's morbidity and premature mortality (OSG, 2023, p. 31). This is the most current alarm bell for a problem that has had many decades of growing concern. We are more isolated and alone than ever before. We are now neck-deep in the unprecedented experience of grouped isolation or crowded loneliness. Like never before, we need deeper relationships, but we are too busy and pulled apart to maintain them. The barren base seems to be increasing. For the individual person, this is a dangerous state to continue in, and for the leader, it results in more than just health concerns. The lonely, isolated state for a leader can spell doom for any serious quest in life.

We know that we are living with a barren base when:

Chapter Three   Leader, Where Art Thou?

Our self-talk is consistently, "It's me against the world."

We have no one who comes to mind when asked, "Who would we call, when our life implodes, or disaster strikes."

In the words of the poet Robert Louis Stevenson, a kind of love becomes present for one's own voice. This, according to Stevenson, is a kind of imbecility.

We feel acutely the greatest disease of our age, loneliness.

Our foray into the world is brief, sporadic, and carefully scripted to maximize avoidance and minimize encounter.

It may be that a personality leaning is part of this chosen base condition, but it is being overdone to our detriment.

The Shallow Base

The shallow base condition varies from the barren state in that this base is populated but the quality of relational investment is weak or shallow. This is the Facebook friend condition of having many "friends" but the gang is a thousand miles wide and barely an inch deep. This base provides little if any sincere care or challenge to one's life. This base could also be framed by the word "random." The random aspect is driven by the "polyvocality" of our current time. More and more voices but less and less wisdom and clarity. The lack of substantial connection is due to shallowness intensified by randomness.

It is strange to think back on the promise of the internet and the promise of social media; we will have a connected world like never before. Nicolas Carr has been at the forefront of both the celebration and critique of the new hyperconnected reality of our webified world. There are enthusiasts and there are critics. He notes that the enthusiasts herald a new golden age of access and participation, while the skeptics bemoan a new dark age of mediocrity and narcissism. Carr tilts his hand in his title, *The Shallows: What the Internet Is Doing to Our Brains*. His premise is that both our brains and our belonging are being profoundly affected, and it is not towards the deep end but sadly to the shallows (Carr, 2010, pp. 2,3). To think that we are going to find both deep and broad relationships in the shallows of social media and a web-based world is like looking for love in all the wrong places.

In the shallow base we suffer from "partial deprivation," a term coined by Roy Baumeister and Mark Leary in their research on our need to belong. This was their way of capturing a monumental problem in today's relational world (Baumeister & Leary, 1995, p. 511). We have people, we need interaction, but we also need caring and support. The partial deprivation comes when we have people and some interaction absent caring. Many people admit to having people, but the interaction seldom leads to true care, greater insight, and better flourishing. The coin of this realm is marked by relational currency of low value. It is a partial deprivation that is better than the barren base, but it still takes a toll.

Instead of true belonging, we have transient connections. An apt image for the randomness of the shallow base is the experience of "hoteling." People in hotels strike no roots. Edward Verrall Lucas notes, "the French phrase for the chronic hotel guest even says so: they are called dwellers *sur la branche*" (Cohen & Prusak, 2001, p. 85). More than ever, we can give actual counts of followers and friends, but rooted connections, rich relationships are few or none. There is nothing wrong with living in a hotel, but most of us know the empty feeling of such living after a week or two. Daily room service is nice, but it lacks roots or any potential for permanent embrace and enrichment.

We know that a shallow or random base condition exists when:

> *The people we consider "our people" don't engender confidence or provide consistent support in times of need.*

> *We have a base of acquaintances but no true friends who will stay in our life through thick and thin.*

> *Our social environment is populated but richness of relationship is absent.*

> *Our circle is a merry-go-round of different people at different times, and seldom for the long haul. The ride lasts for a short time and when done we ask, "Who's next?"*

The proof of the shallow base is revealed when people are asked, how many confidants do you have? In the 1980s, the response to this question was, on average, three. By 2004, when a research project asked the same question, the answer was none (Hari, 2018). For lack of any other base than barren or shallow, we suffer from more than a support deficit; we feel both bad and insecure in isolation. Such isolation, in Hari's estimation, leads to the epidemic of depression in our current world. What further deepens this problem is treating it with everything other than what is at the center, a loss of human connection. The quality of our base matters.

The Pseudo Base

A further expression of partial relational deprivation is the pseudo base. Some relational improvement can be found for the barren or shallow base dweller by upscaling to the pseudo base. With a pseudo base, we make much of our connections by way of "who is who" in our relational zoo. The problem is that like a zoo, our base mates are for viewing. Their presence carries a false sense of strength or power to lift us to higher heights or deeper insights.

The distinction from the shallow base is the portrayals we give and the posing we engage in with our pseudo base. We give the impression that our relational world is amazing. We have a network that is vast and of great value. However, in moments of honesty we begrudgingly admit, the quality of relationship is thin—sound and fury signifying very little to the living of our life. The coin of this realm is play money. We display and exchange currency but there are no real coins of value. It serves to make us feel "as if" we are in an environment where value is found, but at the end of the game, the paper money or coins go back in the box only to be pulled out another day for the next round of posed and pretend relating.

To spot the pseudo-base condition look for:

> *A kind of bravado when it comes to who we know and who knows us, but in truth it is a display case of relational strength with no real connection.*
>
> *A lot of reference to our network or our bench or our vast contact list.*
>
> *A low-grade worry about our score, our follows, our likes, our friends list, and our re-posts. With genuine friends we don't keep score; with pseudo friends it is the only calculus we can*

> *find to gauge some kind of value proposition for having these people in our life.*
>
> *We kid ourselves into believing we have a team around us that will raise our game, when in fact the team is unaware of their role or responsibility to do anything on our behalf.*
>
> *We experience a kind of "crowded loneliness." We have numbers to brag about but little true companionship to share.*

In this base condition, the partial deprivation can involve interaction, but it lacks the giving of genuine care and support. The pseudo base may even give us a sense of power and influence. Mattias Desmet notes how loneliness and atomization is not a minor problem in our culture. It can create isolated people who under the influence of media and social media narratives, suddenly coalesce into a new kind of group: a mass. The mass is a pseudo collective. "This kind of group formation makes people radically incapable of thinking critically about the stories presented to them, willing to radically sacrifice everything they hold dear, and deeply intolerant of any voice that deviates from what the masses believe in" (Desmet, 2023).

The pseudo base also lacks the vital ingredient of rigorous thinking and robust conversations that wrestle with what is true and not true. The marble count may be high in such a base, but like marbles in a bag, the quality of interaction is quick and nothing much happens beyond the micro contact points. Desmet does pose a question in all of this: "What can transform the lonely masses into a society in the true sense of the word? A group of people connected from person to person; where the collective does not destroy the individual but guarantees a space in which to flourish as a singular being" (Desmet, 2023). Basecamp settings can be such a place for such transformation and for catalyzing a safer and more flourishing society.

The Contested Base

A fourth condition is the contested base environment. This is the environment where the inhabitants bring comparison, negativity, angst, and stealth like forms of toxicity. This base of relationships is not about connecting; it is about contesting. People walk in with their hidden ladders and measuring tapes, taking score, hoping their score is higher than others. The smell in the room is that of comparison and competition. Why would we ever allow such a condition to exist? It turns out, far too many of us get drawn to such places and people. This base arises for two reasons. On the one hand, for men more than women, there is a bravado that views most of life as a contest. Men seem more drawn to deal friends and have little time for real friends. On the other hand, we are simply undiscerning as to the nature and quality of the people we hang out with. In such environments, there is a currency in circulation, and the most-valued coins of this realm are grievance and grumbling and never-ending comparison.

Our circles can be places where we happily gather but we secretly harbor a hierarchy within. We seldom leave our ladders at home. We bring with us some kind of gauge to determine where we are on the measuring rod of success. Our laddering or measuring mitigates against our circle ever being or becoming a circle of trust and benefit. It is hard to trust or benefit in relationship when taking and keeping score is of higher priority than giving and receiving care.

Donald Nicholls in *The Testing of Hearts* tells the story of a priest, Father Aiden, doing a stint of chaplain care with a university faculty. Father Aiden was curious to know what theologians in a seminary daily exchanged with one another. One day the penny dropped, and it hit him, the coin of this realm was "grievance" (Nicholls, 1989, p. 50). Like blood circulating through the human body, grievance flowed through their conversations, interactions, and perspectives on the wider world. I referenced this story several times with leaders in my stint as a professor and wondered aloud if this currency was in certain ways true of our own institution. This is a sobering depiction of the toxic base condition. The cautionary tale in such a story comes down to this: whatever you put into circulation is what comes back to you every time.

Here is where we must be alert to Hebb's rule: cells that fire together wire together, or more formally, "any two cells or systems of cells that are repeatedly active at the same time will tend to become 'associated,' so that activity in one facilitates activity in the other" (Keysers & Gazzola, 2014, p. 5). This is applied to neural plasticity but can also be extrapolated to the gains and losses in relational connections. Crowds are fascinating but when they are a mob that fires together, or with our metaphor, freely exchange a certain kind of negative currency, the results can be catastrophic. Such exchanges fuse people's thinking into a concert of opinion and at times vicious vitriol and negativity.

A sobering exercise is to consider the wider influence of our so-called connected world with the rise and flood of internet and social media influence. Has our society begun to look more and more like a massive, contested base of relationship? The emotional and social contagion of vitriol, contempt, and outright destruction has fueled a relational currency exchange like none other in human history. Every micro=second, deposits of negativity surge from platforms destined and perhaps designed to form a tsunami effect. These have also been set up for non-stop flow with tools that fuel our addiction to its prompts.

Jaron Lanier, a Silicon Valley insider, who was there when the platforms and plans for the internet were being devised, implores us to radically take stock. The title of his book says it all, *Ten Arguments for Deleting Your Social Media Accounts Right Now* (2018). I shared this book with a leader in an organization because of what I had witnessed and experienced first-hand by leaders within my own profession. I believe I used the word "despicable" to capture the sense of what was being spewed out on many X feeds (formerly known as Twitter). For those who observe and research such things, our online world is a connection pool where emotion is amplified, and if we are not careful, this amplification technology creates a societal base that turns toxic. In Lanier's assessment, much of social media has become an AAT—an 'asshole amplification technology." There is a powerful yet loose federation ever seeding daily toxins into our system of thinking and feeling. As Victor Klemperer states, "words can be like tiny doses of arsenic: they are swallowed unnoticed, appear to have no effect, and then after a little time the toxic reaction sets in after all" (Klemperer, 2006, p.14) When online, we are seldom, if ever, our better self.

We have raised the social media picture in the treatment of this base condition to note how the toxic base is easier than ever to inhabit. Without realizing it, we can daily occupy a kind of base through social media that captures our connective tissues. Our world of followers and the followed becomes our most visited and occupied space. This world is also the realm of our greatest time investment. As we will see, every base is about a when, a where, and a whom. Time, space, and people audits need more care and attention than ever if we are going to get to a place of flourishing and fully taking on our quest in life.

Chapter Three Leader, Where Art Thou?

This toxic base condition is a simple acknowledgment of how socially and emotionally contagious our world is. We are catching things all the time and we catch the most from the close circle we inhabit or from the close circle that we permit to inhabit our daily space. Most of us are far too undiscerning.

You know that you are living with a toxic base condition when:

> *We find our mood and posture leaning more to the negative. Our place in the world is "against" rather than "for" or "with" people.*

> *An increasingly negative view of the world that looks for reinforcement from the voices of vitriol. Thus, the most sought-after personage in life is the scapegoat. In Sacred Fire, Ronald Rolheiser portrays this tendency as "the ridiculing of someone or something that is so different from us that in effect melts down our differences and brings us into harmony with one another in our mutual distancing from it." He goes on to add, "This is not an abstract concept at all. We do it all the time" (Rolheiser, 2014, p. 158).*

> *We seldom stop to look at the currency of our realm. The idea of what I put into circulation rarely crosses our mind, and grievance, critique, complaint, and attack seem okay because everyone is doing it.*

> *Toxicity spreads to almost every area of our lives due to the contagion of others, and the viral agents are left unexamined.*

> *We find we more and more split the world. There are those who think like us, and then there are "the others" who are simply wrong, bad, and evil. Toxicity breeds superiority every time.*

> *We experience the group polarization effect without knowing how to define it. This effect is in play when people who hold negative and caustic perspectives in a closed group tend strongly towards those perspectives becoming more and more extreme. This is a social and emotional contagion that can deaden and destroy one's life.*

The toxic base is more than deprivation; it is devastation. There is surely much that is missing in a toxic base, but what is added leads to an aggressive kind of negative doom loop. Toxicity enters the pores through the presence of others, and we do become much like the five people we hang out with the most.

The Secure Base

It is well worth our time and effort to get at when, where, and with whom we are based. The late Jim Rohn, a success motivation speaker, was famous for pointing out, "We become very much like the five people we hang out with the most." This adage was his wake-up call to ruthlessly assess "our five" because life is contagious, and we catch what others carry. We do so as readily as a cold virus spreading in a VW bug filled with sneezing and wheezing friends. Some have expanded this best five pursuit to include an economic consideration. Our income will most likely be the average of the five people we hang out with the most. This one is scary and raises for some of us an immediate need to find five new friends. There is also a voice theory that can be added to the mix. The quality and character of my inner dialogue and self-talk will be a direct reflection of the five voices I give the most airtime to in my daily journey. For our focus in the Basecamp Manifesto, the secure base is our "five."

So, when and with whom do we exchange coins of relational richness? Where in our world can we find and foster genuine belonging? How can the gain in finding, shaping, and nurturing a secure base be more fully realized? Henry Cloud, in *The Power of the Other*, seeks to direct people to a place of genuine connection. Instead of a base analogy, he notes the potential corners we may inhabit (Cloud, 2016, p. 41). The powerful and life-giving corner is, in Cloud's terms, the *genuine* corner. In the Basecamp Manifesto, this corner is the *secure base* condition. In contrast, Cloud's *empty* corner is his way of capturing our barren base condition. The *false* corner represents our pseudo base condition, and the *bad* corner points to the peril of the shallow-to-toxic base conditions. In Cloud's experience, which he shares by way of two anecdotal surveys among nonprofit leaders, there is a sobering reality about which corners are most populated. The genuine corner or secure base condition was found in less than 20 percent of his audiences. When he asked a group of leaders, "Do you have someplace where you can be 100 percent honest and vulnerable as to what you are going through in your leadership role, where you can totally be honest about struggles, conflicts, needs, or weaknesses?" shockingly, 80 percent of the leaders surveyed said, "No, I have no place like that" (Cloud, 2016, pp. 37,38). With the follow-up question probing whether these leaders had a setting where others were committed to their growth or supportive of them when experiencing anything emotionally or psychologically that rose to "clinical proportions," the level of only 20 percent was also affirmed.

> *Don't join an easy crowd; you won't grow.*
> *Go where the expectations and demands*
> *to perform are high.*
> Jim Rohn (Coleman, 2019, p. 61)

Cloud's appeal is for leaders to ask the question, "Where is our setting for genuine connection?" For our focus in the Basecamp Manifesto, our query is, "Where would we point to describe and identify our secure base in a volatile and scrambled world?" Our relationships are more than a pile of bricks. The missing piece in the barren, shallow, pseudo, and contested toxic bases is "good mortar between the bricks" (Heffernan, 2015, p. 26). Good mortar is at the core of this Basecamp Manifesto, and what follows is our portrayal and practical guide for relationships that can save our life and leadership in a scrambled world.

A Better Way

So, with these base conditions in view, it is time to set forth a better way. Enter the secure base environment. The secure base is a metaphor that finds a home in a cross-section of domains. Everywhere from the smallest circle of parent–child attachment to the rugged and dangerous terrain of war. The back-story chapter to follow provides the history of the theory behind the secure base and is provided for those who may be skeptical about the intellectual rigor behind the basecamp idea. In essence, the secure base is that environment that fosters both safety and support along with challenge and risk-taking. It provides caring while at the same time prompting daring in the living of one's life. It is a far richer environment than most of life's relational settings, but like any healthy garden, it will not yield good fruit by chance or by luck. It will require intentional care, nurture, and watchful eye.

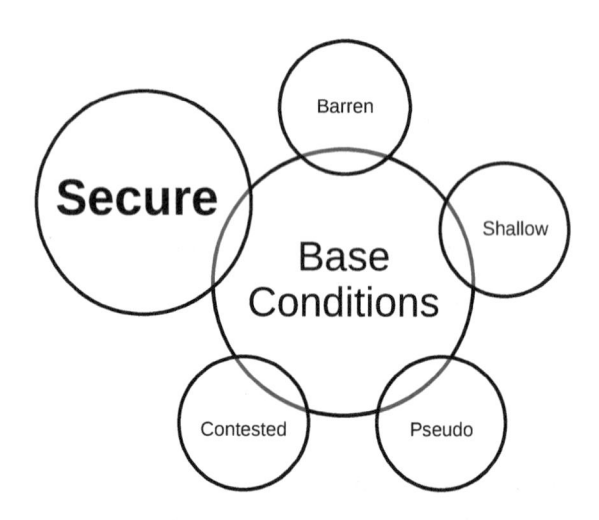

[Diagram: Five overlapping circles around a central "Base Conditions" circle, labeled: Secure, Barren, Shallow, Pseudo, Contested]

The next chapter is a journey into the secure base history and the genesis of holding environment theory and application. It does involve a deeper dive into what informs this manifesto. The basecamp is our chosen metaphor, but it has a strong theoretical foundation in the work of researchers, thinkers, and practitioners in the realm of human connection and well-being.

So, Leader, Where Art Thou?

Most of us walking the earth today have one of these bases in play. So, leader, where art thou? Which one most describes our current reality? Be honest. Now, be truly honest. If needed, have a good cry, or get angry enough to find another way. Let's acknowledge that our life to date may have been filled with relational bases absent true caring and daring. In the words of Keith Ferrazzi, "It is time to stop shopping for milk in a hardware store" (Ferrazzi, 2009, p. 145). It is time to stop looking for love and leadership challenge in all the wrong places. The good news is that there is a better way to happily, and healthfully, base our one and only life.

CHAPTER FOUR

The Basecamp Backstory

There is nothing so practical as a good theory.
Kurt Lewin (Bowlby, 1988)

All models are wrong; but some are helpful.
George Box (Box, 1979)

John Pollack, former speechwriter for President Bill Clinton, was guided by the maxim, "in many arguments, whoever has the best analogy wins." Analogies and metaphors capture our attention because they make the unfamiliar or distant familiar and closer to mind. They help our minds navigate new terrain by making it resemble terrain already known (Gallo, 2018, p. 193). It brings beauty and richness to a concept that may be cerebral but not memorable. It was a metaphoric masterpiece that captured the heart and mind of Warren Buffett, who upon hearing it, said, "these words took me out of my seat." Those words were from Martin Luther King Jr., who declared, "Truth forever on the scaffold, wrong forever on the throne." The use of metaphoric power soon became the hallmark of Buffett's career. He became a master of making the complex simple by way of metaphor. In the HBO documentary, *Becoming Warren Buffett* (2017), he compared his early investment approach to a cigar butt. You look for companies that may look like a discarded cigar butt; they had one more smoke in them. The key is buying the company at the right time to take advantage of the last smoke.

In the beginning of the Basecamp Manifesto, we made it clear that the basecamp is a metaphor, and one image is being utilized to provide a rich picture of another. The other we are dealing with is the secure base concept, and an encampment of climbers and adventurers engaged in an exploration is our rich picture. It carries a meaning and experience that mountain climbers grasp intuitively. The basecamp is the place from which a quest proceeds. The encampment provides support, resources, reconnaissance, and preparation for persons engaged in or anticipating an exploration or adventure. Is it the best metaphor for capturing what leaders need for their quest to be optimized? This may be up for debate, but for our purpose we believe it is a rich picture worth exploring and capturing. The challenge is always out there. The best metaphor often wins.

Shutterstock 171375845 – Enhanced License Permission

Everest basecamp is a familiar scene to anyone who reads about Everest expeditions. The basecamp pictures of Everest capture a foreboding landscape with the summit of the grand mountain in the background, beckoning those who would dare climb it. It is a rich picture of teams on a daring quest. The shared mission is to summit Everest and to then return intact to tell the story. We are utilizing the basecamp image to capture the power of relational constellations that serve as a secure base for life and leadership. Our quest, our life purpose is best tackled out of a place of support, resourcing, and challenge. This rich picture will be central throughout the Manifesto.

> *When discouraged it is close to*
> *impossible to be encouraged by oneself.*
> *It is almost always necessary to have*
> *another person,*
> *rekindle the spirit*
> *that has lost courage.*
> Albert Schweitzer

This chapter is a journey through the field of study, research, and conceptualization that serves as background for the metaphor we have chosen. We are taking some time to trace the quest for good theory. Over sixty-plus years, researchers and writers have observed life in the hope of arriving at a grounded theory of caring and daring relationships. Such theory has arisen out of longstanding studies of human experience as it exists in social contexts, and not in a data set, abstract statistics, or artificially concocted environments. This real-world exploration is, "the difference between watching a pack of lions hunt on the savannah and seeing them get fed from a bowl in the zoo" (Madsbjerg, 2017, p. 17). Grounded theory arises out of observation and involvement in the real world, often resulting in a rich picture of lived experience.

The Journey to Basecamp

For our purpose we will engage in a chronological journey through the shaping of the grounded theory of people in connection with one another and then link these findings to the basecamp concept. Like a series of directional markers from

Nepal's Katmandu to the Everest basecamp, these theories, rooted in robust research, will underscore the place, power, and promise of relational settings. Such settings are referenced via different words and phrases, but collectively make the case that we as human beings travel best when we travel together, with a trusted few.

From Homefront to Battlefront

The subtitle for the Manifesto gives a hint as to the theoretical roots of the basecamp portrayal. The base in basecamp is drawing upon a theoretical framework called the secure base. This secure base concept hearkens back to a six-decade old human development theory called *holding environments*. The term *holding environment* was first coined by Dr. D. W. Winnicott in the early 1960s and arose from his careful and slow observation of mothers and infants. He came to describe the parent–child attachment dynamic as that of providing an environment in which the child could be "held." This holding base fostered exploration, creative adventure, and provided confirmation to a child in times of danger (Winnicott, 1965).

Against the backdrop of this early attachment research, Mary Ainsworth, who studied infant care in Uganda during the late 1960s, coined the term *secure base* to describe the security of children who engaged in unworried expectations, trusting their attachment figures to come to their aid should problems arise (Ainsworth, 1967). Her work on attachment theory served as the foundation for much of the current work on this area of our development and its impact on life navigation. Early life attachment patterns are carried to a certain extent into later life navigation. As the old saying goes, the most valuable and important things passed down to children are not found in the will.

In the late 1980s, John Bowlby would carry the secure base idea into his work and provide further development for the secure base concept (Bowlby, 1988). He framed the rich picture of the secure base in the context of soldiers in battle. A secure base role is played by an officer commanding a military base from which an expeditionary force sets out and to which it can retreat should it meet a setback. Much of the time, the role of the base is a waiting one, but it is nonetheless vital for that purpose. It is only when the officer commanding the expeditionary force is confident his base is secure that he dare press forward and take risks with soldier deployment (Bowlby, 1988, p. 11). For soldiers, it is the provision and assurance of a secure base that prompts them to engage more fully in the fight. Without such provision, soldiers fight differently because absent a secure base they know they are essentially on their own.

For Bowlby, the secure base was also a feature of good parenting. A good-enough parent provides a secure base from which a child can make sorties into their world and then return to their base knowing they will be welcomed when they get there. The extension of this caregiving and secure base provision to other relationships was noted by Bowlby as an essential component of healthy interaction between relatives, colleagues, and friends who take the role of caregivers when comfort, encouragement, assistance, or material aid are required (Bowlby, 1988, p. 11).

To the Therapist's Couch

The holding environment and secure base frameworks in time found their way into the field of psychotherapy to describe the context of a patient–therapist relationship. A therapist is often viewed by a patient as an experienced parental figure. The therapist sees their role as that of providing conditions or a context for exploration. The counselor/therapist has a five-part task, according to Bowlby (1988, pp. 138–139).

1. Providing a person with a secure base from which to explore painful aspects of life, many of which would be difficult to reconsider without support, encouragement, sympathy, and guidance.

2. Assisting a person in the explorations of relationships, expectations, and unconscious biases. This exploration is often in need of prompts and questions.

3. Helping a person explore the specific relationship with the one who is helping them, the therapist.

4. Encouraging a person to consider how his or her current perceptions, expectations, feelings, and actions may be the product either of events and situations encountered in childhood and adolescence, especially

with those of parents. There is never not a history impinging upon the present moment.

5. Enabling a person to recognize their images or models of themselves and of others, derived either from painful experiences or from misleading messages emanating from parents or past influencers.

In summary, Bowlby notes, "Unless a therapist can enable his patient to feel some measure of security, therapy cannot even begin. Thus, we start with the role of the therapist in providing the patient with a secure base. This is a role very similar to that described by Winnicott as 'holding.'" These elements of caregiving and attachment are seen in all supportive and educative relationships (Heard, 1982, p. 114). In therapeutic work, it is important to note, the terms containment and holding ordinarily refer to the symbolic ways in which a therapist manages both the patient's feelings and their own. This is not easy work when you are with others who feel lost in familiar places. The holding work may seem to represent an ideal of consistency and stability, but it is much more fluid, characterized by the way in which failures can be used as learning (Shapiro & Carr, 1991, p. 54).

Over time, the main contributors to the secure base concept worked to depict the best qualities of holding environments. The early theories were enriched by further and deeper thinking. This ongoing work on the secure base concept adds to the robust nature of today's use of this concept for healthier and more resilient living. Every holding environment has its own relative quality of support, caregiving, and attachment. In Winnicott's earliest work on the holding environment, he noted that caregivers must be neither negligent nor perfect, and that good care is all in the balance. The tension between showing sensitivity to another's needs for being held and being free represents the gift to their growth (Winnicott, 1965). This kind of caregiving enables a client to understand and cope, within their capabilities, with the situation that aroused attachment seeking behavior in the first place (Heard, 1982, p. 105).

Sometimes a holding environment is healthy, but at other times the environment can be unhealthy. The starting premise is that perfect holding environments are not found in an imperfect world. The relational dynamics of life, whether parent-to-child or patient-to-therapist, involve infinitely complex variables, which make perfect caregiving or perfect attachment impossible. Research has revealed caregiving that brings satisfaction to both parties and diminishes the intensity of attachment behaviour lies in a blend of proximity, accessibility, physical protection, appropriate interaction, and access to necessary resources (Heard, 1982, p. 104).

Over time a robust framework for a "good enough" environment has emerged. This is an important insight for basecamp shaping and nurturing. It is never a perfect environment because no one can perfectly provide all that is required. The practical goal is one of shaping the "good enough" environment to provide a base that can be healthy and robust (Whitaker, 2016, p. 187).

On To the Workplace

The need for attachment and care that comes in the form of "holding" does not stop in the home or the place of therapy. The search for a secure base, "while most obvious in early childhood, can be observed throughout the life cycle" (Bowlby, 1988, p. 27). The concept of the secure personal base, from which a person explores and to which a person can return, is a concept crucial for understanding how an emotionally stable person develops and functions all through life (Bowlby, 1988, p. 46).

Those who later interpreted the work of Winnicott saw it as an approach to human development rooted in cultural terms that offered promise for understanding the psychodynamics of organizational culture (Van Buskirk & McGrath, 1999, p. 807). Though this take followed his work by thirty years, it was not too far from Winnicott's understanding of development and holding as necessary for later life. The quality of such holding determines the extent to which the person can become a genuine, creative individual. From parent to child relationship, to therapist and client relationship, the secure base and holding environment picture made its way into organizational life. This serves as a third major trail marker on our way to making our case for basecamp formation.

William Kahn, a professor of organizational behavior at Boston University, is perhaps the most prolific writer applying the holding environment concept to the wider world of work and organizations. "The secure base concept offers a particularly useful way to conceptualize relationships in organizations in which members experience themselves, at various moments in their work lives, as lost, confused, frightened, anxious, or threatened" (Kahn, 1998, p. 42). This move takes the concept of the holding environment and applies its principles to caregiving within organizations. Echoing the "good enough" dimensions of a quality holding environment, Kahn states, "The effective care-giving attachment figure neither intrudes nor abandons, in other words, is neither unresponsive (when others seek proximity or help) nor overactive and impinging (when others need to explore and operate on their own). Maintaining such a stance requires sensitivity to the needs, signals, and experiences of others. It requires meeting their reasonable dependency needs while letting them conduct their own journeys of growth and development. It means metaphorically holding others while neither letting them go (abandoning) nor pressing too tightly (intruding)" (Kahn, 1996, p. 162).

The presence of psychosocial support and conditions in which people are "held" in organizational contexts is a benefit both to the individual and the organization. William Kahn, as the father of holding environments in organizations, was fascinated by the potential for better caregiving in organizations. Based upon extensive field studies within teams and organizations, he has concluded, caregiving and the provision of a secure base are ultimately in the service of organizational effectiveness. "Organization members, when they are personally engaged in their work, give of themselves to varying extents, emotionally and intellectually as well as physically" (Kahn, 1996, p. 166). His curiosity was how this engagement could be improved. In an empirical study, Kahn (1990) explored the psychological conditions of personal engagement and disengagement in the workplace and discovered the dimensions of meaningfulness, safety, and availability as critical to the fostering of personal engagement. These dimensions were dependent on the kind of environment fostered by those who dwelt within a team or organizational setting.

There is no better way to apply an inquiry into the "good enough" holding environment theory than to see people holding or not holding one another in an actual organization. Kahn engaged in an intensive study of social workers and a system-level perspective on job burnout and the quality of caregiving relationships. This exploration revealed eight behavioural dimensions of caregiving and five possible patterns of caregiving flow. These dimensions represent the qualities present in an environment wherein workers are appropriately held. The behavioral dimensions of caregiving that characterize healthy emotional resources for others are accessibility, inquiry, attention, validation, empathy, support, compassion, and consistency. These dimensions indicate that organizational caregiving is "witnessing others' journeys—enabling others to experience themselves as joined, as seen and felt, as known, and as not alone" (Kahn, 1996, p. 165).

We may wonder why these characteristics matter within a team or organization. For a social work agency, they are the very qualities that cascade to those being served, or if absent, touch those being served in a way that diminishes help. "The extent to which care givers are emotionally 'held' within their own organizations is related to their abilities to 'hold' others similarly" (Kahn, 1993, p. 540). In view of basecamp development and assessment the vital dimensions are framed below in the form of eight questions:

1. In terms of **accessibility**, are we remaining in one another's vicinity, allowing time and space for contact and connection?

2. In the arena of **inquiry**, are we asking for information or insight necessary to provide for other's emotional, physical, and cognitive needs? Are we probing wisely for other's experiences, thoughts, and feelings?

3. As far as **attention** goes, are we actively attending to one another's experiences, ideas, self-expressions, showing comprehension with verbal and nonverbal gestures?

4. To provide **validation**, are we communicating positive regard, respect, and appreciation to one another?

5. Regarding **empathy**, are we imaginatively putting ourselves in one another's place and identifying with our experiences? Are we verbally and nonverbally communicating our experience of one another?

6. In terms of **support**, are we offering information, feedback, insight, and protection?

7. To assess our **compassion**, are we showing emotional presence by displaying warmth, affection, and kindness? As with the ancient Hebrew concept of compassion, are we turning towards one another in mercy?

8. Finally, to gauge our **consistency**, are we providing an ongoing, steady stream of resources, compassion, and physical, emotional, and cognitive presence for one another? (Kahn, 1996, p. 164)

These eight characteristics are pertinent to our framing of a basecamp environment by providing a means of gauging caregiving quality. For a forming or formed basecamp, a check on these characteristics can prompt course corrections when one or several are lagging. This is a practical way of raising our care and support environment to its most robust level. In the mutuality of a secure base environment, imagine the power of three to five people bringing these qualities to a gathering, a basecamp fire circle, or a vocational covenant group. These are often the missing gifts in relational life and the reason why more and more people confess to an aloneness on the front line. We are hungering for what we call a robust hospitality. This hospitality gives welcome and comfort, but it also allows tension and discomfort to be in the room. Without such a base, it is difficult to impossible to face and follow through effectively on the fulfillment of one's quest.

The importance and need of social support for individual development is more acute than ever due to the increase in situations that trigger potentially debilitating anxiety. The provision of an environment that calms, appreciates, understands, and helps is essential for regaining equilibrium (Kahn, 2001, p. 260). If individual development requires the gradual strengthening of capacity to handle environmental challenges, we need a different conversation around the matters of self-care and leader-care in organizations.

We also need a reframing of human resources in organizations as the provision of an overall secure base from which people can work and live more sustainably. Debra Rowland portrays every organization as a container wherein containment leadership makes the difference, especially in leading change. Containment leadership is "acting as a non-anxious container for others, strong and secure enough to hold and guide us through difficult emotions and painful transition, while not taking over. This is one of the most precious roles we can take on for another human being, or human system. It demands us to be present. It calls on our compassion. It brings out our dignity. It can also bring out the depths in us as we learn to confront our own insecurity and darkest fears. It is a transforming and generous act" (Rowling, 2017, pp. 146, 147).

Holding and containment leadership can be helpful or hurtful. The research of William Kahn provides a fascinating portrayal of the conditions that either facilitate the creation or threaten the effectiveness of any holding environment. At our website, **basecampenviro.com**, we have provided several basecamp

Chapter Four   The Basecamp Backstory

resources for your reference and use. You will find there a table outlining the holding behaviors that help or hinder the shelters to which people, caught in storms, find their way (Kahn, 2001, p. 268). The irony at an organizational and personal level is that when such environments are most needed is often when they are most difficult to create and sustain; times of high stress, disequilibrium, and anxiety (Kahn, 2001, p. 273). These observations are pertinent to our basecamp formation because of the present challenges for leaders in complexity, stress, ambiguity, role confusion, and increasing expectations.

The great need for many leaders is finding "functional relational systems" that have the potential to contain and assist all members, offering lifelines that they can grab and then be pulled into shore by others not as intimately involved in the anxiety-arousing situation (Kahn, 1998, p. 42). Every leader needs the provision of anchoring relationships in which co-workers, teammates, managers, and employees create a space for appropriate relational work to occur. This space is the wonderful provision of both survival in the storm but also the prompts and prods for us to thrive and return home at the end of the day in one peace.

A small digression is in order here as most of you think I meant to say we return home in one piece. After giving a talk on Living in Peace several years ago and making a play on the phrase of 'living in one peace,' a wonderful artist, Linda Rempel, made an artistic representation of this phrase by placing it in a window box with these words suspended on the inside. It is a great memory of a kind gesture and her way of capturing a unique way of being in the world. It is a good thing to be in one piece at the end of our day, but it is qualitatively different to be in one peace. We all want to keep it together, but what does it mean to be kept together by a presence and power not our own? I leave this as a point to ponder.

A former hostage negotiator turned author, George Kohlrieser, has recently provided a concise portrayal of the power and promise of secure base relationships within organizations. In *Care to Dare: Unleashing Astonishing Potential Through Secure Base Leadership*, he calls for the shaping of highly developmental environments where daring is meshed with caring (Kohlrieser et al., 2012). The highest potential environments give optimum attention to both challenge and support, and this kind of secure base produces optimum results developmentally. In our web site, **basecampenviro.com**, we have provided Kohlrieser's full portrayal of the characteristics of the secure base environment. Once again, these characteristics of secure base behaviors can be utilized in a forming or formed basecamp to gauge the quality of both our caring and daring while together.

> *Can you imagine a place where a group of*
> *friends or colleagues evidenced,*
> *staying calm, accepting one another,*
> *seeing potential, listening / inquiring,*
> *providing a clear message, focusing forward,*
> *encouraging risk taking, inspiring*
> *intrinsic motivation, and signaling accessibility?*
> *These are the secure base qualities that*
> *blend caring with daring.*
> Summation of Kohlrieser's Care to Dare

Kohlrieser's work is a robust picture for a basecamp environment. For some who read his work, there may be a sense of going soft with a focus on the "care" dimension. However, the "care to dare" is what makes the full picture so elegant. Caring is foundational to daring. Dare is the robust and consistent challenge needed for taking on life's quests. Care is the support, resourcing, and encouragement needed for keeping on in life's quests. Whenever a dare is bold and sourced in peers who care deeply, we receive and respond in exponential ways. These qualities make for a great basecamp, but they also apply to good parenting, effective supervision of employees, shaping a great team, and leading any enterprise that wants to be a great place for people to flourish and succeed. These two overarching characteristics, caring and daring, are directly applicable to basecamp inhabitants in terms of what we each bring to our circle. Caring with daring envisions a circle dance of relational richness. These qualities can also be utilized by a basecamp group to gauge the presence or absence of these qualities and to make necessary course corrections. At times a basecamp can lean into caring at the expense of daring. At other times we can lean into daring without the provision of caring. The wonder is in keeping an elegant tension between the two.

Chapter Four   The Basecamp Backstory

In the final coverage of the basecamp backstory, we are providing other conceptual phrases and metaphorical frames that seek to capture the richness of the secure base. These portrayals are the hope-filled depictions of life-giving relationships. This is what is at the heart of the Manifesto. We are surrounded by much that invites us to surrender and give up. What we need are invitations to triumph and carry on. This is the basecamp invitation. In the words of Sydney Girard, "Every day we issue unique and powerful invitations to one another. Invitations to triumph or surrender, to live or to die." The Basecamp Manifesto is an invitation to live and triumph by finding, shaping, and nurturing our secure base for a better life and stronger leadership.

The Secure Base – AKA

What follows are other conceptual frameworks synonymous to the secure base concept:

Circles of Trust – For educator Parker Palmer, circles of trust are needed more than ever due to the erosion and diminishment of trustworthy environments. Loss of trust is endemic in the "scrambled" reality where misinformation, disinformation, and outright propaganda fill the airwaves. A circle of trust is needed to provide a greater and better measure of truthful interaction and perspective (Palmer, 2004, p. 73). Palmer adds, "The relationships in such a group are not pushy but patient; they are not confrontational; they are filled not with expectations and demands but with abiding faith in the reality of wisdom and in each person's capacity to learn from it. This way of being together, in the words of the poet Rumi is a promise, 'a circle of lovely, quiet people who become the ring on my finger'" (Palmer, 2004, p. 59).

Communities of Practice – The settings bearing this depiction are groups of people who share a concern, a set of challenges, or a passion about a topic, and who deepen their knowledge and expertise in this area by interacting on an ongoing basis (Wenger, 2002, p. 4). Such communities are a specific type of social structure with a very specific purpose, and their application to the basecamp community is of great value. The definition of community that guides these guild-like structures is that "such community involves a limited number of people in a somewhat restricted space or network held together by shared

57

understandings and a sense of obligation. Relationships are close, often intimate, and usually face to face. Individuals are bound together by affective or emotional ties rather than a perception of individual self-interest. There is a 'we-ness' in a community of practice, one is a member" (Bender, 1982, p. 8).

Ecosystems of Potential – In wrestling with how we realize greater potential in life, Shawn Achor, in *Big Potential*, puts forward the need to, intentionally and carefully, shape our ecosystem of potential. After a decade of research, he challenges leaders with this maxim, "We can be exceptional, we just can't be this alone" (Achor, 2018, p. 68). What we need is a constellation of positive, authentic influencers who support each other, reinforce each other, and make each other better. Achor's work can serve as a rich resource for any formed or forming basecamp. The book frames how to create a virtuous cycle of potential by planting SEEDS in our life. The first seed is SURROUND, or the people and system around us. In the words of John Wooden, the legendary NCAA basketball coach, "The main ingredient of stardom is the rest of the team" (Achor, 2018, p. 84).

Developmental Sanctuaries – Another portrayal of a group of committed peers is a psychosocial environment that holds or fuses those in the group while also letting them go or allowing them to differentiate from one another. Such "developmental sanctuaries" offer a place to belong, a space for one's whole self, a rest from the results-driven work world, and an opportunity to pay attention to personal thoughts and feelings in the company of others who understand (Hodgetts, 1996, p. 299).

Home & Crew – In the most recent work of Robert Kegan, *An Everyone Culture*, the image of home is employed to capture the secure base dimension in the mix of developmental settings (Kegan & Lahey, 2016, p. 108). In the overall equation of development, home is linked to "edge" and "groove." We will not develop without an "edge," or aspirational challenge. We will not develop well without a "groove," or sense of clear developmental practices. The home is the environment of developmental communities where we find our crew. This equation is based in the prior calculus of Kegan in his pioneering work on adult development in the early 1980s (Kegan, 1982). At that time, he portrayed the holding environment and secure base concepts by framing the adult development journey as our movement through "cultures of embeddedness" (Kegan, 1982, p.

257). Such cultures occur across our entire life course and are hopefully present to hold the person for a time in equilibrium, supporting and releasing us as we grow. Our most intimate and impactful culture is obviously "home."

Lifeline Relationships – *Who's got your back?* This is the title of Keith Ferrazzi's book and his call for every business leader to be able to clearly identify their lifeline relationships. These lifelines are mindset-directed peers who bring generosity, vulnerability, candor, and accountability to your life and work (Ferrazzi, 2009, p. 41). His challenge is to build our own inner circle who can help us identify what success truly means, gauge our focus and long-term plans, and assess the most robust strategies for moving ahead. Such relationships are also needed to help us examine and identify what we need to stop doing to move forward in our lives, and to be the people who can help us sustain the changes needed to transform our lives from good to great (Ferrazzi, 2009, p. 29).

Musters – We referenced earlier the work of John Bowlby on the secure base as applied to soldiers in war. He framed the idea of the "muster" as the soldier's haven for support and security. Jocko Willink and Leif Babin, have more recently authored two books, *Extreme Ownership* and *The Dichotomy of Leadership*, to call leaders to the highest levels of development, and for them the "muster" is also in view. Their final word in the *Dichotomy* work captures their motivation, "We have learned that leadership is the most important thing on the battlefield – the crucial factor in whether a team succeeds or fails" (Willink & Babin, 2018, p. 293). Wanting more than a rah-rah, feel-good book and follow-up with seminars and podcasts, they called leaders to a "muster." In the military, muster is the term for calling together troops for inspection in preparation for battle. Their musters were formed for leaders willing to engage in a humbling and brutally honest look at themselves and where they could improve in their personal and professional lives (Willink & Babin, 2018, p. 294).

Resonant Relationships – In *Resonant Leadership*, Richard Boyatzis and Annie McKee put forth a mirroring of the secure base through the idea of resonant relationships. They characterized such relationships as evidencing hope, mindfulness, and compassion. Their observation is that most leadership settings potentially diminish these qualities through what is termed "the sacrifice syndrome" (Boyatzis & McKee, 2005, pp. 62, 207). Many leaders sacrifice hope, mindfulness, and compassion for survival in the middle of the fray. One of the critical factors in combating this syndrome is finding "resonant relationships," or settings of support where there are others who bring hope, mindfulness, and compassion to a relational environment. These relationships are a life-giving resource and a contrast to dissonant relationships that can arise in times of stress and challenge. Dissonant relationships reflect environments that have become overwhelmed by relentless stress absent fresh infusions of hope, mindfulness, and compassion.

Safe Havens – Meryl Louis puts forward the need for well-bounded places of safety for leaders that can serve as protected spaces during stressful situations. Safe havens have both individual and organizational implications as they serve as islands of calm in the stormy seas of work and life (Louis, 1996, p. 225). A cove of interaction is far better than a cave of isolation. What we need are coves not caves. We need a safe harbor from which we can then sail the vast seas of influence. Amy Edmondson, who was named by Bill George as one of the top leadership influencers in 2024, writes and speaks as a champion for the psychologically safe work environment. Her main premise is that our hunger for psychologically safe environments is greater than ever. Her research also makes clear the difference this safety makes to productivity, creativity, and engagement (Edmondson, 2019). In contexts where fear abounds, her hope is that safe contexts and places of trust and support, can become fearless. Her premise is that such psychological safety will serve as the foundation of robust relational systems and prove the difference between engaged and disengaged people in the workplace.

Sanctuary –Lance Secretan proposes that we need much more as leaders than information troughs from which to feed; we need sacred communities of shared values or sanctuaries. "A sanctuary is not a place; it is an attitude, a state of mind, a set of shared values among people. A sanctuary is a safe environment. We may not be able to change the world around us, but we can change ourselves. In this way, though the world around us may be crazy or dangerous, in the sanctuary of our sacred relationships we are secure. A sanctuary is like a shield, repelling the toxicity around us. Sanctuaries are formed by groups of like-minded individuals who meet, share values, love and trust one another, and safely tell the truth among themselves. They trust and respect one another and enjoy a common code. A sanctuary is a holy relationship, an association where we give reverence to the people and things within it. It is a group of people connected by their souls, among whom a sacred code is practiced, and members live in grace, serving and honoring one another" (Secretan, 2004, p. 29).

Scaffolding Relationships – The image of scaffolding relationships came out of a frank admission by Rosabeth Moss Kanter in her work, *Think Outside the Building* (2020). There was a key element Kanter, and her team, had not factored into their model for "advanced leadership." It was the peer group. The safe setting of a few peers processing learning and experience is what provided the scaffolding to bring together the other factors of development they had framed. Their model involved bridges or people who carry us over the gaps in our work: clubs or informal settings and gatherings, and ashrams or intensive teaching and learning environments. Their surprise was where these bridges, clubs, and ashrams found enrichment. It was in peer group conversations and interactions. Kanter confessed, "We missed the sheer magnitude of the overwhelming importance of the peer group or primary group on its way to being a major reference group" (Kanter, 2020, p. 77). Scaffolding relationships made the difference.

This has been a chapter loaded with background theory and concepts. It is important for the simple reason that it gives a robust foundation upon which a secure base can be framed and built. This is not a concept pulled out of the air. It has roots in recent history and finds confirmation in ancient tradition. We are wired, created, and designed to function and thrive in community. So, whether we appeal to the last six to seven decades of research into parent–child attachment, the rich ancient traditions of guilds, or the military use of musters, the conceptual trail is rich and abundant. For our purposes we continue with the rich picture of a basecamp, the secure base from which we can venture out and more fully take on our life and leadership. The gifts we give and receive in our encampment are of great value. To these gifts we now turn over the next five chapters.

Around the Fire

In the five chapters to follow we have provided some prompts for a "campfire" conversation through the image above. Researchers have discovered campfire gatherings to be fascinating environments for better health and engagement. If we gather around an actual fire or even have a big-screen TV with a crackling fire, the sight and sound has a calming therapeutic effect, acts as a de-stressor, and results in lower blood pressure. The researchers on campfire influence propose "we defray the costs of the social brain through fireside relaxation." (Lynn, 2014, p. 984). In a forming or formed basecamp, we could build a fire and gather around it or use the screen version. Simply make sure to have the sound up as this was found in the research to be a key to the beneficial effects of gathering around a fire. The sound and sight of a bubbling stream or trees being blown by a good wind have the same effect, so we have options.

Looking Ahead
Chapters Five to Nine

The Basecamp Advantages

- Sharpening Our Clarity
- Improving Our Agility
- Strengthening Our Durability
- Heightening Our Generativity

THE BASECAMP ADVANTAGES

CHAPTER FIVE

Sharpening Our Clarity

*Sense making is the solitary work
of leadership, you cannot do alone!*
– Karl Weick

If we could eavesdrop on a circle of leaders discussing what they know for sure these days, what would we expect to hear? The "know for sure" zone for more and more leaders is a shrinking realm in the face of today's complex and uncertain conditions. It seems for many that certainty is scarce, and uncertainty is abundant. Making sense of it all is perhaps the greatest challenge being faced in settings small and large. As John Kay and Mervyn King posit, *Radical Uncertainty* is upon us like never before (2020). The subtitle captures the dilemma – we must make more and more decisions beyond the numbers. Uncertainty is raising our ambiguity score to astronomical proportions.

Not a day goes by for most of us, in which the questions – What is going on? What is really going on? – aren't somewhere in the air. We are grasping for clarity and simply hoping it is of better quality than guesswork. Throwing guesses at ill-defined and little-understood problems can often lead to greater and more tangled problems. But what to do? I am a leader, and I am expected to know, even the unknowable.

Sir Winston Churchill captured the dilemma well in his epic multi-volume work, *The Second World War*. His leadership experience had led him to declare, "Statesmen are not called upon only to settle easy questions, these often settle themselves. It is where the balance quivers, and the proportions are veiled in mist, that the opportunity for world-saving decisions presents itself" (Churchill, 1948, Vol 1, p. 284). This phrase, "veiled in the mist," is where leaders, especially in senior positions, find themselves. Yet, we instinctively know, it is in such mist that most important decisions and opportunities are found. Decision-making is harder than ever, and it is here where we need a shift of perspective. Since the era of World War II, a sea change has occurred in the study of decision-making. There is now a marked bend in the road. The bend is to be less in thrall with decision-making and more adept at sense-making (Drath, 1994). Sense-making and paying attention are the newest and most needed literacy, especially when the entire scene before us is more nuanced than ever before.

It is very hard to see the picture,
when you are inside the frame.
It is impossible to read the label
when you are inside the bottle.

But life, we have a problem. In a world flooded with more noise than signal, we have massive investments in more information but mounting deficits in clarity. The doctors and diagnosticians who study modern life define this malady in creative yet sobering terms. Ed Hallowell calls it, "continuous partial attention," or the steady state of mind where attention is divided, diffused, and distracted. This good doctor also puts forth the peril of our seemingly society-wide attention deficit trait called the "F-State." Our shared pseudo ADD is the state of being "frantic, frenzied, forgetful, flummoxed, frustrated, and fragmented, to name a few." For Hallowell, most of us are suffering from "a severe case of modern life" (Hallowell, 2006, p. 57).

Many of us admit to a loss of clear focus. Our field of vision is full of more horizon, but our focal vision has been diminished or damaged. Johann Hari frames this dilemma as "stolen focus," or the incessant successful attack on our attention such that something precious is being stolen from us, and not

Chapter Five   Sharpening Our Clarity

without willful and malicious intent (Hari, 2022). Life has become miles wide and inches deep and our attention and focus has suffered accordingly. Gervase Bushe speaks of "the mush" that often exists in organizational settings through the lack of good awareness, description, curiosity, and appreciation (Bushe, 2001). Instead of clear leadership clarity, the environment is mired in mush.

In the life of climbers on Everest, the basecamp is a place and time for careful reconnaissance. What do we know about the mountain? What have we learned from those who have just come down the mountain? What are the conditions anticipated in the days ahead? What is the current reality? This matter of current reality was central to the leadership philosophy of Max DePree, former CEO of Herman Miller. "The first responsibility of a leader is to define reality. The last is to say thank you. In between the two, the leader must become a servant and a debtor. That sums up the progress of the artful leader" (DePree, 1989, p. 11). Today's challenge is where and how to find help with the clarity challenge in the face of so much that keeps our current reality veiled in the mist.

Clarity Killers

In the scramble, we now face an ever-expanding world of complexity, uncertainty, and ambiguity. We find ourselves navigating *distruction*. This is a newly devised term in the Manifesto to capture the "distractions" that bring "destruction" to our work in the world. This fuzzy sense of *distruction* results from a combination of conditions that collude to make attentiveness and clarity hard to attain or maintain. However, we may also struggle with gaining clarity because the things we know for sure can form a predictability that blinds our eyes from seeing more of what's around us or ahead of us. In a world of distractions, sameness, and the increasing scramble, we sense the need to sharpen clarity on current reality, but so many of our problems sit before us ill-defined and therefore poorly perceived. The risk is we may simply trudge ahead or speed ahead not knowing where we are or where we are going. Clarity is illusive and the reasons are clear. There are forces at work that cloud and kill clarity. We look at these forces next.

The Fog of Ambiguity and Complexity

Clarity suffers whenever conditions change; our clear skies turn to clouds and then have the audacity to descend. On a clear day we can see forever but in a fog bank we can barely see the ground beneath our feet. The sunny scene of basecamp is well known from crisp depictions of the Everest landscape dotted with orange and blue tents. In the bright light of day, it looks like some sort of staging area for a clear-cut mission. Yet, more often it is enveloped in conditions that block the sun and erase the mountain from view. This challenge of diminished visibility doesn't just begin at basecamp. For those who get to basecamp, they share the trek of forty winding miles from Katmandu to the major starting point for the climb up Everest. Most tell stories of finding themselves in nasty fog banks and crossing streams that suddenly appear out of nowhere due to melting ice from somewhere they cannot see. On the way to basecamp, these will not be the last fog banks or surprise water flows encountered (Hayhurst, 1996, p. 43). Every time there are only two questions that matter. The first is, where are we? This is taking bearings for the sake of care and safety. The second is, where are we going? This is goal remembering for the sake of mission accomplishment. Both questions are vital. What happens to some in the fog is that they become stuck on the first question and lose sight of the second. This is all about the need for ongoing calibration and collaboration on a quest. We have a goal, and now in the fog and flow, we must walk more carefully but we must keep walking with our crew. The presence and perspective of fellow climbers becomes the invaluable resource as we collectively answer the two questions above.

For those of us who will never climb a mountain, we have known the experience of walking through a forest. The experience has become a metaphor we draw upon when clarity is missing in action. How many times have we declared in frustration, "I can't see the forest for the trees?" Common wisdom denotes "the trees" as the enveloping surround on every side, shadowed by canopy, leading to the sense we are deep in the woods with little idea of where we are. In the Rocky Mountains where I live, the fog is made of fir trees – tall, dense, and dark. On forest floors, all sense of the whole, or "the forest," is lost and in this place of diminished perspective and vision we can panic and end up more lost than ever. A common symptom is worry, but we can fool ourselves into thinking that even worry is a badge of hiking honor. In the trees we worry, our heart rate rises, often we panic. We have lost our sense of where we are and recognize our need to somehow get above it all.

> *The worse things are, the happier designers become.*
> *A good situation is not interesting, a bad situation is good,*
> *a terrible situation is inspirational.*
> Bruce Mau (2020, p. 90)

The only way to address this need is to get to a perspective point from where we can see the forest. Bruce Mau, a masterful design architect, notes the upside of this dilemma by noting, "being lost in the forest is the furthest extreme of creative ignorance" (Mau, 2020, p. 236). For Mau, it is lostness that opens up pockets of possibilities, but the presence, in his terms, of a "design team," is what makes the difference. We all need a place and a space where we can geolocate to gain a renewed sense of which way is east, west, north, and south. Being lost can be a strange gift, finding perspective with and through others that leads us to seeing things we could never have imagined before.

The Onslaught of Distractions

We also suffer from an ever-growing cascade of distractions. Our clarity suffers because our attention is ever being drawn away from what truly matters. We now make ourselves ever interruptible and then wonder at the end of the day why we seem to have gone nowhere. Greg McKeown frames distractions as the cataracts of the mind. Our vision becomes clouded, and our way becomes unclear. The countermove is to embrace the power of "essential intent," or making the one decision that makes a thousand other decisions easily and without hesitation. This is what his "essentialism" is all about, but the enemy is the onslaught of distractions and the absence of the disciplined pursuit of less (McKeown, 2014, p. 128).

Welcome to the world of superficial inputs. The loss and absence of meaningful solitude and deep relationships leave us with inputs that are by their very nature superficial. Bite-sized, moment by moment, prompts on what to wear, buy, eat, visit, watch, or experience hit us like confetti. These inputs hearken back to the previous words on distraction ruling the day. "These inputs distract the mind to no end, tying it down to the mere surface of thought, like a thousand Lilliputians" (Kethledge, 2017, p.xx). The deeper toll is untapped inspiration and thwarted serious thinking. Our response to these superficial inputs generates as much thought and inspiration as swatting at flies. They deaden our soul and stultify our minds. Rich inputs lead to flourishing and enrichment. Superficial inputs lead to floundering and eventual poverty.

An apt metaphor for today's distracting inputs would be invasive species that choke out rich and diverse foliage leaving only noxious weeds. In the province we now live in, it is common to travel stretches of highway and see nothing but yellow flowers covering the roadside areas. Invasives have been introduced, and they have done their work of taking over. The natural species of varied plants and grasses are left to struggle for existence or are gone entirely. The yellow chickweed rules the ditch. If we are not careful, our lives can become a cautionary tale about flourishing invasives. When inputs are dominated by mini sound bites and mindless texts or tweets, we are well on our way to superficiality on a grand scale.

Distractions and invasives are intention and attention derailers and destroyers if they are not acknowledged and mitigated. This dilemma of multiplying distractions in our world is evidenced by the number of writers raising the alarm on this front. As I write these words, I am distracted, but in a beneficial way. On my shelf are books with titles that make the case for our modern-day dilemma. Doing some work in the past year on getting the right things done, I explored numerous works on time, energy, and life management. I noted one word that kept coming up in recent titles. These works raise the alarm on our increasingly distracted existence.

> **Deep Work** – *Rules for Focused Success in a Distracted World by Cal Newport*
>
> **Driven To Distraction at Work** – *How to Focus and Be More Productive by Dr. Ed. Hallowell*
>
> **Indistractable** – *How to Control Your Attention and Choose Your Life by Nir Eyal*

Chapter Five Sharpening Our Clarity

Stolen Focus – *Why You Can't Pay Attention and How to Think Deeply Again by Johann Hari*

Crazy Busy: *Overstretched, Overbooked, and About to Snap! by Ed Hallowell*

Hyper Focus: *How to Manage Your Attention in a World of Distraction by Chris Bailey*

It is clear, we now live in a world of distractions, or in our terms, *distructions*.

You clearly get the idea that our acquired attention deficit disorder, the AADD put forward in Dr. Hallowell's work, *Crazy Busy*, is tied directly to a noisier and more distracted world. The distractions are winning, and the vital dimensions required for healthy living are ending up in the loss column. With the loss of attention on the essential, the urgent has taken over. The road we now travel is being designed with more and more lanes of traffic with more and more off-ramps, so every day becomes a crazy journey through the land of distraction.

Distraction from distraction by distraction.
T. S, Eliot, Four Quartets, Burnt Norton, Stanza III

The battle is for our attention. In a basecamp setting, a few questions to pose are, "What are we most paying attention to right now?" or, "What is filling our field of vision right now?" The power in these questions and our response are the degree to which they reveal much about our current state of mind and life. As Amy Krause Rosenthal puts it, "For anyone trying to discern what to do with their life: Pay attention to what you pay attention to. That's pretty must all the information you need" (Kleon, 2019, p. 121). In our distracted and distracting world, it is more important than ever to do regular attention checks. On Everest, you can't afford to let distractions enter your field of vision. In our own quests, we are often not as vigilant.

The rolling distractions and superficiality phenomena have also flooded our culture of quick relating. The thinking that everything in life can somehow be microwaved or fast-tracked or hacked is common. We imagine there is a way of avoiding a slow walk over the long arc of relational processing. Parker Palmer, in making his case for deliberately and carefully shaping "circles of trust," notes the contrast in so many of our current relational settings. We resemble a group of people noisily and recklessly running through a forest (Palmer, 2004). Adding to the very nature of the forest as a hard place to get one's bearings, we make it exponentially worse by quickening our pace, hoping for an easy way through and out of our confusion. The picture of Doug the Dog in the movie *Up* comes to mind. We are running around ever distracted, stopping every few meters and shouting "squirrel."

In the late 2010s, I noticed this theme of lost attention and heightening distraction not only on bookshelves but in the stories of friends and colleagues. Our shared encounters with the distraction dilemma have gone viral as we search to find our way through and out of increasing ambient noise and momentum. The Manifesto is putting forward a way through and above it all via a quieted circle of friends regularly seeking clarity in the scramble of a distracted world. Remember, it doesn't take much to lose focus these days. Our role together in a basecamp is confronting the distractions to get back to defining well our current reality. Doing wise reconnaissance as if our lives depended on it, because in a very real sense they do.

The Stupor of Sameness

Clarity can surprisingly suffer from an infatuation with sameness. If distractions pull our attention in all directions, sameness narrows the focus of our attention to a narrowed circle that blots out all else. Karen Martin, in *Clarity First*, notes her amazement as to how common lack of clarity has become in enterprises large and small. This missing clarity is the main symptom of seeking to be more of what we have always been. In her engagement with a greeting card company, the simple question, "What do you do?" brought minutes of silence and then answers soaked in "sameness." We create and sell greeting cards, with quality paper and good design. They had been doing this for years, but their business and their brand was in trouble. Martin's objective was to wake them out of a slumber of sameness and renew and refocus their clarity about what it was they truly did. In time, the team woke up to the fact that they connected people to one another in the middle of life's greatest joys and sorrows. This clarity breathed life back into a legacy company suffering from sameness. For years they had participated in the greeting card business and had become like every other greeting card company. They were at best a slight variation from all the rest (Martin, 2018).

We don't often think of sameness as a problem to clarity of thought and forward navigation. Sameness can be a great comfort, a stable place of calm in a world crazy about change. The danger is in the stupor state of being half awake or half asleep while on our quest. Rather than alertness and scanning our horizon for opportunities or danger, we narrow our sights to the ground at our feet because we know the terrain. In a basecamp setting, we are prodding one another to take little to nothing for granted. We are taking time to explore the aspects of our work and craft that have become routine and mindless. We are checking for stupor conditions and giving each other a whack on the side of the head. In sameness conditions a wake-up call can be a great gift.

If you stay doggedly at the work,
you will deceive yourself.
Leonardo da Vinci

Bruce Mau again provides fascinating insight into the nature of all endeavors in life. Every endeavor, process, strategy, brand, and innovation are like musical notes. There is the strike where the sound goes out from whatever instrument is struck or played. There is the sustain where the sound carries forward, but then there is the fade, the point where the sound is heard no more. We tend to forget everything is subject to the rule of being new, becoming familiar, and eventually being taken for granted. Nothing carries on in the way it began. Yet we think our idea or process or way of doing what we do will sustain through time with the freshness in which it began. A mutual call to ongoing clarity is a resistance move against the slumber of sameness.

Around the Fire

Right now, what is our greatest challenge? Is it, finding clarity in some area that is presently covered in fog? Is it, getting out from under the onslaught of distractions? Is it waking up from the slumber of sameness?

*A few other questions: What is **most** on our mind these days? What are we paying attention to? Where are we most stumped when we ask "What is really going on here?"*

Clarity Seeking

Clarity seeking is learning how to navigate with others through the fog and flow of reality, the siren calls of distractions, and the tyranny and drag of sameness. This entails a willingness to be a person who is truly hungry for clarity. Adam Bryant, after scores of interviews with successful and effective leaders, found a common trait: they almost all had a passionate curiosity (Bryant, 2012). They were clarity pursuers. *The Corner Office* research was conducted by Bryant to explore the perspective of leaders in corner offices. His finding matched the discoveries of Karen Martin, who defines three categories of clarity people. There are clarity pursuers, clarity avoiders, and then the clarity blind. Avoiders are of three kinds. First, deceitful avoiders are those who put self above all else. Second, strategic ambiguity avoiders are those who shun clarity so as to not have to take a side or stance. This type can be often found in the realm of politics. And third, willfully ignorant avoiders seek to skirt troubling situations or ever dampen the pressure to take some action. Those who are clarity blind simply choose a willful blindness to problems and represent the type of leader who buries their head in the bush (Martin, 2018). We often refer to people who stick their head in the sand as acting like an ostrich. This is not what ostriches do when afraid. They more often find a bush and hide their head in the branches. If I can't see you, you can't see me, or so they think.

Chapter Five   Sharpening Our Clarity

Clarity is the hoped-for outcome in all sense-making. Sense-making is work we often do alone, but in its best form, it is work we do in concert with others. Where are we? And where are we going? represent our crucial questions. The basecamp is a place and time for getting to high ground for clarity seeking. In the Manifesto, we layer in another metaphor for how we best give and receive the gift of clarity. It is, in a phrase, getting on the balcony with one another. If clarity is missing in our world, then some form of perspective-taking must be in play. Enter the concept of "the balcony."

> *Leadership does not begin with vision.*
> *It begins with getting people to confront*
> *the brutal facts and then,*
> *acting on the implications.*
> *One of the greatest ways to*
> *demotivate people is to*
> *ignore the brutal facts of reality*
> Jim Collins (2001, p. 89)

A few years ago, I stumbled across David McKenna's book, *Never Blink in a Hailstorm*. The title was drawn from the homespun wisdom of President Lyndon Baines Johnson, who declared, "Being a leader is like being a jackass in a Texas hailstorm, sometimes you just need to stand there and take it!" (McKenna, 2005, p. 35). McKenna's wisdom is a collection of short insights drawn from long experience of leadership in contexts of great complexity. It was this complexity that prompted a chapter titled "Never Lead Without a Balcony" (McKenna, 2005, pp. 61–71). It was his way of framing a simple yet vital discipline that every leader must develop: the discipline of taking time to discern larger movements in one's context, thoughtfully, slowly, and critically.

Ronald Heifetz and Marty Linsky echo the need for the balcony discipline in their work on adaptive leadership, *Leadership on the Line*. They point out how easy it is to get caught up and taken away by the whirl of everyday action. We get captivated and captured by the motion on the dance floor and quickly lose sense of wider movements in our context (Heifetz & Linsky, 2017, p. 51). These days, the dance floors of our lives have fog machines. At the core of adaptive leadership is this advice: if you are going to be a wise adaptive leader, you must get on the balcony ... often!

Around the Fire

Right now, how would you describe yourself? Are you a clarity pursuer, a clarity avoider, or a clarity blind person? What makes a robust pursuit of clarity challenging for you?

Clarity Intensifying

In view of our personal challenge with seeing our contexts and lives more clearly, there are two pivotal questions that move us from a solo clarity-seeking stance to the force multiplier of clarity seeking in concert with others:

- Do we have a balcony? If our answer is "yes," this is a good sign that we are clarity pursuers.
- Do we have a band of brothers or sisters who can share our balcony? If the answer is "yes," you have made a pivot towards greater clarity pursuit. If your answer is "no," then a fresh pivot is needed if you are to move to greater clarity.

In reflecting on the power of navigating from the balcony, I once proposed to a few colleagues that the regular practice of getting on the balcony *changes everything*. Some, who heard this claim, thought it was a bit over the top, so a few qualifiers were proposed. Perhaps a balcony practice *could* change everything, or *should* change everything, or *might* change everything. I realized my bold claim needed a bit more clarification. The balcony discipline, when practiced with focus and regularity, changes the way we see, make sense of, and then engage our world. This perspective-taking changes how we navigate our leadership and

Chapter Five   Sharpening Our Clarity

can extend into every nook and cranny of life. I am still of the mind that this discipline, when practiced with care, regularity, and a practical guide, literally changes everything. The greatest change is the area of enriched sense-making leading to wiser action in life.

The second question represents the personal challenge: Will we allow others to share in our perspective-taking? The basecamp or secure base is a potentially rich balcony-sharing environment and can be an intensifier for gaining perspective. It is bringing our personal balcony-musing into the light, inviting others to hear and see what we sense we have heard and seen. It is allowing a few trusted friends a full view of our life and leadership realities plus the fog, the distractions, and perhaps our state of sleepwalking through sameness. It is admitting to others that confusion reigns and clarity is needed. Someone, please, help me!

Enter the potential gift of a secure base and the power of shaping and sharing our balcony. Robert Wick provides insight into how the personal and the social weave the best tapestry for clarity. It is both personal and collective mindfulness that brings the personal within the social and then defeats the peril of mindlessness that has so inflicted our lives and society (Wick, 2014, p. 17). Mindfulness can serve as a concept synonymous with clarity. It is the state of being wide awake, present, aware, and able to focus attention on the vital. The challenge with the mindfulness fascination of late is the "what" and "how" of effective mindful attention. In other words, the mindfulness challenge requires clarity as to what our minds are to be "full" of. Ron Heifetz and Martin Linsky round out the analogy. Our balcony is above the "what" and "how" of our current dance floor. From this vantage point, we see the full extent and existence of the floor, the dancers, the musicians, the lights, the exits, the stairwells. For each of us, we inhabit a distinct and unique dance floor. Taking time to fully detail our dance floor realities gives us a fuller focus for effective versus random mindfulness.

In my own life, the balcony discipline as a life-check, work-check, and context-check has been a profound leadership practice. It has often been my greatest small win in my weekly rhythm. If you go to our website, **basecampenviro.com**, we have provided a "dance floor" guide for the three checks noted above. It is a good way of seeing the forest, getting above the scramble, and taking back our own focus and attention from a world hell-bent on stealing it away. It is also a good of seeing **our** dance floor realities from a vantage point where our attention is slowed down enough to discern the movements that matter and require our most careful attention and action. Together, the attention and action lead to a dance that has both focus and fulfillment. One without the other is like dancing on one foot. It is the practice I cannot live without, and it has changed everything. On the website we have also provided a practical how-to guide for implementing the balcony discipline into your weekly rhythm of leadership.

> *When we don't know what to do*
> *we know exactly what to do;*
> *we learn.*

For years, I have put forward the balcony discipline as essential for every leader. However, in working with the basecamp essential, a light bulb went on in terms of the secure base as a balcony-sharing opportunity. In a peer network where colleagues gather to process life and leadership, we may walk in the room having done a lot of clarity-seeking from our individual place on our balcony. In conversation, we can make our personal and very subjective balcony muse explicit to others who can then share the view. They may be entering our fog bank, but what a gift; at our side, we have others who hear our wondering and worrying about where we are and where we are headed. This opens the potential for a second or third opinion on what might really be going on. This balcony-sharing dimension is a clarity multiplier and, in today's environment, an essential for making it through the fog and confusion that often exists in our endeavors.

Around the Fire

What for us is a balcony kind of practice or discipline? How and where do we get some sense of perspective on the bigger picture of our life and leadership?

Chapter Five   Sharpening Our Clarity

What do we sense gets in the way of our willingness to share our balcony thoughts and ideas with one another?

How would we describe to others the current state of our dance floor realities? What have some of our most recent reflections on our life and leadership revealed to us about our greatest area in need of clarity?

Our Shared Clarity Work

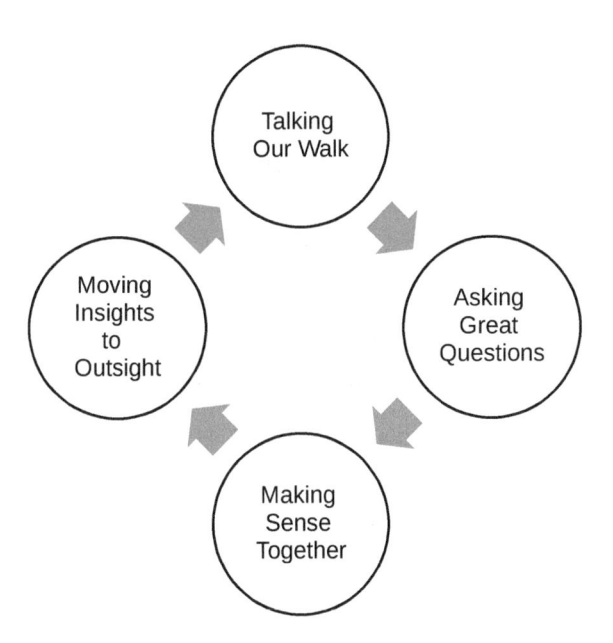

```
          Talking
          Our Walk

Moving                    Asking
Insights                  Great
to                        Questions
Outsight

          Making
          Sense
          Together
```

There are four aspects in the basecamp setting that extend the gift of clarity to those who gather on a regular basis. They are variations on a common theme. We need help with gaining better clarity. We do so by talking our walk, asking great questions, making sense together, and then moving our insight to outsight for the quest ahead.

Talking Our Walk

In our culture, we greatly honor and value those who walk their talk. If someone declares what they are in character and then shows up in the world accordingly, we know we have before us a trustworthy person. As the philosopher Seneca taught, any teacher who is not modelling what they teach, can't benefit us any more than a seasick pilot in a hurricane. All declarations absent consistent action prove meaningless. A flip on walking our talk comes from Karl Weick, the father of sense-making. For Weick, we get a better sense of our world by "talking our walk" in full view of trusted others. "To talk our walk is to be opportunistic in the best sense of the word. It is to search for words in the presence of others that tease out some sense of our current walking. This current walking is our adaptive journey for reasons that are often not clear" (Weick, 2001b, p. 120). In other words, we are fulfilling the need to complicate ourselves by making explicit what may be veiled in the mist. Why is this important? It is important because problems these days are too complex for individual minds to comprehend. When we let others hear our bumbling articulation of where we are stuck or where we are going these days, they can sometimes see the path in clearer or different ways than we can. They can act as clarity filters in our confusing scramble.

> *There ain't no use in running,*
> *if you're only running blind.*
> Randy Travis (2004)

Sometimes a country and western lyric captures the long experience of life in a single line. Randy Travis makes the point that much of life is running. Some of us are running from things, while others are running to things, but you're wasting your time and energy if you're running blind. The basecamp is a place to slow down and at times stop entirely.

Our dilemma these days is the degree to which most of us have been socialized to keep moving, go it alone, stand on our own two feet, and act as the chief and solo clarity finder. This soloing, combined with our tendency to "tunnel," a concept put forward by Dan Heath in *Upstream*, leads to a narrowed and quite limited perspective on matters that are often complex and ambiguous. The tunnelling tendency is bearing down and boring through whatever we are facing. Heath adds, "It is a terrible trap: If we can't systematically solve problems, it dooms us to stay in an endless cycle of reaction. Tunneling begets more tunneling" (Heath, 2020, p. 62). This well-established habit affects our vision because we are head down with only the ground in front of us in view. With no horizon, we see "right now" and remain blind to any "after now" possibilities.

This has also been called "the spotlight effect." This effect is our tendency to quickly place the spotlight on our problem and then direct the spotlight on our quick fix while the rest of the room goes dark. We miss signals and signs in the room of perhaps a different take or way of dealing with our conundrum. From this "enlightened" place, decisions are made, actions taken, often with dire consequences, all for a lack of a second or third opinion. The beauty of a basecamp is the prompt of others to tilt the spotlight, to make it more mobile, to consider other ideas or paths. Making better sense of life and leadership is imperative in every setting, and it is magnified when the "share" is encouraged *or* dampened down when the "share" is missing.

It is vital to note that this sharing work is not relieving one another from our front-line work. It is "pointing, as with a finger to a vein in the mine, and to let each one dig for himself" (Lowney, 2003, p. 115). This is a concept that Loyola, the founder of the Jesuit order in the 1600s, intuitively grasped and what every competent therapist or coach or personal developer of people understands about self-discovery. It is also what every quality manager understands about motivation: the switches are on the inside. Talking our walk fuels wiser understanding, clearer attention, and more effective action on our next moves. Thinking out loud with a few trusted friends is qualitatively different than the faux friend sphere of casual friendships or the shallows of social media.

Asking Great Questions

The only way to better clarity is through wiser inquiry. Wiser inquiry is not based in throwing out answers. It is best based in asking better questions. In a basecamp we are learning to track together. Leonard Sweet and Michael Beck, in *Contextual Intelligence*, make the point, "tracking requires community … every context has a scenius, which is shorthand for the 'genius of the scene.'" They note, visual artist, Brian Eno coined this term to refer to "the intuition of a whole cultural scene. Scenius is the communal form of the concept of genius" (Sweet & Beck, 2020, p. 137.) The cultivation of contextual intelligence is less the effort of a heroic solo leader and more the work of a community.

However, most of our upbringing, schooling, and socialization in business has shaped us to see through solo eyes and silo-hardened lenses. We are lured into the goal of being a "genius" but have little sense of what it means to be engaged in "scenius." So, we observe, interpret, and intervene solo hoping to be recognized as a genius. It rarely happens because when we are solo, we lack the multiplier effect of others. As Sweet and Beck conclude, "Observation without conversation issues in a deprivation of innovation and fosters nothing but a motivation for conservation" (2020, p. 137). Sounds like a motivational fridge magnet, but it carries a world of insight into the weave needed for fostering human connection that leads to clarity.

The greatest tool for opening the scene is the use of great questions. Not nice questions or good questions, but great questions. It has been said, the difference between a great question and a good question is the difference between lightning and a lightning bug. Our challenge is our relative inexperience in knowing how to ask great questions. My leadership philosophy was heavily weighted toward the leader as the bringer of answers. Followers ask questions; leaders produce answers. This is a faulty view of leadership, and beyond heroic in a scrambled world. Questions that are more beautiful are like a stick in a campfire; when the embers are glowing, a simple poke stirs up the flames.

Great questions are also called the crown jewels of mentoring as they prompt insight rather than provide basic information. Any question that solicits information gets information. Our pressing need in the scramble is insight, which is qualitatively different than garnering more data. *A More Beautiful Question*, as Warren Berger writes, "is an ambitious yet actionable question that can begin to shift the way we perceive or think about something, and that might serve as a catalyst to bring about change" (Berger, 2014, p. 8). Some of the most valuable work a basecamp gathering can engage in is to frame our own most beautiful questions. On our website, **basecampenviro.com**, we have provided a set of campfire questions that can serve as a beginning resource for framing our own set of great questions. Reading together the work of Berger or taking time with Michael Marquardt's work, *Leading with Questions* (2005), can also inform and inspire this work. Getting to better clarity is often a search for ways through the fog; great questions can stir the flames, create more light, and hopefully dissipate the fog.

A set of simple but great questions can also open up the scene of our individual lives and leadership. A basecamp can place in the middle of conversation *the experience cube*. The experience cube, developed by Gervase Bushe, draws upon four simple questions. In full view of others, we can process the following: In our current context of life and leadership, 1) What are we observing? 2) What do we think about what we are observing? 3) What do we feel about what we are seeing and thinking? 4) What do we ultimately want to see as a good outcome? (Bushe, 2010, p. 73). These questions help us to clarify our experiences in the presence of others and, in Bushe's words, clear away the mush. Once again, we have provided an overview on **basecampenviro.com** of the cube and the four aspects of what we are doing in this simple exchange. We are doing something that is rare in most circles of conversation and in settings of work and business. We are caring enough to ask more than two questions. Dan Allender notes how "psycholinguist, those who study how we talk with each other, tell us that it is rare for a person to ask more than two meaningful questions of another person, especially it that person is in distress" (Allender, 2006, p. 113). Taking the risk of more than two questions, increases the possibility for the clouds to lift and the high level of angst we feel in ambiguity and uncertainty to be tempered. Struggling well with great questions is one of the best gifts we can exchange in our basecamp setting.

Making Sense Together

In doctoral research I conducted in the early 2000s, I came across a surprising discovery around the greatest contribution made in, what at the time I called, a "peer cluster." For people who had spent several years engaging with a small cohort of peers, they were asked the question, "What were a few of the greatest gifts you received from your circle of peers?" The number one response was "making sense" of things or, to use the more common phrase in the research, "sense-making." This was a surprise because the people interviewed were all a part of a leadership development program or system that touted their focus as "developing you as a leader." None of the leadership development systems mentioned sense making in any of their promotional material. The surprising gift turned out to be the gain of better clarity. Their almost unanimous discovery was that being a better leader was not possible without the shared work of sense-making.

The greatest gain in these committed and consistent gatherings was receiving added perspective on matters that confused or confounded these leaders. What made this added perspective possible was the "ground truth" that these peers, working in a similar vocation, shared. Ground truth, a phrase coined by the US Army, refers to the complex reality of authentic experience, as opposed to generalities, theoretical models, and official pronouncements. In the army, ground truth is what soldiers encounter on the ground, in a real battle, in the full fray of a military operation. In our organizations, we learn ground truth in our daily work and in the actual hard decisions made in solving a problem, serving a customer, handling our promotions or demotions. Some of these ground truths are working practices; some are values and norms in real-world situations; some are pressures and crises that heat up the crucible of our lives and leadership (Cohen & Prusak, 2001, p. 62). The provision of some place and time for this truth to be shared was and is a great gift.

> *Discovery consists of seeing what everyone else has seen and thinking what nobody else has thought.*
> Albert von Szent-Gyorgi

Ground truth captures the idea that soldiers get it; that is, they get what it is like to be in combat, face an enemy, be under fire, and feel all that is felt in such conditions. When peers share ground truth, they grasp what is being said about a given situation without having to hear all the details. It is this ground truth that needs to be shared far more than is presently being experienced by many in higher levels of leadership. For most of us, our ground truth is our hidden, and private reserve of sight and sense-making. Uncertainty in such a reserve breeds stress, and for this reason, we are ever scrambling to find clarity. Alone, clarity becomes elusive. In a basecamp, the elusiveness can fade if we invite and allow others to share our sight and sense.

It is important to remember that the secure base environment and experience is not about getting to certainty. Realistically, it is about seeing as much as we can, knowing we will never see it all. What a secure base then provides is a kind of multiplier effect. To what we see is added what others see. They can

Chapter Five   Sharpening Our Clarity

see with us because they share a degree of the "ground truth" in our industry or calling. Another set of eyes and ears can add further insight to the nagging question we all wrestle with, "what is really going on here"?

Sense-making is a vast field of study and well worth the time and energy to explore. We do it all the time but seldom use this term to describe our moment-by-moment way finding. In a basecamp, we are doing one form of sense-making. This is reflecting with others after-action or before-action to gain clarity about what has happened or to gain better sense as to what might happen ahead. There is another form of sense-making that is during-action, and this is a different aspect of observing, interpreting, and intervening as events unfold in real time. The basecamp is of most value for the after-, before-, sense-making process. However, this sense-making process and practice translates into sharpening our skills for during-action reflection.

Karl Weick refers to the entire process of sense making as the legitimization of doubt. With decades of research and experience with sense-making, he reminds us, "Successful sense making is more likely when people stay in motion, have a direction, look closely, update often, and converse candidly. People need to act in order to discover what they face, they need to talk in order to discover what they think, and they need to feel in order to discover what it means. The 'saying' involves action and animation, the 'seeing' involves directed observation, the 'thinking' involves the updating of previous thinking, and the 'we' that makes all of this happen takes the form of candid dialogue that mixes together trust, trustworthiness, and self-respect" (Weick, 2001a, pp. 96–97). There is no better summary of sense-making in a basecamp than these ninety-seven words.

Moving Insights to Outsights

The purpose in talking our walk, asking great questions, and making sense together is to help us move forward. Clarifying our thinking is a good thing, but it proves meaningless absent action. What we are doing through our clarity work is deepening insights that can lead to enriched and focused outsight. I first came across this word "outsight" through the writing of Lewis Smedes. He framed insight as the power to see potential reality inside what already is, while outsight is seeing a reality beyond the reality we see and touch. In a word, it is "hope." "With outsight we see beyond the way things are to the way things

87

ought to be: beyond present misery to future joy, beyond present pain to future healing, beyond present evil to future good, beyond present problems to future possibilities" (Smedes, 1998, p. 16). It is this outsight that directs our next steps.

Taking what we gain as an insight is turned outward towards possibilities and innovative directions. The goal of reflection is to frame forward action. It is turning insight into outsight. In a later chapter, we will tackle in detail how our secure base relationships help with a hope-based presence and practice by heightening our generativity. We do not engage in wiser and more effective work in our world without clarity. If clarity is seeing through messes and contradictions, seeing futures that others cannot see, finding a viable direction to proceed to see hope on the other side of trouble, and then our mutual goal is to become better noticers, better questioners, and better sense-makers for one another (Johansen, 2009, p. 32).

Around the Fire

When it comes to "talking our walk," we are simply telling our story. What is a brief story of our journey in recent days that captures what we have been going through?

When it comes to "asking great questions," we often struggle with what to ask. In the resources section of **basecampenviro.com**, *there are some campfire questions. Which one's would we like to be asked more often?*

When it comes to "making sense together," what is one circumstance or situation that we need help making sense of?

When it comes to "moving insight to outsight," what is one area in our life in need of hope and some sense of how to practically move forward?

In practical terms, how do my secure base mates help with clarity and perspective-taking? We might think in general terms of encouragement, a few points of insight or advice, perhaps a few well-placed questions that clear away some fog for a moment or two. The deeper gains are confusion processing, insight gaining, focus renewing, and next-action wisdom. Perhaps at our best, we get to a place where we gain some clarity about, what my friend Jungle Jim Hunter calls, the WIN Principle: **W**hat's **I**mportant **N**ow?

Hearkening back to mountain climbers in the fog, what are we to do when the fog rolls in? We don't stop; we keep moving but we do so differently. We slow down, we anchor well to our surrounding crew members, we raise our question asking skills, we note more carefully our path and our periphery, and we take our next steps with care and hope. A basecamp is by its nature a reduced speed zone. The slower pace of conversing and thinking about the conditions being wrestled with allows us to discover deeper insight and hope-filled outsight. This is all in the service of our quest. Absent such opportunities, we can freeze in place or trudge ahead at full speed, at higher risk, and most often, the quest suffers or is threatened; all for a lack of slowing down our attention in the presence of trusted others.

The Clarity Advantage

- The increasing ambiguity and complexity of life and leadership heightens the necessity for greater clarity.
- Clarity is not the same thing as certainty. Certainty is not possible in most of today's adaptive challenges.
- Talking our walk, in view of trusted peers, is to open ourselves to multiplied perspective.
- Every basecamp is a balcony environment where we bring our individual balcony musing into the light for others to see, hear, and challenge.
- Great questions are far more valuable than brilliant answers.
- We must remember that sense-making is that solitary activity we cannot do alone.
- Tracking in concert with our basecamp is doing wise reconnaissance that deepens our insight and focuses our outsight.
- Every quest requires greater clarity.

CHAPTER SIX

Improving Our Agility

He who would travel happily must travel light.
Antoine de Saint Exupery Wind, Sand and Stars, p. 122

Todd watched as Erin, his nine-year old son, prepared for another day. Like a hiker heading to the trail head, Erin focused on filling his backpack with the essentials that would get him through his day. His prized possession was a new camouflaged green and brown canvas backpack with cavern-like features. The inside had pockets and pouches with hooks and slots. The outside pockets and side loops granted additional carry capacity when the cavern was full. As an amateur scholastic backpacker, Erin had yet to discover the full carrying potential of his prized possession.

For Todd, this school-boy ritual had begun to signal for him a mirror image of his own life at thirty-five. He too was a carrier. His backpack, however, was unseen, and the contents were kept under careful wraps. Most days, the carrying capacity was maximized. Todd knew that recently the weight seemed to be increasing. At a personal level, he carried the keys to life – car keys, house keys, boat keys, and vacation home keys – but he also carried the debt for all. At a broader level, he carried the marching orders for success, and the weight seemed to be growing exponentially. One of his tricks for all of this was to utilize the add-on features of the backpack of his soul. These capacities, in recent days, were things like "midnight oil" and tapping adrenaline reserves. He also reached for more energy drinks and a few unnamed substances that, for a time, seemed to help him feel invincible. Little Erin would return at the end of the day with a bit of a kink in his neck but leave his backpack at the front door. But Big Todd would end his day with his backpack still in tow but invisible to those around him. They couldn't see the load, but they increasingly felt the ripple effect of a laboring and overburdened husband and father. Todd was living with the disturbing awareness of miscalculation. Miscalculating his abilities while also miscalculating the relentlessness of life's add on capacity. Rolling over in bed had become more challenging of late. The lumpy, noisy, and overcrowded backpack made it so.

Every leader who walks out the door in the morning senses the carry. Call it responsibility or routine or the race to the top, it all leads to something being carried. On our quest, we hope we are agile and carrying only the essentials, but a few moments of reflection raise concern that agility has been waning of late and there seems to be a lot more on board than is necessary. However, there is more to the loads we carry than routines or our race to the top, and it this "more" that requires honest attention. The "more" has to do with the totality of what life brings. Life, it turns out, is additive. We add and add, or others add in bits and bytes, daily or weekly or monthly, and we don't notice the heavier burden until our knees buckle, back muscles fire, or our nerves shatter. As any day hiker or extreme hiker will tell us, it isn't the load that brings us down, it's the overload. The danger of our present moment is how the overload is stealth like; it sneaks up on us and so often catches us unaware.

Agility Threats

In the early years of my leadership journey, I came across the insightful teaching and motivation of Denis Waitely. In *The Psychology of Winning*, he noted how most of us are "POWs." Over time, we become prisoners of ways, worries, wounds, words, wants, wishes, and on and on. We become captured and burdened by these Ws, and we walk out the door every morning with a load on board (Waitely, 1986, p. 26). The difference from an actual prison is the unawareness of our incarceration. The camp, the cells, and the bars are invisible, but we are still captive. We carry our worries, tucked carefully away in some

Chapter Six   Improving Our Agility

hidden region of our being. We carry words, spoken by family members, or friends, or foes, and sometimes their weight is a joy, at other times the words are heavy and heartbreaking. We wear the prison garb of wounds, unable or unwilling to let them go, and in time these wounds metastasize, and our entire body keeps score (Mate, 2014). Turns out we cannot separate our psychology from our physiology.

Without awareness and stock-taking, we multiply the danger of this imprisonment and unexamined carrying. We become prisoners and purveyors of more and more. As carriers, we need perspective, but where and how do we assess the full measure of our life load? The Basecamp Manifesto frames the secure base environment as a robust yet gracious place for weighing all that we are carrying. A safe place to add it up, look in the backpack, and get real about the full measure of load and overload. In a secure base, we can take time to remind one another of the vital equation of our weight to energy differential. We all have a quest. We also have a limited supply of energy. If our weight bearing is excessive due to all that we are carrying, then the quest is compromised. On most days, we end up feeling done by noon. Our weight to energy differential tells us there is no more terrain to cover. The honest processing of current carrying is something a great many people have never experienced. For most of us, we get on the scale with the bathroom door closed and we keep the number to ourselves. In our basecamp, we open our door, point to our number, and ask for wisdom and counsel from trusted peers on how to better manage the load and realize greater agility.

In *The Things They Carried*, Tim O'Brien provides a distant mirror for today's overload dilemma. With soldiers in view from the Vietnam War, his story unfolds a kind of meditation on war, with one question posed to veterans on all sides, "What did you carry?" (O'Brien, 2009). The question was simple, but the repeated queries brought deeper insight into what soldiers fully carried in combat. It was more than the obvious, visible things. The heaviest cargo was internal, emotional, and historical. Like these hardened veterans of war, it may be truer now more than ever that most of us, like them, are only three queries away from tears.

This question, "What do you carry?" would prove to be a fascinating exercise for any vocation. For the police officer, educator, health practitioner, politician, carpenter, salesperson, pastor, technician, entertainer, or pilot, the surface load would easily flow out first. Upon deeper reflection, every vocation would surface deeper and weightier matters. What are we to do with this load-carrying and the challenge of bearing well what is essential, while also dealing with other loads we must let go of? The tragedy for many is the lack of any safe relational base for such assessment towards lightening. In military terms, the muster, or what we are describing as a secure base, is essential to facing and processing the full measure of the load of life. Every vocation needs help with pack lightening. It may be the myth of self-care as solo work has won the day. That our own load management should be done in the confines of our basement office after the family has gone to bed? It could be that such myths prompt us to simply trudge on as best we can, but much of the load remains.

In *Breaking Free*, David Noer tells the story of a supervisor who had served as a marine commander. From time to time, he would tell David that he had another rock for his backpack (Noer, 1997, p. 59). One day he realized his boss was using the metaphor from his US Navy Seal training wherein training involved the constant companion of a backpack that would be loaded with rocks to strengthen the soldier for the real thing in combat. "Another rock" was Noer's perfect expression for what happens every day to leaders and change agents. There always seems to be another rock that is added by a boss or our own hands. Over time, the pack becomes heavier than we can bear. For Noer, it is in settings with like-hearted people where we best do the vital work of pack lightening. In his words, "Pack lightening is a communal activity. Individuals cannot empty their own packs. If we are to lead productive lives and help our organizations cope with change and transition, we need to forge organizational cultures where it is not only an acceptable practice but a required activity to engage in mutual pack lightening" (Noer, 1997, p. 62). We will get to this wonderful provision in a bit, but first we will link this dilemma to the experience of agility and lightness of being.

Packing for a trip is an exercise in values clarification.
Belden Lane, Backpacking with the Saints, p. 87

What does this have to do with agility? Ever noticed how differently you feel and move when you are at your optimum weight. My tipping point is at fifteen pounds over my ideal weight of two hundred and five pounds. It is at the upper limit that problems multiply – a touchy back, stiffer and sorer knees, a diminishment of well-being, and the loss of a skip or two in my step. These are my agility warning signs that tell me I am carrying extra load on my physical frame. If a simple physical reality can do this, imagine what happens when we carry more mentally, emotionally, and relationally. When our work world complexities add up and sit next to our increased personal world issues and challenges, there is a soul-level weight gain. Add to this a macro or external world load that comes from a globe in crisis, incessant drive-by-shoutings from the chaotic human weather of social media, ramped up political and ideological contempt, and a myriad of other rocks from our wider world, we have the makings of weighed-down life where it becomes harder to move let alone be agile and light on one's feet.

In my own season of "the deep sigh" referenced earlier, I took little stock of all that I was carrying in that moment of my journey. Looking back, I now see the additive nature of my life taking a toll that eventually led to bringing me down. The backpack of my soul was crammed with past hurts, personal demons, leadership expectations from self and others, performance drivers, and a host of internal messages that morphed into life sentences to do more, do better, keep on, and hold the environment as perfectly as possible. My own lack of a secure base at the time further increased the load as I had no one, other than a counselor friend, to wake me up to all that had gone on and was furiously going on inside my weary soul. I was almost too tired to even make the cry, "Someone, please help me." Lacking a secure base, I experienced lowered agility and with that an increased inability to help others.

Pack lightening is a communal activity.
David Noer

We need help with the equation of life and the necessity of traveling with greater agility. Every one of us is a living system equation, and none of us get exemption from this calculus of life. This equation is a reminder of our daily challenge to retain enough energy and slack to be creative while also having enough reserve in the event of emergencies. This equation was popularized by Dr. Richard Swenson in his work, *Margin* (1992). As a medical doctor, Swenson found himself in the early 1990s noticing more and more patients evidencing symptoms of illness that seemed to have roots in something other than a virus or a physiological malfunction. The roots, he observed, were tied to the decrease and deficiency in margin. When people were carrying more load in life than they had resources to manage that load, the negative margin that resulted was leading to breakdown in physical health. Some people were habitually in negative margin and the living system equation kicked in, telling them it was time to stop, adjust the load, find resources, and recover.

Around the Fire

A basecamp conversation can be ignited by a series of simple questions? First, **what are we carrying right now?** *Get on the scale, open the backpack, take stock, and provide one another a sense of the inventory of contents, discontents, responsibilities, concerns, and the Ws mentioned earlier. Second,* **when do we know we are in or near the danger zone** *of overload? My warning signals are not yours. Your signals may be very different from mine. This awareness is a step toward better self-awareness. We all have signals and warning lights that may have been ignored in the past but can be life savers in the future. Third,* **how is our current weight-bearing affecting our quest?** *Remember, the quest requires focus, energy, stamina, and a lightness of soul. If our weight to energy differential is skewed by excessive load, recognize the toll taken on quest fulfillment.*

Climbers on Everest do not, will not, carry excess weight. What they carry is essential and what they might like to carry must stay in the tent. The three questions above are a way of honestly acknowledging the reality of overload and the indicators of negative margin. It can also be an encouraging indicator that positive margin is also a reality, and remembering the difference between the two states becomes a helpful reference point for reading our own gauges in a better way. We can also explore our mode of operation in our red zones. What do we do when we are in overload? What can we sense we can do differently to reduce load and/or increase resources? How is our overload state linked to how we play our hunger games and deal with the temptations of life? These are all option-thinking skills that make our load awareness and management more astute. The conversation zone is where learning and wisdom can be gained for the path ahead. We can also remind one another that our quest pursuit absolutely requires a higher agility factor.

So, What Do We Carry?

In my season of "the deep sigh" referenced earlier, I spent a lot of time reading up on the puzzles of leading well and the conundrums of being in a leadership position. Light bulbs flashed on through the work of Daryl Conner. I was struggling with how to get a handle on the bundle of weight I was carrying on the inside. His titles may have been the draw. Anyone writing about *Managing at The Speed of Change* and *Leading at The Edge of Chaos* must have been reading my mail. Taking the prediction of Alvin Toffler that our future would be one of future shock, framed as the constant and overwhelming experience of never-ending change, Conner noted, future shock usually occurs because of the aggregate impact of three domains: our micro, organizational, and macro worlds (Conner, 1992). These three domains gave me a way to see the pieces of my overloaded backpack and a practical way for assessing the load I was carrying.

```
        Our Close-to-
         Home World

  Our Wider            Our Work
   World                World
```

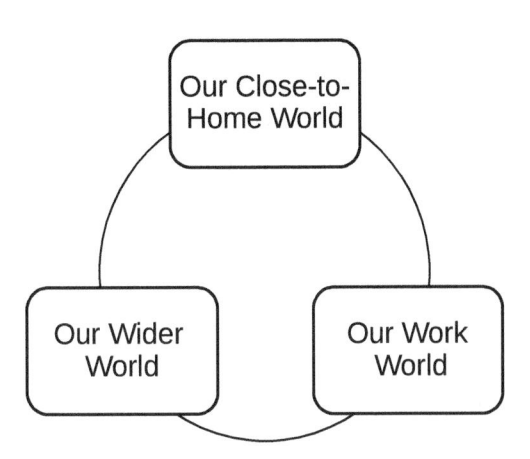

For the Manifesto, we are adapting these domains as our close-to-home world, our work world, and our wider world. We have added a fourth dimension:

our internal world where the influence of the other three worlds goes to dwell. This final world, the internal world, will be covered in the chapter to follow.

Our Close-to-Home World

First, we are all carrying things from the micro world of our close-to-home reality. Think of everything that is in our close-to-home world, and you have a multifaceted array of people whose burdens, causes, circumstances, dreams, and crises that end up in our arms and in our hearts. We think about them, worry about them, and step in to care for them in times of need and distress. This is part of our life load, and it is important that we care about it. This caring is what makes human community so rich and essential. Without such care, we are all alone and life is unlivable. Yet, this carrying dimension requires time, energy, resources, plus physical, mental, and emotional strength. None of these are infinite or inexhaustible, and when the load exceeds our resources, this micro world can bring us to a point of overload and dangerous burnout.

Our close-to-home world is ever in flux. The load we carry is not some dour burden but often sits in our hands and hearts as a joy, an honor, and a sweet part of life's gift and responsibility. Yet, load is load, and at times, the home front brings a heavy rock or two that involves heartache, trauma, or adversity that must be borne. The load at times becomes too much and we feel the weight. Yet, our wider world of work prefers this home world to be left at home. As much as employers want an unburdened worker, everyone walks in the door with a load on their back and mud on their shoes. They may want their employees to carry the organizational vision with 100 percent of their energy, but the meter is already reading less than this as they lock their car and walk in the front door of their workplace.

In the early 2000s, I found myself journeying with my wife Deb, two teenage boys, a growing career with exponentially expanding responsibilities, and an aging father and mother. My father was more than a decade into his journey with Parkinson's disease, and I was the only Young in town to help with the physical, emotional, and familial drama as it unfolded. For the space of a few years, I had added shifts helping my father get into bed at night and assisting him on many mornings to get ready for his day. Looking back, I now know why I felt a weariness that defied explanation or description. I was carrying more load in my micro world than ever, while also packing along more load from the other domains of my life. On top of this, I had no place to open the backpack in the presence of trusted friends. I lacked any perspective or prompt during this time to help me assess my overall load or find some added resources. I was a solo carrier, on a quest, trudging uphill some days while losing ground on most other days.

When was the last time you paused to see the full sweep of your close-to-home world? To sit with the simple question, "what am I carrying these days" in my family and relational world? We may be carrying all of this well or we might note added strain and stress in need of attention. This is the work of self-awareness and opening the pack in the presence of trusted others could bring valuable insight and shared wisdom, since all our base mates share this challenge.

Around the Fire

Let's take some time to unpack together what we are carrying from our close-to-home world. How has the load increased recently? What have we learned about keeping the close-to-home world in clear view and avoiding the temptation to avoid, neglect, or run away from some of these responsibilities? What are some resources we have found help with the load on the home front?

Our Work World

Our micro world of family and friends is the close-to-home world that we all encounter and seek to honor. But there is more. We also carry the things of our organizational or work world. Thinking on this domain, we can fill a page or two of roles, responsibilities, goals, problems, and the scramble in our work environment. The additive and subtractive nature of work responsibilities occurs weekly. Yet, we sense far more additions than subtractions. The boss rarely pops his head in the door to ask if there is anything he can take off our shoulders. So, the load waxes and wanes but wax seems to win over the long term, and we bear these loads while also bringing the close-to-home load with us when we walk in the door every morning. This was Henry Ford's frustration in the early 1900s as he brought the automobile to the common citizen through the innovative system of the assembly line. He was known to have exclaimed, "All I want are two hands, but instead the whole person walks in the door." We never walk in the door with just two hands. We bring with us a home, kids, bills, illnesses, and minds preoccupied with realities having nothing to do with our organizational life.

We want to receive our paycheck, but for some, according to Jeffrey Pfeffer, more and more people are dying for that paycheck. Ominously, Pfeffer writes of this in a literal way as the work and organizational worlds become increasingly complex, ambiguous, and toxic for their human occupants (Pfeffer, 2018). We also have a work world that measures productivity as visible activity. In the words of Malissa Clark, we can then end up *Never Not Working* (Clark, 2024). Our ever-on culture invades our work life, and, in her terms, this is bad for business and life. Our front-line world can be ever on and in flux. For this reason, mindfulness on this front is essential.

When we took time in chapter five with the shared work of sharpening clarity, we presented the balcony discipline as a game changer when engaged in with regularity. In the resource section of our website, **basecampenviro.com,** there is an overview of the balcony discipline and a resource on *Questions for Gaining Perspective on our Dance Floor Realities.* An important aspect of our dance floor realities are these four context check questions.

- What are my roles?
- What are my major objectives and goals in the near and far term?
- Who am I responsible to encourage, equip, and lead?
- What is on the near and then distant horizon that I need to think about?

A regular take on these questions can sharply focus our present thinking and future action on load, specifically what is most important to carry and then what needs to be let go of. We want to carry our work world with efficiency and effectiveness. A mindless or careless approach only leads to trouble.

When was the last time you paused to see the full sweep of your work world? To sit with the simple question, "what am I carrying these days" in my career or vocation? A regular balcony discipline focused on this dimension of life is

Chapter Six   Improving Our Agility

quite revealing but it can also be a lifesaver by providing perspective for much wiser priority setting. It can also give insight into how and where our margin has diminished and what may be the next wise move for decreasing current load or increasing future resources to gain healthier margin. It might be we are carrying all of this well or we may note added strain and stress in need of attention. This is the work of self-awareness and opening the pack in the presence of trusted others to bring valuable insight and shared wisdom, since once again, our base mates share this challenge.

Around the Fire

What are we carrying these days from our work world? How has the load increased lately and what resources can help us better manage this load? What have we learned about managing more wisely the demands of our work world?

Our Wider World

The overall load we carry, it turns out, is a bundled lot, and there is even more. Added to the two domains of home and work is a third source of load: the macro world of our surroundings, the goings-on of our community, city, country, and world. We are citizens of a wider world, and this world bumps us, strikes us, and often jumps into the backpack of our soul. The macro world heaviness is aided and compounded by the 24/7 surveillance of suffering that comes via news and social media. If we choose to do so, our windows to the wider world can now be constantly open to take it all in. The angst, anger, and, at times, awfulness of events thousands of miles away add to the weight that we carry in our souls.

This third domain affected our margin equation in a way unprecedented in recent history. From the early days of 2020 to the later months of 2022, the three worlds of home, work, and wider world merged in ways never experienced before. In normal times, our wider world stood at a distance from our home and work world. With COVID-19, racial controversy, political polarization, economic uncertainty, and the shared experience of chronophobia (fear of the passage of time where no end appears in sight), all these wider world storms had direct bearing on home and work life. This had a unique wider world impact across the globe. In a pre-COVID 2020 world, we took in events that were episodic and came at us from time to time. We took on the load of such events, but we were able to bracket them and handle them as we handle a day or two of bad weather. The left-hand depiction is pre-COVID, and the right-hand portrayal shows the mesh of what we carried in the time of COVID and perhaps beyond.

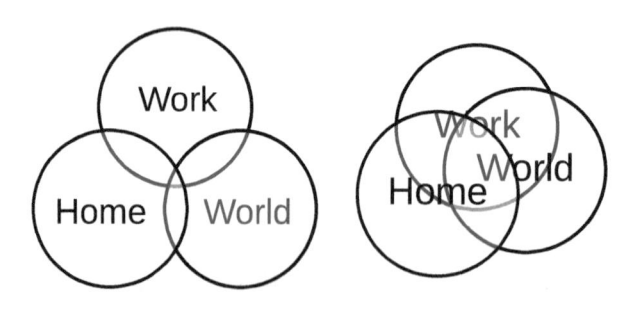

The COVID storm of 2020 and beyond had an event structure unlike anything in our past. We found ourselves in a total reframing of how work intersected home and to add to the complexity, how the macro world collided with our work world. This disruption came home to our dwellings where we used to find sanctuary from the wider world and our workday world. An updated observation of Jeremy Rifkin reminds us, the experience of the 2020's was not new, but it was a greatly intensified form of confusion and disorder on our watch.

Each day we awoke to a world that appeared more confused and disordered than the one we left the night before. Every time we thought we'd found a way out of a crisis, something backfired. The powers that be continued to address the problems at hand with solutions that created even greater problems than the ones they were meant to solve.
Jeremy Rifkin (1980, p. 3)

Chapter Six   Improving Our Agility

This complex mesh fractured everything. It brought divides to work teams, families, congregations, organizations, and communities. It did not create new-found elements of fractured attention or decreased agility; it simply supercharged what was already there (Hari, 2022, p. 272). COVID was a reminder that a crisis does not create newfound capacities and capabilities; it only reveals what was already present, only more so. The shared life experience of COVID has given us greater literacy on how load intersects and interacts, but it also explains what most of us felt: a level of weariness, anxiety, and complexity that was both new and strange.

Around the Fire

What do we find ourselves carrying from our wider world? What has been added lately and how is this affecting us? How much of this wider world load can we control or change? What are we learning about handling a world on fire with more volatility and uncertainty?

Improving Our Agility

Alone, we face a dilemma in increasing our agility and improving our margin equation. A little objectivity is possible; total objectivity is impossible. As much as we might try, subjectivity and self-protection blind us from what is really going on. Add to this, the human tendency and proficiency to ever live in a state of denial wherein our sense of current reality becomes stunted. To admit that we are in an unhealthy place of overload is to many an admission of weakness or failure. The word on the street is, "Strong leaders and good leaders handle overload; they aren't taken down by it." This is living by denial. Living as if the law of gravity doesn't apply to us, we trudge ahead, but gravity still does its thing. The living systems principle of margin is our gravity. All the denial in the world leaves its force unchanged, and in the end, it always wins. We may also suffer from a kind of unreflective pessimism. Our previous attempts to move into a more balanced or healthy life have proved difficult to impossible so why bother now.

In the words of Dan Heath, we just keep tunneling. "This is a terrible trap. If you can't systematically solve problems, it dooms you to stay in the endless cycle of reactions. Tunneling begets tunneling" (Heath, 2020, p. 62). We put our head down and bore through whatever is in front of us, hoping for a breakthrough that never comes. We also experience the sacrifice syndrome that stems from our ignoring, denying, or pretending that we can live with constant sacrifices without let up. In time, this syndrome manifests itself in the breakdown of the body's immune system and results in an increased susceptibility to genetic predispositions. The power and peril of chronic stress is now confirmed in the field of medicine and psychology. Overload is not to be trifled with (Boyatzis & McKee, 2005, p. 52).

As the years of my life have rolled along, I have come to a brilliant conclusion, I only have so much energy. With good training and disciplines, I can improve and increase my energy store, but there are still limits to human endurance. For this reason, becoming a wiser and stronger carrier is crucial. We can only use so much energy and only do so much work. We must steward this with much greater care. As we will see in the chapter to come on the gift of durability, we can help one another in our basecamp to grow in our ability to carry more. Jim Hayhurst, in *The Right Mountain*, telling his story of climbing Everest admits, at first, we can't carry our sixty-pound load. This is why sherpas step in and hoist one-hundred-pound bundles of our stuff on their shoulders as if they were filled with nothing but air. But later we can carry more because we have become acclimatized and become stronger from the carry of the lesser load (Hayhurst, 1996, p. 56).

Our basecamp challenge to one another is to learn how to expend energy wisely and on the essential, and to not expend energy on the non-essential, the unimportant, and the residual. We can provide the promise of both light and listening, frank analysis, resource surfacing, and creativity on load lightening. We must also remind one another of the additive nature of our lives. The peril of additive living is, over time, the adding of more to what we carry without any gatekeeping or filtering. Before we know it, the backpack is full, the add-on features used up, and we wonder why our life has become a slog.

Chapter Six   Improving Our Agility

The critical question for a basecamp gathering is, "How can we meaningfully help one another towards greater agility?" Traveling light is more than a nice saying or aspiration. It is a vital piece in taking on our quests in life. If we are habitually or chronically overloaded, the quest suffers. So, what do we do with the loads we carry? First, we get honest about them with our secure base colleagues. We gather around the fire and talk our walk as it relates to the backpack. Second, we wrestle together with where to find the needed resources to address the load. The way to positive margin is not complicated; we must reduce load or increase resources *or* do both. The basecamp setting is the mutual outworking of this journey towards better agility. The longer-term goal is in helping one another navigate the margin equation wisely over the long term.

The basecamp can be that safe place for encouraging, resourcing, and inspiring one another to travel light. Let's not forget how our base condition either exacerbates the peril of a life in negative margin. How we are based can reduce or produce agility. A barren base brings no help other than self-help. A pseudo base offers a faux hand up in the pack-lightening work of life. A shallow base leaves us alone at the very moment we most need help and then shows up when we are carrying the load of life with ease. The contested base climbs on our back and makes things worse. The Basecamp Manifesto is setting forth the proposition that we discover our greatest help and hope in a world of overload when in the presence of a secure base that prompts us to find and fuel greater agility.

The Agility Advantage

- Every basecamp is a weigh station where we can bring into the light the full measure of what we are carrying.

- The human systems equation wherein load minus resource equals margin cannot be ignored. It applies to everyone and everything in life.

- We must remember, load lightening is best done as a communal activity.

- Exposing all that we are carrying in view of trusted peers is to open oneself to multiplied wisdom on decreasing load and/or increasing resources.

- Every quest requires an awareness and honoring of the load to energy differential equation.
- Agility is essential for any sustainable and successful quest. If we are overloaded without adjustment or change, we will eventually be overtaken by weariness and breakdown.

CHAPTER SEVEN

The Deep Threat to Agility

There are many things we carry well out of sight.
These things have a special kind of weight.
They are often the heaviest things in the backpack of life.

T. C. Young

Todd, the thirty-five-year-old backpack carrying dad we met in the previous chapter was never not carrying the three domains of his family, work, and wider world. In addition, he was carrying the added weight of things carefully housed in his internal world. This stealth-like "other" dimension was formed in large part by his interactions and encounters with home, work, and world. Todd's internal world was where his life experiences, voices, recorded scripts, and inner doubts went to dwell and then exercise powerful guidance and control. We are Todd. All of us know, our outside world has a way of entering our inside world forming a kind of chamber of never-ending mental and emotional loops. The experiences, voices, scripts, and doubts of life accumulate and add weight at the heart level. If we could frame a "bearing score" or metric for the weight of these inner loads, we would be astounded as to their effect upon our lightness and agility. Our agility can be affected by the things we carry from our external world, but the deeper threat to our agility comes from what we carry on the inside, well out of sight of others.

The internal load of life is unseen by others, but it is intimately known by each carrier. We all have a public theater of operations, but with this we also have what Manfred Kets deVries frames as our "inner theater" (Kets de Vries, 2006, p. 11). Our inner theater is the noisy and sometimes messy place well known to us but invisible to people around us. It is a crowded space of experiences, voices, scripts, expectations, and dialogue accumulated in our growing-up years and along our life course. The marvel is the stealthy nature of this theatre in the deep recesses of our soul and mind. We carry it all, but no one sees any of it directly. They only see the outworking of behaviors, emotions, and attitudes, while the origin of this outworking remains a mystery. How we show up in the world is largely the manifestation of what is really going on in our hidden world.

How often have you observed someone's actions or bizarre behavior and wondered, what in the world is going on? What is most often going on is the inside showing up on the outside. The dilemma is, we have little to no idea as to what is behind the public stage performance. If we knew the depth and weight and darkness of their internal load, we would most likely take a different tack than criticism or foreboding. For all of us, there is far more going on than meets the eye, though what meets the eye is directly linked to what is going on in our internal world. Our noisy and crowded theater of life experiences, inner voices, memorized scripts, and wardrobes of doubt and shame are simply making themselves known in ways that surprise even us as the actor.

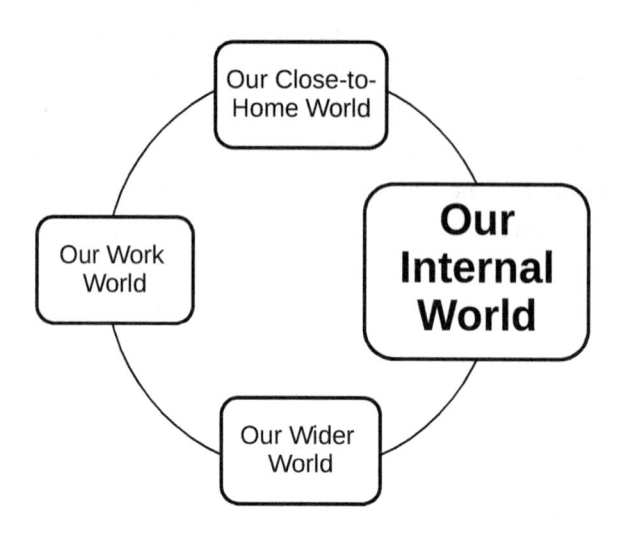

Chapter Seven   The Deep Threat to Agility

When it comes to agility or lack thereof, the premise of the Basecamp Manifesto is that our lack of lightness has to do with matters on the surface but also matters well out of sight to others. The hidden load, like so many tennis balls in our hot tub, require precious energy to keep under the water, lest others see what is really going on beneath the surface. The heaviest things in life are ever matters at the soul level. Street-level load is one thing, but soul level is where our most important work needs to be done. But where do we go to face and process the out-of-sight dimensions of our inner world? What do we do with this "inner theater" that we know exists but keep locked up from public viewing?

Tending to the outer things is easier, and perhaps that is why we gravitate to the loads we can share with others in response to the question, "How are you?" The internal loads are much trickier because most of this load is learned, absorbed, deeply embedded, and kept under lock and key. We more easily talk about how hectic it is with kids, family, and friends. We quickly note the craziness of our work world. We don't hesitate, chiming in with opinions on the flow of political vitriol and world angst that is on our screen's moment by moment. Our friends, however, would cringe if we exposed the raging rapids of our inner dialogue and the inside turmoil we are rafting through. In most relational settings, we have an unspoken rule, "Let's keep things at the gently flowing stream level. No one needs to know about our level four rapids." We pull out our TMI card, too much information, when someone breaks this rule. So, we conclude the inner theater is for private showings, and there is one person with a ticket, slumped in the middle of row eight, and we can guess who that is.

Our internal world is a theater filled with all that any play or Broadway production brings to life. The drama centers around life experiences, the heaviness of things done to us or not done for us. The voices represent all that has been said to us and about us. Scripts have then been written and represent the lines we have memorized. They are the burden of "life sentences" we have come to adopt and follow. The deep thematic thread in our theatrical plot line is often centered around doubt and shame, the nagging sense that we do not have what it takes. The heaviness of this doubt comes from our own conclusions, the imagined conclusions of others, and assumed conclusions about us from the wider culture.

Opening our inner theater to a caring core is a potential life-changer. It is also frightening. Unlocking the door for a tour through our inner theater involves turning the house lights up for others to see what to date has been hidden in the shadows. The Basecamp Manifesto puts forth that an honest acknowledgement of these heaviest of loads is vital for a life of agility. The path to greater agility and the wonder of travelling light is found in sharing these experiences, voices, scripts, and doubts with a band of trusted friends. We believe that when a secure base relationship becomes a reality, we grant one another the potential for much greater agility. But first, we need a deeper dive into the load of our internal world. The portrayal to follow is a way to capture the makeup of our inner theater.

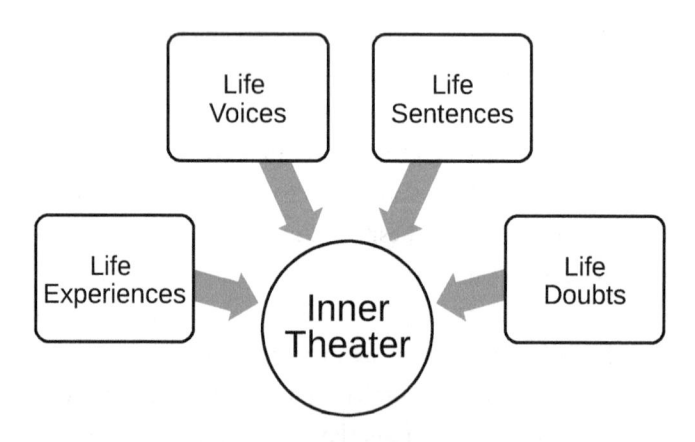

The Experiences of Life

In the realm of our internal world, we have the experiences of our life-long journey. The triumphs, tragedies, and traumas are given home. Our experiences are both delightful and disruptive; some are life quakes while others are transformational. The best way for a basecamp gathering to share the trajectory of life experiences is to take the time to shape a decadal storyline. If you have never shaped your storyline, we have provided an example of a decadal story-line guide and a link to a few resources for doing this work at **basecampenviro.com**. It is a way to capture our stories, noting the good, the bad, and the ugly sprinkled through our personal narratives. We all carry internal residue of past adversity, suffering, and trauma. We also carry rich deposits of blessing, affirmation, and triumph. Who we are on the inside is in large part the mix and mesh of life experiences. Getting this story down for our own sake, and to then hold it out for others to see and hear becomes a wonderful way to turn up the lights in our inner theater.

A healthy balance in sharing life experience is to talk about the experiences of both triumph and trauma. Trauma can become a fixed condition whereby the wounding's of life can become the master story we tell ourselves about ourselves and others. Trauma strikes us and even enters our bodies, and we are not taught about what to do with the residual of negative life experience. In the space of fifteen minutes, we could fill a page with what trauma and adversity we have experienced. Triumph on the other hand is also formative and should have more play than is often give in our inner theatre. We have victories, accomplishments, and blessings, but these seem to have less stage time. This may be due to the characteristic inherent in humankind that bad is stronger than good, the negative has more draw than the positive. This is strange, but all we need to do is watch the news to see the proof of this human tendency. We need a way of balancing perspective on our life experiences.

Around the Fire

Take a page, draw a line down the middle, and on one side record our consolation experiences. Consolation experiences are those experiences that have been the good deposits into who and where we are. On the other side, detail the desolations. Desolations are the dark valleys, seasons, events that have made their marks on our memory such that even the recall brings pain, guilt, or anger.

In our lifetime, what is one difficult and one delightful life experience we remember from each decade of our life to the present day? How have these experiences shaped our life?

What can we do with this record? What do we often do? Remember, we are more often drawn to adversities than to advantages. We must learn to walk together down the middle of our page or through the decades of our life, looking both ways and taking time to honor and give thanks for the consolations and then be honest and thoughtful around the desolations. Whenever I have led a group of people through a storyline exercise the deepest growth and development has almost always been found in the disruptions, the dark places, and the life quakes within people's stories. The telling was painful and difficult but in time people almost always noted the advantage in their disadvantage. It was Booker T. Washington in his work, *Up From Slavery*, who coined the phrase "the advantage of disadvantage." His insight on life was that when we sit on our cushions of advantage, we fall asleep, but when we experience disadvantage, we wake up, move, learn, and endure. This is perspective-taking on life experience in a wise way among trusted friends. It is also much better than rehearsing our story alone in the middle seat of row eight.

Let's remember, the common life bases we portrayed in the early pages of the Manifesto provide little to no help with processing our life experiences. Barren, shallow, pseudo, and contested base conditions have little time or interest in hearing our life story. So, we are left to brood, bottle, and then manifest our behavior rules for managing or mitigating the fall out of our histories (David, 2016). The basecamp can be a wonderful gift as we tell our stories and turn our ruminations about our life experiences into reflections for future growth. In the presence of care and challenge, we may experience the first provision of a healing conversation that allows the experiences to be seen in the full light of day. In the telling and then gracious listening of trusted friends, we can process our stories in a way that can lighten the weight of experiences that have, for too long, been given place and power over our lives. It can also be a prompt for us to draw more fully from the consolations within our story that can serve as resources for the road ahead.

A particular challenge with life experiences is the problem of resentment and bitterness. Most of us have had things done to us that have taken root. The rest of us simply don't want to talk about it. In the text of sacred scripture, there is a warning, "See to it that no one misses the grace of God and that no bitter root grows up to cause trouble and defile many" (Hebrews 12:15). The bitter root troubles us as individuals and left undealt with spreads the toxin to many others. Resentment is one of those conditions that also acts like a renter being given space in our head, but the renter never pays the rent. We as the landlord pay. This is where we need a loving but firm prompt by others to "let it go." This may sound like a shallow cliché, but it carries with it ancient to modern wisdom in

Chapter Seven The Deep Threat to Agility

three words. Hanging on to hurtful life experiences is a never-ending tax burden only the carrier pays. We may try to tell ourselves to let it go, but we best hear it from others. In a basecamp gathering, it comes from those who love us enough to challenge us with the necessity of lightening our load. We need someone to get in our face and space and remind us, we will never climb our mountain with the heavy weight of resentment on board. Bitterness and resentment are a special kind of burden. We cannot steward our dream while straddling a grudge. We will never achieve our quest with our feet stuck in a quagmire of resentment. We cannot keep our eye on our goals and dreams if we carry deep down an insidious preoccupation with the past.

We all carry the experiential hurts of things done that should not have been done., but our hurt may also be of a developmental nature; something was not done that should have been done. We needed the time and presence of a dad who was absorbed by work and success. At a time of need our friends were out to lunch in the crunch and left us high and dry when we needed them most. The organization told us how valuable we were and how they would support us in our career development, but the support and development help never showed up. The hurts that are developmental are voids and missing pieces that over time can fester and infect us if undealt with. Whether experiential or developmental these life experiences create memory, and memory can be a seed of bitterness taking root as resentment. Over time, such roots grow and wind their way underground, but the poisonous tree in some way grows up and out. The trouble comes personally but it also spreads relationally. A gentle yet firm prompt to "let it go" is an invitation to lighten our load to travel more freely and lightly.

Experiences accumulate as we travel our life course. Agility is not a given. The load internally from life experience can be a resource; it can also be a heavy burden. Knowing the difference and doing work in a secure base of relationships on load assessment, management, and release can bring a lightness of being for our quest. Absent such a process, we may exceed our weight to energy differential, and the pace slows, the back strains, and more deeply, the heart flags.

At an early point in my leadership journey, I found helpful perspective in a book by Gordon MacDonald, *Restoring Your Spiritual Passion*, in which he profiled seven conditions of the soul due to life experiences (1986). At the time I treated them as a personal checklist. Was I drained, dried out, distorted, devastated, disillusioned, defeated, or disheartened? These can be the toll taken by life experiences. What turned the corner for me was Gordon's chapter, "For Those Who Bring Joy." He noted how much we need loving and gracious help with the experiences we carry. I needed to find those who could bring me joy. For a time, I found such people, but as we will see, such relationships must also be nurtured and not just found. A basecamp can be a place and time for processing well and wisely the experiences and conditions of life. A specific aspect of this processing will no doubt raise the challenge of voices. There is no inner theatre without a cacophony of voices. To this dimension of deep threat to agility we now turn.

The Voices of Life

Embedded in the experiences of life are the voices of life. There is not a day that goes by that we don't hear voices. The outside theater is filled with actors, jesters, protagonists, enemies, hecklers, encouragers, and lifters. The inner theater takes these in and gives them ongoing roles in the play of our lives. There are things directly said to us and about us, and the many "you are" statements we hear often become our deeply ingrained "I am" conclusions. They can take on a life of their own and be granted a shelf life with no expiry date.

A basecamp environment can provide a safe place for sharing our respective voice remembrances and recordings. Our field of influence is full of the following voices. As with life experiences, these voices can bring consolation. They can also deliver desolation. What are we to do with these voices?

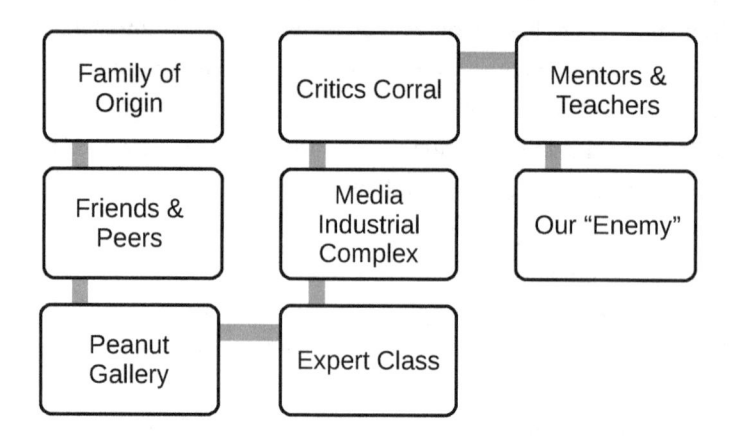

```
┌──────────────┐   ┌──────────────┐   ┌──────────────┐
│  Family of   │   │              │   │  Mentors &   │
│    Origin    │───│Critics Corral│───│   Teachers   │
└──────────────┘   └──────────────┘   └──────────────┘
       │                  │                  │
┌──────────────┐   ┌──────────────┐   ┌──────────────┐
│  Friends &   │   │    Media     │   │              │
│    Peers     │   │  Industrial  │   │ Our "Enemy"  │
│              │   │   Complex    │   │              │
└──────────────┘   └──────────────┘   └──────────────┘
       │                  │
┌──────────────┐   ┌──────────────┐
│   Peanut     │   │              │
│   Gallery    │───│ Expert Class │
└──────────────┘   └──────────────┘
```

Chapter Seven   The Deep Threat to Agility

All of us inhabit a field of influence filled with words. To give perspective on the variety of voices in our field of influence, we have identified at least eight voice localities or *vocalities* (our word) for consideration. These make up what is now called our world of polyvocality. Many voices making up the ambient din and noise of our world. Multiple voices coming at us at the same time with little let up in sight. Some of these voices bring life. At other times, these voices bring death. The stories of words, now decades old, from a father, mother, or sibling, reveals the power of now emblazoned or embedded words or phrases. At times, like a gift from on high, these words encourage us and inspire us. At other times, these words are like terrorists embedded in our neighborhood where they stealthily attack, hide, attack, and hide. You never know when the terrorist will appear and do damage, disrupting a peaceful moment in a heartbeat, by bombs or bullets in the form of hurtful and caustic words spoken decades earlier. What do we do with this contest of voices in our souls?

Some of our voices are very loud, while others are mere whispers. The volume is not as important as the source. Some voices come from people who hold huge sway, and a mere whisper can echo in the deep recesses of our memory for years. Other voices hold very little sway because we know we would never seek or care about their advice in the first place. A basecamp setting can be a safe place to surface and assess the voices we have heard and still hear. The goal is greater agility and lightening our load involves naming and releasing the weight that has come with the voices we now define and describe.

Family Voices

On any given day, we can experience the impact and effect of voices from our family of origin. We all have words that have been said to us in our growing-up years, and they still reside deep down in our souls. When my father was growing up in Boone, Iowa, my granddad as a coal miner was an old school type of father. My dad remembered him saying to him on occasion, "You'll never amount to anything." That five-word phrase stayed in my father's mind, and I believe a part of his work in the world was an attempt to prove his father wrong. What is intriguing about my father's story is how, in his teen years, he had another man in town who one day said to him, "Lowell, I think you're going to do great things in the world." It was a counter voice to the voice of his father, and, again I believe, his life became an embrace of this affirming message. Yet, his life, like ours, can be a contest between voices heard at home and other voices that bring a counter message. In my dad's case, his life was a contest between these voices. He did do great things in the world and perhaps both voices played a part. One voice drove him and the other voice called him.

The family of origin words that our fathers and mothers and brothers and sisters and aunts and uncles and grandparents say to us are immensely powerful. Sometimes they're incredibly life-giving and inspiring, but sometimes they are life-destroying and inhibiting. I remember well doing a workshop with a group of leaders in British Columbia a number of years ago, and during one of the breaks, an elderly gentlemen came up to me and said, "I've been married for sixty-plus years and not a week has gone by in which I have not had to help my wife in some way deal with the voice of her father." Her father, long ago dead, was still alive in her memory in the never-ending loop of messages she heard as a little girl.

Peer Circle Voices

We also navigate a world where friends and peers offer their voices to us in the form of the good, the bad, and the ugly. Sometimes they voice words of encouragement to take on the challenge. Sometimes they say things that seek to pull us back from what we're doing in the world. We can apply the wisdom of Jim Rohn to voices. He declared that we become like the five people we hang around with the most. This is why we must choose our friends more carefully. On the voice front, our inner voices will echo the voices of the five friends we hang around with most. A good question to ask of our friendship circle is this, "What do they put in circulation and what is the coin of their realm?" If it is grievance, negativity, criticism, or discouragement, it is time to find a new circle of friends.

The friend zone can be a rich source of encouragement and support. It can also be a disheartening zone. To be wounded in the circle of our friends is a double burden. We are not surprised when harsh or hateful words come from our enemies, but when such things come from friends, it adds a heavier load in need of careful treatment and relief.

Chapter Seven   The Deep Threat to Agility

Peanut Gallery Voices

The peanut gallery is the never-ending cacophony of voices that we find at street level or in the bleachers who seem to think they know better than we do, how to live our life. In our social media–driven world, the peanut gallery is larger than ever and represents nothing but "chaotic human weather" that now goes with us everywhere we go (Lanier, 2018, p. 2). For this gallery of voices, we need to develop much better filters to limit and mitigate their presence in our lives. Johann Hari calls for an attention rebellion whereby we take back our attention from the everywhere present attention bandits (Hari, 2022, p. 272). These forces are bent on stealing and destroying our attention and in so doing make life a kind of perpetual merry-go-round; movement going nowhere, but fooling us into thinking, "wow, what a ride." We're not spending much time focusing on these voices here and neither should you.

Critics Corral Voices

The critic's corral is populated by the voices of those who always seem to have a negative word about what we're doing, where we're headed, what we think, what we believe, and how we live. In our fully connected world, we can now find a critic in a heartbeat. This corral is made up of people who do not like you and delight in leveling their dislike via never-ending *critiquiness*. I came across this term "critiquiness'" a few years ago while reading Miroslav Volf's, *For the Life of the World*. As a professor of theology at Yale University, he noted how the critics corral has infested the supposedly pristine world of theology. He and others have noted how progressives, in particular, relish critique. They interrogate and unmask; they trouble and problematize; they expose and subvert; they demystify and destabilize (Volf, 2019, p. 54).

Hang around the world of progressive ideologues or young progressive leaders and even theologians long enough, and you will see these tendencies up close and in spades. The problem is that, as a rule, they offer no positive alternative. In the absence of a positive vision, their voices devolve to mere griping, knocking things down. Not able or willing to attract with a good vision, they attack with gross vitriol. "Their supposed unmasking gives the impression of intellectual profundity, and their griping offers the cheap thrill of understated self-righteousness. These voice characteristics are also found in the progressive side of the political divide, and the corral is now louder than ever. Change in our world, will come from 'I have a dream' speeches, not from 'I have a complaint' speeches" (Volf, 2019, pp. 54, 55).

Let's search out and find the voices of dreamers and distance ourselves from the screams of complainers. Critics have a drive to spot flaws, name failures, and blow out the candles of others. Their very existence centers on being the world's watchdogs, and they believe they are not doing their job unless they are attacking something or someone somewhere. The best reminder on this front comes from Theodore Roosevelt: "It is not the critic who counts; nor the man who points how the strong man stumbled or where the doer of deeds could have done better … far better it is to dare mighty things, to win glorious triumphs even though checkered by failure, than to rank with those poor spirits who neither enjoy nor suffer much because they live in the gray twilight that knows neither victory or defeat."

If someone likes you, you can spill hot soup in their lap, and they will still like you. If someone dislikes you, the way you hold your spoon infuriates them.

The critics of our world obsess over what is wrong. They are masters of outrage at spoon holding. Just as we will never win a puking contest with a buzzard, we will never win an argument with a critic whose mind is made up and whose arsenal of destructive critique is mindlessly unleashed. We need reminding, critics create nothing, and their voices are best kept corralled and then dispatched from our thinking. In a basecamp setting, in the time it takes to put a marshmallow on a stick for roasting, we can all repeat a recent or ancient criticism we have spinning in our minds right now. We must never let such voices roam free or add weight to our souls.

Media Industrial Complex Voices

When it comes to the newfound power of the media industrial complex, we are desperately in need of a strategy for handling the onslaught of these voices. Naomi Klein notes how almost everything in our culture is now mediated via screen. She calls this our "screen new deal." (Klein, 2020). In the past few decades, we have been embracing a vision of the future that started as a trial run but has ended up as a crash course in the perils of invasive technology. This deal is the never-off engine of our newfound polyvocality, the experience of multiple voices coming at us at the same moment in time. The result is a newfound hypervigilance resulting in raised stress levels, fragmented minds, and shattered thinking. We now live, if we choose to keep the screens open, with an ambient din, noise ever present, and voices coming from every angle vying for an ear to hear.

Taking back our attention is no small matter when the media industrial complex is hell-bent on stealing our attention. As basecamp members, we can prompt one another to join the resistance and take back our attention or "daylight." James Williams, former Google strategist, in a conversation with Johann Hari, framed the term "daylight" and our loss of it through the distractions and noise of our current culture. In framing three forms of attention, he noted how spotlight attention is needed to keep our focus on immediate conditions and actions. The second form of attention, starlight attention, is needed for maintaining our line of sight on long-term goals and purpose. Daylight attention is what makes it possible for us to sense what is really going on. It is only when a scene is flooded with light that we can see current reality most clearly. William's observation is that we have been losing our daylight through the onslaught of disruptive and distracting media technology. It is leading to a "decohering" of life (Hari, 2022, p. 265). A basecamp is a time and space for recovering our daylight.

It is an ominous turn when we stop making sense to ourselves and become obsessed with the petty and insignificant (like endless retweets of nonsense). We cannot find daylight without sustained periods or reflection and deep thought. We cannot refresh and refocus our starlight when we are on the spin wheel or captivated by the shiny lights of tiny screens. Without clear starlight and daylight, our spotlight attention gets set on random. Our basecamp can be a reminder that our resistance towards the voices of the media industrial complex is a key to taking back our life. It is also a move towards greater agility.

Expert Class Voices

The expert class is an intriguing element of the voices that we hear. We are very much beholden in our culture to those we believe are the experts. Experts are those in the know. They know better than we do. They know more than we do, but in fact, the research on those who put themselves forward as the intellectuals shows us that we should be very careful about listening to the expert class. Experts are most often area specialists with a very narrow zone of thorough knowledge. They are people who live in their system of parallel trenches. "Everyone (in the expert class) is digging deeper into their own trench and rarely stands up to look in the next trench over, even though the solution to their problem happens to reside there (Epstein, 2019, p. 13) The dilemma with today's news and media approach is how experts in one area of knowledge are featured as experts on broader issues. Their range is limited, but they are interviewed as if their wisdom is broad and final. They come out of their trench to comment on the broader field of which they know little.

David Epstein, writing on how the generalist triumphs in a specialized world, makes the case for surrounding ourselves with broad thinkers rather than the expert class. "The challenge we all face," he adds, "is how to maintain the benefit of breadth, diverse experience, interdisciplinary thinking, and delayed concentration in a world that increasingly incentivizes, even demands, hyper-specialization" (Epstein, 2019, p. 289). I have often reminded leaders to value and respect the wisdom in the room where they gather. Too often we discount our own wisdom, sensing our perspectives are merely low level or low brow compared to the rarified air of the expert class.

A more cautionary word comes from Paul Johnson. In his classic work, *Intellectuals*, he concludes by saying intellectuals should not be easily or quickly trusted. He makes this point by declaring in the final page, "A dozen people picked at random on the street are at least as likely to offer sensible views on moral and political matters as a cross-section of the intelligentsia. But I would go further. One of the principal lessons of our tragic century, which has seen so many millions of innocent lives sacrificed in schemes to improve the lot of humanity is – beware intellectuals" (Johnson, 1988, p. 342). We too easily pull up our chairs and listen to these voices without further thought. It is good to remember that a basecamp gathering is where breadth, slowed concentration, and patient conversation can yield rich wisdom and insight. There is great wisdom in our tent and around our campfire if we take time to let it emerge.

Mentor's and Teacher's Voices

Then there are the voices of mentors and teachers. For many, this can involve a positive rehearsal on the voices of our life instructors. They said things that

Chapter Seven   The Deep Threat to Agility

trained us, taught us, corrected us, and shaped us. We're very thankful for these voices in our lives and their provision of a catalyst to make us better. On a darker turn, mentors can dangerously and destructively alter a life course. Adolf Hitler in his early years wanted to be an artist, but his father's voice and the voice of his mentor turned him to a different path. Hitler's associates all agreed that Hitler revered alcoholic playwright Dietrich Eckart more than any other colleague. It would be Eckart who would greatly shape the young mind of Hitler, and antisemitic hatred and power were his major themes (Tyson, 2008). Tyson begins his work with the summation of Ernst Nolte, "To understand Nazism we must restrict ourselves to the most prominent racist writers, the central figure of which, among those surrounding Hitler, was Dietrich Eckart" (Tyson, 2008, p. 1). This is the darkest confirmation of our premise that words change worlds. Hitler would go on to send out his voice through his 1925 writings on "his struggle." It is staggering to note that for every single word in his *Mein Kampf*, seventy-five people lost their lives in the Holocaust. This should leave no doubt as to how words of a single mentor can change worlds.

Sometimes the harsh or dismissive evaluation of a teacher can put us on the path of sad and settled conclusions about who we are and what we can do. Teachers can also be world changers by granting words that give us life. In my Grade Eight year at Milton Williams Junior High, Fred Ring, who would go on to be the Principal of Western Canada High in Calgary and then a top executive of WestJet Airlines, voiced confidence in me after a failed attempt to present a simple five-minute speech. After standing to deliver my well-prepared speech on "Principles of Success," I froze in place, lips paralyzed, with tears of fear about to fall. To my chair I returned, not having shared my "Principles' that no doubt could have changed the life trajectory of that entire Grade Eight class. Fred Ring, post my humiliating failure, encouraged me and then at the end of the term exercised his full authority to grant me a high grade for the class that some students objected to because of my success speech failure. I still remember his voice. For a while, I carried a voice that whispered, "never speak in public again." But in time I remembered the affirmation of Fred that I could write a great speech, and that delivery would in time work its way out. Thankfully the whisper lost out, as I entered a vocation where speaking in public was my weekly reality and over the decades I have prepared and presented nearly three thousand times before gatherings large and small. A basecamp can be a wonderful processing environment for these voices and a place to retain and rehearse the good words while jettisoning all voices that have brought doubt or pain.

Enemy Voices

The final dimension in this portrayal of voices is the spectre of our enemy. What are the voices that oppose us? Our nemesis will be unique to our own story. It is a wise question to ask, Who or what is our nemesis? For those who follow faith traditions, the enemy is called the father of lies, the deceiver, and the accuser. For others the enemy to be named may be those seeking to drag us down and take us out. Whatever our enemy, we need to be aware of the impact of the voice of the one or one's who oppose us.

Such voices can reside at some level inside our heads and navigating them wisely is essential if we are ever to take on and realize our quest in life. In my early years of leadership, I had a mentor who one day said, "Terry, I have found in my leadership experience, the greatest tool in the arsenal of the enemy is words." His point was that these voices are never intended to help but only hurt and if we let them in, they discourage, distract, and derail us from our work in the world.

> *The human mind is a noisy*
> *parliament of competing factions.*
> Steven Pinker (2009)

Wise leaders learn how to navigate with voices. We must travel through our present, past, and long-past voices, because untreated and unchallenged, these voices add tremendous weight inside the backpack of our souls. The beauty of a basecamp environment is that we have others who can hear the voices that we've heard and may continue to hear. We can help one another check the validity and veracity of these voices. We can prod and prompt each other to embrace and amplify those voices that are true, good, and profitable. We can also help one another take the voices that have been untrue, hurtful, harmful, and destructive and to dampen their volume or mute them altogether. Our basecamp gathering also provides a chorus of different and new voices speaking a different narrative about who we are, what we're about, what we can truly do in our quest in life.

Chapter Seven   The Deep Threat to Agility

Around the Fire

Of all these voices, which one is the loudest, strongest, and most in control of our life right now? (the good or the bad) What has been said in the past that stays with us to this day? (the good and the bad) What have we heard in recent days that is reverberating in our head right now? (the good and the bad)

Whenever I have processed the power of voices with a group of leaders, or with students during my professor days, I always came away with a staggering conclusion. Words form worlds. The words of others form our personal world. We form the worlds of others by our words. Once again, the sad take is that negative is so often stronger than positive. The bad seems to drown out the good. We find it easier to remember the verbal blasts we have taken and harder to remember the blessings we have been given. This calls for much-needed help in voice management because most of life involves voices. Voice management is best done in concert with others. A basecamp gathering can be a safe place for voice processing and navigation; turning down the voices that can take us down and turning up the voices that can lift us up.

The Sentences of Life

Bringing the voices of our lives into the open for others to hear is vital for traveling lighter on the road ahead. The din of voices, when left to themselves, bounce around inside our heads, and in time become our "life sentences." Unaddressed, the voices become a kind of script that we fight with and yet follow. In a sense, we go through our days with an imagined teleprompter in front of us showing us the words said by others. Henry Cloud, from long experience of counseling and coaching leaders, notes how the scripts of life contain the lines laid down by others and how these go through a magical process of internalization (Cloud,

2016, p. 166). Our great need is to discover new material from new voices to lay down a better script. It is also the move of giving to a few trusted friends the role of editor to help us with our bad scripts. Permission given to bring out the red pen can be the pivot needed to strike from the page words too long tolerated. Such words do not leave easily or without a fight. Sometimes we need to have others help us with the red pen to delete what are often bold-faced, upper-case statements that have too long dominated our teleprompter.

Steven Zaffron and Dave Logan in *Three Laws of Performance* note the need for most of us to get out from under our "life sentences" (Zaffron, 2009, p. 151). These sentences are all the things we tell ourselves about ourselves. The sentences are often picked up or plastered on during our growing up years and then beyond. The things we tell ourselves about ourselves show up in how we think and then live. Imagine the power and potential in making these sentences explicit with a small group of basecamp friends. Such transparency would let a secure base in on how we see the world, not as it is but as we are.

We all need some good editing. We need terministic screen cleaning, and there is no cleanser better than "another" who calls it for what it is; life applied disinformation about who we really are. The hard part is in seeing how much weight these sentences place upon our souls and minds. The most negative of these things hinder and hamper movement and freedom. They are agility killers, and thus we desperately need the gift of a secure base for the processing and appropriate releasing of life scripts that weigh us down.

Strangely, we avoid the move of letting others into our inner theater to read the script by which we live. We hesitate or even hide from revealing the deep-seated to-do's and to-be's that govern our actions and reactions. Parker Palmer notes, "Everything in us cries against the inner journey." He then adds, "That is why we externalize everything. It is easier to deal with the external world. It is easier to spend your life manipulating institutions than it is dealing with your own soul. It truly is. We make institutions sound complicated and hard and rigorous, but they are a piece of cake compared to our inner workings" (Palmer, 1990, p. 5). We tend to outer things because these are easier. The first three circles of home, work, and world are easier reveals. This fourth circle of our internal world takes us beneath the external loads. A vibrant basecamp should resist the externalizing of everything and insist that honesty and transparency become the code. Revealing our cover stories won't be enough for getting to

Chapter Seven   The Deep Threat to Agility

greater agility. We must dare to go inside and lift the cover to reveal the deeper scripts in play. Our quest requires freedom from life sentences that weigh us down and keep us from traveling light.

But where do we go to lay such burdens down? I can tell you, having inhabited the halls of a university for nearly a decade, most students don't know where to go with this inner script, and so the play carries on and the memorized lines dominate their waking hours and haunt them in their sleep. For lack of a secure base, the gift of trusted friends goes unrealized, and life sentences go unchallenged and unchanged.

> *We have to tell the truth about our "life sentences" and what they are designed to hide.*
> Steve Zaffron

A sampling of life sentences has a way of helping us spot a few candidates for our secret teleprompter. Often, they are scripts on the required to-do's and to-be's if we are to be seen in the best light by everyone in our world. Some of us carry a life sentence, "I must care for everyone around me. I must be that person whose funeral tribute will be, 'He or she gave their shirt off their back and the shoes off their feet.'" Others of us have an internal prompt that says, "I must have all the answers and always be right about things. I can't be wrong or seen to be wrong." If we carry an internal script that says, "All of the wrongs in life must be righted," we will likely be the kind of person who seems ever on edge, quite angry, and driven by a resentment that defies reason. We could go on about the internal messages of "I must … be liked, be in control, be perfect, never show emotion, be ever available, prove that I am capable, or prove my father or mother wrong." These are the script samples from our inner theater, and they can be a very heavy load in the backpack of the soul. Their weight is inestimable for some and, if left unacknowledged and unaddressed, can be the weight that brings the hiker down.

We all have a tribe of internal thought vectors. We have thoughts, memories, and self-concept descriptors that stand like dominoes in our mind. Some thought vectors are more powerful and perilous than others. One sentence can take control and become dominant over our entire life. Chris Bailey wonders,

"What thought vector is the equivalent of a domino in a line of ten to twenty that once it topples over initiates a chain reaction that accomplishes great things OR demolishes possibilities and potentials?" (Bailey, 2018, p. 44). Thinking and repeated thoughts have second- and third-order consequences, yet we seldom examine the script we are following now or have been following for years. We need time for an examination of our life sentences. It can be a personal exercise, but the force multiplier is when the script is handed around a secure base of relationship. It is attending to our scripts in concert with one another.

A basecamp or secure base can be the place where we become safe enough to expose our shy souls and shed the weight of the heavy lines in our drama. Think of the impact of sharing in time our scripts, our life sentences, and the internal dialogue that drives us on most days. Think of the power in a friend who helps with much-needed editing of that life script, someone who confronts the lines in our play and proposes a re-write so we work on different and better lines to rehearse, remember, and recall in the days ahead.

Around the Fire

What are a few of our life sentences? (Good ones first, then a few of the other ones)

In recent days, where have we seen a life sentence or memorized line from our past affect your leadership?

What is a life sentence we wish we had heard more of growing up?

What is a life sentence we would like to speak to those closest to us right now?

The Doubts of Life

In 2022, I joined a cohort of people from across North America for a learning experience sponsored by the Modern Elder Academy. MEA, as it is more commonly referred to, is the brainchild of Chip Conley. After a long run of building a boutique motel brand, then serving as a board advisor at Airbnb, Conley planted a retreat center for "elders" in Baja, Mexico. His cause is that of encouraging and inspiring "elders" to live their lives fully rather than accepting the cultural default setting of sailing off into the sunset. In one of the sessions, he noted a triple threat to people in the years past fifty or sixty. As I considered this triple threat, I noted my own struggle with these threats, but I also noted how these three dilemmas are found throughout every decade of life.

The triple threat coalesces around one word, doubt. The triple threats are self-doubt, other doubt, and context doubt. Self-doubt is our struggle with who we are and why we are here. When asked, "Who are we?" many of us respond, "Not much." When asked, "Why are we here?" most of us respond, "Not sure." We doubt ourselves, and this is a threat to full living in any decade of life.

Other doubt is our imagined take on what we think other people think of us. We fear going public with what we're thinking of doing next because we're convinced shock, surprise, or cynicism will come pouring out. Other people doubt us, or so we think, and this becomes another threat to any new or ongoing endeavor in life.

Context doubt comes at us as expectations and default settings we accept from the wider world. Culturally we discover ideas and expectations that seem automatic when it comes to our life stage, whatever it may be. For those starting the second-third of life, it can take the form of thinking the whole world thinks we're too young, too inexperienced, or too aggressive. For people in the third-third of life, the culture doubt convinces us that we should think of decline rather than incline, retirement instead of refinement, settling down in a great armchair rather than setting out on a great adventure. Context doubt is a threat across our lifespan, and it stops many of us from moving forward past the doubt into a life of declared intention and dedicated service.

We have framed the final dimension of our inner theater as doubt. Doubt is often wrapped together with the peril of shame. Shame is the deep sense that we do not have what it takes to live life well. We don't have enough to endure this season or moment. Doubt and shame prompt our actions of shrinking back, going silent, or just giving up. What then follows are attempts to mask, medicate, and mitigate our sense of "not rightness." This kind of shame and doubt are more common than we think. Oprah Winfrey, after interviewing over thirty thousand famous, successful, larger-than-life personalities, made a stunning observation. Almost every one of her interviewees were still searching for validation. Some of the richest people on the planet were still thinking the price tag on their own sleeve reflected very little in terms of real value. People the masses worshipped were going around with a profound and hidden sense of low worth. It may be that doubt and shame covers our world. The hunger and search for validation is something everyone, everywhere is engaged in, and yet we seldom talk of it with others. Our struggle with this triple threat of doubts remains locked away in our inner theater.

In my work over the last decade of journeying with graduate students in an educational institution, I framed a "brand story" for our work in the professional graduate program I chaired. A brand story takes the work we do and seeks to frame an overarching narrative that can guide the work we envision. Donald Miller, in his work, *Building A Story Brand*, notes, in every story, there are main characters, a villain, some form of guide or plan to defeat the villain, and a call to action leading to a better day (Miller, 2017, p. 21). For graduate students as main characters, many were in mid-life and seeking to find a way to navigate ahead in uncharted territory. Many felt lost in familiar places. Others were in a transitional season. Most were wondering about their next chapter. Their villain, as I discerned it, was a shadowy character called doubt. A few did exude confidence upon entry, but most came wondering about who they truly were and what it was they were to do with the rest of their days. The sense of "not quite being right for the part, whatever that part was to be" was a common refrain. Validation was needed and wanted but the request was difficult to articulate. As a shadowy mood, doubt hung like a cloud. The villain was alive, cunning, and stubborn. Our aim was to be a resource and guide for dispersing the clouds of doubt and providing the freedom of hope and lightness upon graduation. In some cases, the doubt was banished. In other cases, the doubt remained. Some students engaged their future quest with a lightness of being, while others still bore the heavy load of doubt that made their quest more difficult and foreboding.

Shame can be a never-ending echo of, "I'm not right for this. I don't have what it takes. I can't measure up." This can become the story we live in. One of the most important questions we must ask ourselves is, "Which story do we believe we are living in?" Is it a story of shame or a story of freedom? The solution to moving to the lightness of freedom out of the heaviness of shame "lies ironically in doing the very thing that shame convinces us is the most dangerous, threatening act we can commit" (Thompson, 2015, p. 114). Shames remedy is vulnerability. Yet this pursuit is challenging since shame produces our hiding instinct. In our hiding we become disconnected, and this disconnection is internal as well as relational, and then "the process tends to snowball, caught in a self-perpetuating loop" (Thompson, 2015, p. 133). Shame has a way of begetting itself. As Curt Thompson describes, "We don't find ourselves shaming others loudly in the staff meeting apart from our own shame telling us we are not enough. We do no embezzle unless at some deep level we believe we are not enough without the money. We continually look at pornography in no small part as a coping mechanism for our inadequacy that long precedes it. … In all these and hundreds of other seemingly innocuous moments, shame begins with a whisper and crescendos to a roar" (Thompson, 2015, p. 130).

Hidden lives carry tremendous weight at the soul level. Vulnerability is the move that confronts shame's primary tactic, isolation. Vulnerability is coming to the place with one another where we open the door of our inner theaters, move out of our solitary seat in row eight, turn up the house lights, and then invite one another to the balcony for a time of honest conversation. Honest and frank vulnerability is about more than letting someone know we carry shame. It is coming to fully acknowledge that the deepest burden we carry is self-doubt, and this is where all the contributors to our internal world have come to focus their power and control. Life experiences are joined by life voices, then captured in our life sentences. These dimensions get twisted together and then trap us in the grips of shame, which until now, is the thing of which we do not speak. The first step toward the lightness of freedom from such things is opening the door of our inner theater to our band of trusted and trusting friends. It is important to note what this is not about, and what it is best about.

The point of opening the door to our inner theater is not:
    to obsess over the directors, actors, and extras in our play
        to replay the entire movie
            to rehash the drama of the darkest scenes
                to give the experiences and voices another showing
                    to get wrapped up in another round of grief or regret
                        to do lengthy readings from our well-worn script.

The point of opening the door to our inner theater is:
   to safely tell our stories and to find in them the good worth keeping
      to help one another release what we must let go of
         to let grief and regret be faced and felt, but also transformed
            to squeeze from our stories the lessons to be cherished
               to begin new chapters in our script.

What are we doing when we find, shape, and nurture a basecamp gathering? At the practical level, we are forming an encampment that provides reconnaissance, support, resources, and preparation for persons engaged in or anticipating an exploration or adventure. At the deepest level, we are moving to an embrace of shames remedy. We are opening the inner theater of our lives and allowing our basecamp the honor of helping us overcome the deepest threats to our agility. We are co-interpreting our stories to date, while also co-editing and co-writing a new narrative for the journey ahead.

Around the Fire

When it comes to wrestling with doubt and shame, how does this battle show up in our life and leadership?

Why do we think it is so difficult for us to come out of hiding on this front?

What should we say to one another when we declare, "I'm just not right for the part I am playing in life."

Life experiences, voices, and life sentences set patterns in how we live and navigate our journey. In the words of Chip Conley, from the Modern Elders Academy, all of us are desperately in need of "pattern interruptions." This is what we do when we sit around the fire or get up on the balcony and share our status quo. We are gathering to inspect and interpret the patterns and plots of the drama going on in our inner theater. Help and healing only come with exposure, by turning the house lights up, pulling out the scripts, the story lines, and the darker shadows of shame and self-doubt. These only receive the interruption and redirection by the presence and prompts of caring and daring friends who sensitively poke the fire or gently sit with us on the balcony of our inner theater. Such gentle presence helps us see a much wider scene and sense the deeper messages in our story that are worth keeping, while letting go of those parts worth losing.

When we presence ourselves in a secure base the lightening of our load is exponentially greater due to the caring observation plus urging by others who ask high-value questions. We need help with the cognitive load that we harbor in the form of thoughts wrapped in much self-doubt. Aaron T. Beck, the father of CBT or cognitive behavior therapy, noted a dominant story is carried when depression is on board. Our cognitive narrative circles around three lines: I am terrible, I live in a terrible world, and therefore the future looks terrible. Cognitive therapy is thought pattern disruption and redirection best done in a caring yet challenging environment. It is not our aim to simplify or thin the richness of cognitive therapy, but to propose the basecamp gathering as a form of CBT in a tent or around the campfire. We provide one another a safe place to acknowledge and address the dominant thought trails that may be leading down a path that makes us less resilient.

We must remember, perspective-taking, way finding, wise resourcing, quest preparation, and caring follow-up are the manifold gifts of the secure base environment. The quest ahead deserves care and diligence to ensure we are carrying the essentials. The non-essential also need acknowledgement, and when named should be left in the corner of the tent or in some cases be taken out to the trash. Our agility makes the difference between carrying on or crashing, moving adaptively or cramping up. In some quests, agility is a matter of life or death.

Imagine being given the gift of a secure base, wise friends who love one another enough to ask the question, "What are we carrying these days?" And then the follow-ups, "How did those things get in there?" "Are we in overload right now?" "What in the world is **that** doing in your backpack?" "How can we help?" If in serious overload, we can assist one another in finding more resources or exploring ways for decreasing our load." What would we receive if we had base partners who would wonder aloud with us about the unnecessary, unhelpful, and ungodly load of shame and guilt being carried from long ago? Agility is the essential gift that comes from circles of trust that permit our shy souls to open the door of our inner theater permitting others to gain a shared perspective. The blend of truth, grace, and patience makes traveling light a wonderful possibility. Our best quests require an agile life, mind, and soul.

The Deeper Agility Advantage

- A basecamp is a place where our story is given space and time to be heard by trusted others.
- Every basecamp is an opportunity to surface and share the most obvious and most hidden dimensions of who we are.
- The deep threat to agility can be mitigated but we must honor the shy soul. We must not go crashing through the bushes to scare out what we carry at our deepest levels.
- A basecamp is the place where we share the daily experience of hearing voices. We need help challenging these voices and in speaking into one another the fresh voice of support and belief.
- We must remember, agility can be greatly reduced by the weight of the inner load of life sentences and the deeply ingrained "I am" statements we carry.
- Every quest is threatened most by those things that are most hidden.
- Doubt and shame are villains in need of vanquishment. A secure base provides shames remedy through vulnerability with trusted and trusting friends.

CHAPTER EIGHT

Strengthening Our Durability

Resilient people run in the company of "a happy few."
Gordon MacDonald (2004, p. 198)

Resilient teams recognize they have only one major asset and that is one another.
George Danzig

A few years back, a group of researchers were curious about the power of a friend at our side. The question they asked was simple. If we are looking at a hill trying to judge how steep it is, does the mere presence of social support around us transform our perception? Their wonderful discovery was, if we look at a hill while standing next to someone, we consider to be a friend, the hill looks 10 to 20 percent less steep than if we are facing that hill alone. Their conclusion was, "Perception of our objective, physical world is transformed by including others in our pursuit of achievement. This result holds even if the friend is three feet away, facing the other direction, and silent. People presence transmits to us the sense of resources and support. So, mentally and physically, mountains seem more climbable, successes more achievable, and obstacles more surmountable with others beside us" (Schnall, 2008). As we look at our quests in life, we have good evidence that there is a vast difference in our resolve when staring at our challenge alone versus staring at it in the company of good friends.

If facing an actual mountain with others reduces the difficulty in our minds by 10 to 20 percent, what are the implications for a basecamp group boldly taking on their life and leadership challenges? The gain is real and, these days, needed more than ever. Those who are most resilient figure out how friendship, kinship, and mutual benefit partnering works for their quest in life. The dynamic of people in concert is unmistakable. Nelson Mandela captured this dynamic as he reflected on his prison experience and noted the mistake made by apartheid leaders: "They kept us together." In his autobiography, *Long Walk to Freedom*, he recalled his almost thirty years on Robben Island noting, "The authorities greatest mistake was to keep us together, for together our determination was reinforced. We supported each other and gained strength from each other. Whatever we knew, whatever we learned, we shared, and by sharing we multiplied whatever courage we had individually. That is not to say that we were alike in our responses to the hardships we suffered. Men have different capacities and react differently to stress. But the stronger ones raised up the weaker ones, and both became stronger in the process" (Mandela, 1994, p, xx)

In extreme situations, our endurance capacity is multiplied when doing so with a trusted band of brothers or sisters. As the ancient proverb of the Old Testament declares, it is iron that sharpens iron (Proverbs 27:17). There is positive friction in shared community that makes everyone better and stronger. To go solo is to remove a vital component for sharpening one's edge and raising one's endurance. Raised resilience is seldom the product of a solo endeavor to become more resilient.

Resilient people inherently know the peril of the lone ranger syndrome. In the mountain climbing world, there are occasional stories of climbers going "pure." Those who go "pure" on Everest or K-2 go into the danger zone solo and disdain the need for supplementary oxygen (Warner, 2009, p. 107). These intrepid adventurers often look down on those who use oxygen, but they are also those known as sooner lost and dead than those who climb with others and use the resources needed to survive and succeed. Anyone can take on their quest alone and go "pure." This is an option, but the possibility of enduring through is exponentially reduced.

Chapter Eight   Strengthening Our Durability

So, what does it mean to be resilient? For many of us, the resilience factor is a conundrum. Myths abound around this quality of resilience or hardiness that cause us to think it is the possession of the strong, or the blessing of a mysterious few. The fact is we all possess resilience. Ann Masten, a lifelong resilience researcher, calls resilience, "ordinary magic." The surprise of resilience research is the ordinariness of the phenomenon and how in most cases it results from basic human adaptational systems. If such systems are healthy, growth in times of trauma is more evident. If the systems are weak, then developmental problems tend to be prolonged in times of trauma (Masten, 2001).

Spend time with any group of people, hear their stories of challenge and adversity, a wonder appears. How is it that we go through deep valleys and dark alleys, and yet, here we are telling one another our stories? We got through, somehow. Not without pain or grief or scars, but we got through to the other side. Time spent in the literature and research on resiliency surfaces a common and consistent refrain: we are all resilient to a certain degree, though the degree may differ according to several key dimensions. Resilience, it turns out, is never static and can be strengthened over our life course. Resilience research also strongly supports the shaping and nurturing of a basecamp in that greater endurance is directly correlated with the strength or weakness of one's relational circle.

The Resiliency Raising Regimen

How is it that social support strengthens resiliency? A way to think on this is to consider the reverse. In extreme situations, absent social support, what do we draw upon? We draw upon our own internal stock of resources. These resources are what we have known, studied, and placed within our personal resilience portfolio. Such resources are important and may help greatly in the face of a life disruption, but if we are in the adversity over a long period of time alone, these resources may run dangerously low.

Social support is the potential multiplier of resources for all that we carry personally. A longtime friend of mine who had worked for years with international workers in a cause called Member Care, noted how in every article or presentation on factors contributing to greater resiliency, there is a repeated refrain to community and tending to your circle of care giving and supportive relationships. In the middle of adversity, when disruptions abound, we can find in others a boost to our durability and a strengthening of our resilience muscles.

What happens to resilience in the presence of support and a circle of trust? Let's first remember our treatment of other possible base conditions. In barren, shallow, or pseudo bases, resilience raising is minimal or missing altogether. In contested base conditions, our resilience is diminished through the influence of negativity. The key point is how resiliency diminishes through negative or non-investing base environments. The wonder of a secure base is how our durability can significantly improve when we have social support that is of higher quality. If resilience is more than survival, and all about growth, what can be done to move an environment from a trauma-enduring community towards a trauma-engaging community? What is it that a secure base brings to the raising of resilience? We are putting forth four moves in a secure base environment that can greatly strengthen our durability.

```
        Assessing
         Our
        Resilience
    ↗              ↘
Refueling         Flipping Our
Our Courage       Scenarios
    ↖              ↙
        Minding Our
          Gaps
```

There may be other resilience-raising factors, but for our purpose, we are highlighting these four as of great value. We must remember that clarity and agility are needed for our quests, and now durability is added to the mix. Every quest seems doable until we face the mountain. Every quest has obstacles that foster potential quit zones. Every climb appears straightforward until the unpredictable conditions unfold within the first hours of the climb. Every fight seems

Chapter Eight   Strengthening Our Durability

winnable until, as Mike Tyson put it, someone starts punching you in the face. To successfully endure, we must do our own climbing, but the gift of a secure base community strengthens our durability if these four important moves are put in play.

Assessing Our Resilience

In a basecamp, we provide one another a safe space for honestly assessing the current strength of our durability. There is an art and science to resilience. On the science and research side, there exists a strong consensus that certain dimensions combine to raise resilience to the highest levels.

During my tenure as an associate professor in a graduate program, I utilized the work of two authors who have invested their lives in the topic of resilience. Steven Southwick and Dennis Charney (2018), two of the most robust researchers on resilience, set forth key factors in play in those who are most resilient or most able to make their way through challenge, adversity, and trauma. One element in the work of a basecamp gathering is checking to see that we are resourced well for the quest ahead. Resilience factors can be mind-mapped to illustrate some measure of progression. The portrayal provided is our way of capturing the essential ingredients rooted in extensive research on resilience and the more recent findings on post-traumatic growth.

This overview can be a source of inquiry within a basecamp gathering. The queries below and accompanying mind map provides a way of honestly probing the factors that give us greater likelihood of making our way through times of testing and adversity. A deficit area can be a rich source of conversation and challenge to one another. We can also consider how to optimize the strong links as assists for our weaker links. Imagine in our basecamp environment asking and being asked nine questions, each one a factor in our overall resilience portfolio. For most of us, the experience would be a first. Seldom have we had someone look us in the eye and inquire deeply along these lines.

1. Faith and Hope Anchoring– Where is our ultimate bedrock?

2. Compass Setting – Do we have a compelling purpose and robust values?

3. Outlook – Is our outlook optimistic and future oriented?

4. Fear Navigation – How are we handling our fears in life?

5. Support Embracing – Are we fully accepting the support of others?

6. Flexibility– Are we learning to adjust and adapt along the way?

7. Role Models – Do we have an inspiring circle of role models?

8. Physical Care and Training – Are we keeping our body strong?

9. Mental Discipline and Training – Are we keeping our mind focused and sharp?

These nine questions raise our perspective on resilience from a vague concept of hardiness to a rich picture of interlacing characteristics. Our resilience, like our physical frame, is made up of skeletal structure plus muscle plus circulatory system and internal organs, all of which make up our health or unhealth. All of it makes for a healthier and stronger person when it is all harmoniously working together. The same is true for our durability and resilience. The fuller picture comes into view when we make explicit with others our relative strength or weakness in each area.

The processing journey within a basecamp setting can be a regular check-in. The diagram below can serve as a guide. We check our life bearings via questions one and two. Then we honestly assess and reveal the state of our lifelines by asking the questions in dimensions three to six. A wrap-up for our resilience assessment concludes by checking the final three life support dimensions. What we are doing with these queries is checking the state of our resilience portfolio. This portfolio could be viewed as nine vital investment areas that, over time, pay great dividends. The key in resilience investment is the same as the key in financial investment. We make choices daily and weekly and monthly that pay dividends for a future we cannot see but we know is coming. Brief check-ins and small prompts to invest in each area today are what build a robust portfolio for tomorrow.

Chapter Eight Strengthening Our Durability

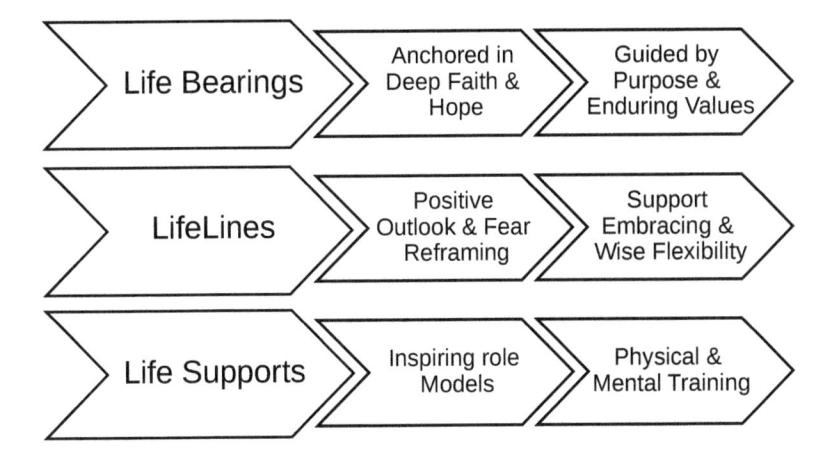

Life Bearings	Anchored in Deep Faith & Hope	Guided by Purpose & Enduring Values
LifeLines	Positive Outlook & Fear Reframing	Support Embracing & Wise Flexibility
Life Supports	Inspiring role Models	Physical & Mental Training

Adapted from the work of Southwick & Charney (2018); MacDonald (2004) and Bolsinger (2020).

This is the inside–outside process of *The Summit Mindset,* laid out by Scott Miller and James Moore (2023). It is the honest work of naming where and how we excel, then where and how we falter. No true tackling of our summit can be done without first taking time to get real about where we are strong and where we are weak. This honesty is not only vital in setting our course, but crucial to saving our life. An unacknowledged weakness needs acknowledgement in the basecamp tent. It is too late to name it when we are on the face of a mountain in extreme conditions.

This overview is given to heighten our resilience literacy, process our current reality, and to then imagine a better future in terms of our overall durability. In my teaching efforts on this front, I had students process each area in terms of current reality and preferred future and to then determine practical steps for optimizing their strong suits and shoring up their weak areas. As Gordon MacDonald reminds us, "Simply talking about the issue of resilience doesn't get one very far. Nor is there much value in taking about how badly everyone else needs it. Resilience belongs to the person who pursues it relentlessly for him or herself … The pursuit of resilience never ends. It is a lifelong, calculated adventure. The search for resilience is dampened if one coasts on his or her natural abilities. The pursuit of resilience is difficult to measure on a moment-by-moment basis. It is a long-term investment in life" (MacDonald, 2004, pp. 15–24).

In a future book in The Basecamp Leadership Series, *The Resilience Dividend*, the fuller portrayal of the resilience portfolio will be explored. The premise is, every day and every week, we are making choices about our resilience investments for a future we cannot see. Investing now in small incremental fashion pays dividends in a future that will come. This is grounded vision where realistic optimism can be applied if our portfolio is being enriched today for what will come tomorrow.

On January 15, 2009, a US Airways plane piloted by Chesley "Sully" Sullenberger crash landed on the Hudson River in New York with 155 people on board. Everyone survived. Sully became the story, and the movie *Miracle on the Hudson*, captured the drama. A pilot under fire, in an impossible situation of total engine failure due to a bird strike on takeoff, gliding a jet to a safe river landing in the heart of New York City. In his interview with Katie Couric on *60 Minutes*, Sully made a statement that bears directly on the need to assess and invest in our resilience. He stated, "I think in many ways, as it turned out, my entire life up to that moment had been a preparation to handle that particular moment. One way of looking at this might be that for forty-two years, I've been making small, regular deposits in this bank of experience, education, training. And on January 15, the balance was sufficient so that I could make a very large withdrawal" (Conley, 2018, p. 237). Once again, every day and every week, we are making choices about our resilience investments for a future we cannot see.

> *Though one may be overpowered,*
> *two can defend themselves.*
> *A cord of three strands is not quickly broken.*
> Ecclesiastes 4:9-11

The basecamp gift for building stronger resilience is moving the discussion to the level framed above. It is posing these questions to one another and listening for a sense of portfolio strength or weakness in each area. It is the pursuit of a calculated adventure that pays the greatest dividends. It is the iron-sharpening-iron work of life-on-life challenge. I can work alone on my resilience muscles and gain some measure of improvement, but the perspective and prompting of others becomes the force multiplier for deeper hardiness and durability.

Chapter Eight   Strengthening Our Durability

Around the Fire

We all have our own resilience stories. Let's share a time when we experienced a time of adversity, and we made it through. Looking back, when were we at our best during this time and when were we at our worst?

As we look over the nine dimensions that contribute to stronger resilience, where do we spot our stronger investment areas and our weaker investments areas right now?

In our weakest area, what would be one investment we could make in the next month to strengthen this area?

Flipping Our Scenarios

Another boost for our resilience is the provision of a safe environment for flipping our scenarios. Every time we enter a setting with a group of colleagues for a time of conversation around our challenges, we come with an array of internal narratives. Often inside our heads are a competing parliament of scenarios, and like parliaments of the world, the voices are talking over one another – lots of noise but no discernible or clear signal. They may be fear-inducing scenarios, and we need help slaying the monsters we have conjured up. They may be narratives dominated by complexity or uncertainty. We also bring tangled situations, conundrums, problems, and aspects of the climb that appear impossible. Most often, our internal talk echoes with "this is … awful, devastating, unbearable, brutal, or nasty." Added to our self-talk is the deeper level of very creative labeling. Situation-labeling and self-labeling go on all the time, and in the face of adversity and trouble, it is amazing how we title the narratives in our heads. Resiliency is tested in the face of labeled realities. The imagined threats prove more challenging than the actual realities, but we need help with the lighting.

The presence of others can illuminate what is real from what is imagined and prompt us to flip the scenarios.

Remember, true resilience is not about magically bouncing against or bouncing back from life's challenges. We must go through our challenges to grow through them. We must face them squarely but truthfully. The question is, how? Early on in adverse situations, we struggle with what "is" and we portray what "is" in normal ways. Our "what is" perspectives are most often neutral to negative in focus, and our scenarios can quickly lock us into a state of negative rumination. Often, we are in a state of down or stuck or wanting to flee. Positive energy networks help us with changing our state of seeing and being.

This is where flipping our scenarios becomes a vital gift in a secure base setting. The flipping involves taking time to name our mindset. Carol Dweck in her work, *Mindset*, notes the difference between a growth mindset and a fixed mindset. A growth mindset, with its focus on development, fosters ideas about challenge and effort, while a fixed mindset, quickly fears challenge and devalues effort (Dweck, 2006, p. 10). Flipping our scenarios begins with showing others our mental frame or the lenses we are looking through. Regarding the stress or strain we are feeling, it can become quickly evident our mindset is positive or negative, fixed or fluid, learning or non-learning. If we wear lenses that see all stress as debilitating, we are likely in a fixed state of rumination. If we wear lenses that see stress as enhancing and a growth opportunity, we are likely in the fluid zone of reflection. Most of us need prompts to move out of negative rumination toward positive reflection. We need people around us declaring, "Don't make it worse than it is. See it clearly for what it is. Then frame it in a way it that moves us forward." Without this kind of prompt, we can stay in our state of negativity, fear, and fixedness. Our brains, being wired to keep us safe induce the warnings of danger, fear results, and the necessary pivot is to have a prodding to better control the brain. This prodding is vital since, as Carol Dweck adds, "my research has shown that the view you adopt for yourself affects the way you lead your life" (Dweck, 2006, p. 6)

A few years back, I stumbled upon the fascinating work of Nick Petrie and Derek Rogers. At the time, the title, *Work Without Stress*, seemed weird to me and quite frankly impossible. Diving in, their claim became more believable. The twist in navigating stress is in our definition of stress. For Petrie and Roger, stress is a result of pressure, challenges, and obstacles when we ruminate rather

Chapter Eight Strengthening Our Durability

than reflect (Roger & Petrie, 2017, p. 6). We live in a stressed-out world because most of us have decided to be full-fledged citizens of rumination nation. We face problems, challenges, and pressures and we choose the road most travelled, the road of negative self-talk and endless rumination. What is rumination? It is the state of mind wherein what-if and if-only dominates. Where events are imagined to be bigger and more consequential than they are. Rumination is our power of magnification when life turns down a dark alley. We see much more than is actually there. It is also where our imaginations become occupied and often preoccupied with what others might think or think of us.

So, let's take a brief test on where we might currently fall on the scale of rumination to reflection.

We know we are first-class ruminator if we:

Catastrophize about how bad things will be if various events occur.

Blow situations out of proportion, making small events seem big.

Are often in emergency mode, as if everything is a crisis to manage.

Believe we will be unable to handle future events, so we ruminate to prepare for them.

Force our teams to over prepare for events that may or may not happen.

Take on other people's emotions or problems as our own.

Fuse our identity with our career, kids, finances, and family.

Hold on to grudges and are slow to forgive and forget.

Relitigate past decisions even when there is no chance of changing them.

We know we are becoming a master of reflection if we:

Put things in perspective by focusing on the values that matter most.

See the day-to-day pressures of work as non-life threatening.

Handle other people's strong emotions without taking them on.

Differentiate between caring (useful) and worrying (useless)

Use humor to break the tension in tough situations.

Know that change is continuous, and we can learn to shape it rather than resist it.

Help those around us surface and let go of what is overwhelming them.

Let go of grudges and forgive quickly.

Are open-minded to new approaches and are not constrained by "how did we do things in the past."

A basecamp that helps participants flip their scenarios is the kind of relational base that shouts, "Everyone, into the reflection zone!" Let's learn together to see, describe, and address our narratives in a way that leads to wiser action and greater resilience considering the challenge. Let's choose fluidity over fixedness, learning over non-learning, growth over staleness, and positive reflection over negative rumination.

Most of us can remember times when we needed a serious check-up from the neck up. Perhaps a good friend confronted us about serious malfunctions in our attitude. Attitude malfunction is why most summits go untouched. Our mindset, outlook, and attitude frame our scenarios. The frame intensifies our fear, and fear by its very nature spawns a much larger quit zone. It slows us down, causes us to look both ways four times before crossing, and multiplies the number of scary expectations in our heads. What might be a small stream on the way to the next camp towards our summit looks much scarier when fear and a negative mindset is in control.

Chapter Eight   Strengthening Our Durability

Around the Fire

Let's use the characteristics noted above as a retrospective on the past month. Honestly, where has our mind been going?

What have we learned over our life course about bringing our thinking and focus into reflection versus rumination?

What scenario do you need the most help with right now?

Flipping the scenario is having others bump us out of our own version of *Alexander and the Terrible, Horrible, No Good, Very Bad Day* towards a positive posture of *carpe diem* or seize the day. The Alexander story is the brilliant portrayal of childhood angst, where nothing goes right, and everything seems wrong (Viorst, 1972). Like Alexander, we can look at life and conclude, our circumstances are awful and all of it is out of control. To flip the scenario, he and we need someone to nudge us to consider what resilience researchers call our agency. Agency is no small matter when it comes to greater durability in the face of trauma or adversity. Instead of focusing on the swirling sense of adversity, the flood waters of stress, or the unfairness of life in our family, the basecamp crew can serve to redirect focus on what is within our control and who we are and hope to be in the storm. It is having help to flip our preoccupation with "this is bad" to a clearer sense of "this is who I am and can be" in the middle of my current story. "I am" is all about agency, while "this is" can be all about the angst.

We all need help with the work of focusing clearly on the challenge while not allowing the challenge to overwhelm our field of vision. At another level, we do not want the "I am" statements we state to be our wholesale declaration of condition or identity. When we declare, we are overwhelmed or we are stressed out, we have put forth an inaccurate and dangerous framing of reality. Susan David's work on *Emotional Agility* makes it clear that, in such statements, we have given a full emotional state coverage over our lives and such coverage is never a true state (David, 2016, p. 36). Flipping scenarios and hacking stress involves learning a wiser conversational approach. It is better to state, "In a certain aspect of my life, right now, I am overwhelmed, or with respect to this situation, I am highly stressed out." These statements pinpoint an aspect of our total field of vision as challenging, while allowing for other areas in our life to be acknowledged as sources of strength, joy, and thanksgiving. The presence of others prompting and clarifying the fuller picture of our life is a good gift and a friendly whack on the side of the head to flip our scenarios.

Helping one another move from rumination to reflection is a pivot for resilience building. We need help with this because, on our own, we often stay in the swirling waters that overwhelm us. Stress can be like a flood breaking down the door and flooding the house of the mind (Roger & Petrie, 2017, p. 80). Our work within our basecamp is moving up to the rafters as the floodwaters boil and roll beneath us. Our term for such rafter dwelling is getting on the balcony, where we do the vital work of more robust perspective-taking.

The presence of others also provides us much-needed prompts to focus outward rather than inward. As Thomas Kolditz and Jospeh Pfeifer (2007) note in their work, *In Extremis Leadership*, self-focus versus external focus is where we often get mired in the bog of negativity (p. 117). Often, a shift of focus is needed, and the presence of companions prompt us to breathe, keep our eyes open, let the situation develop, and act on the environment. In negativity, our own agency becomes blunted, and the prodding of others is what bumps us back into our own agency (p. 131). Agency, it turns out, is a central factor in resilient response to life's stress and trauma. It is the internal posture that embraces the truth that there is a response that we can choose in situations that initially make us feel helpless and powerless.

Another important element in facing and flipping scenarios is providing one another a safe space where our negativity can be indulged. In dangerous contexts, personal responsibility is in such demand that we can't afford to use personal time or energy to complain about an environment that is trying to pull us down or take us out (Kolditz & Pfeifer, 2007, p. 130). We can strengthen our resilience by having a place where the real fear, trepidation, and doubt can be excised and placed in the open. When we do so in a place that helps us hold the fear, we then discern a way through and forward. The *In Extremis* authors note well that emotions are real and important, but the time for emotions to be free to roam is not in the face of emergencies or troubles. A basecamp can be that safe place for emotional roaming, a practice field where scenarios can be run through from various angles.

Flipping our scenarios also falls into the intriguing arena of stress hacking. Stress is often treated as if it is what it is and there is nothing, we can do about it other than try to get it removed. Stress and pressure are a part of life. The good news is stress can be dealt with differently than most of us have been conditioned. We can engage in "a coalition of conversations," as Stanley McChrystal puts it, to bring down our emotion and confusion, see situations differently, and discover the gift of option thinking through the prompts of others (McChrystal, 2015).

Minding the Gaps

The third resilience-raising dimension in a basecamp gathering is a safe vantage point for minding the gaps between our current reality and our preferred future. This gap represents the messy middle or the liminal space where we sense our greatest unease and insecurity. The messy middle is where disequilibrium and terra incognita, or unknown terrain, expands. It is the region where durability and perseverance are needed and where our basecamp peers can be of great help in minding and making it through these gaps. The "minding" dimension is, as the word suggests, a matter of mind management and discipline. It is gauging emotions while guiding actions in the land between. It may be that most of our efforts and lives are spent near or in messy middles. It seems we are always navigating some patch of ground that is not where we were or where we want to be. Thus, resilience is needed to endure and make it through.

Every quest involves scary moments and seemingly impossible situations. There is no climber of mountains who claims, "I have never once been scared." You won't find a business owner on the planet who will tell you they have never felt fear in building or leading their business. Talk with any clergy member or social worker, and they will speak of moments of foreboding and fright at holding well their congregation or clients. Fear, it turns out, is our universal reaction to any threat or danger. It is also one of the most common barriers to quest realization. Our world is littered with stories of people who made it halfway up their mountain acknowledging, "I turned around because I was scared."

Our mutual challenge in the messy middles of life is being honest. Candor about our fears, anxieties, and discouragements is hard for most of us. A legend in the field of organizational leadership, Abraham Zaleznik, tells his own story of writing an article for Harvard Business Review on *The Management of Disappointment* (1967). His deep-down sense was no one would read it. At the time, he believed there were some topics we would rather avoid. He was right. Fifteen years after the article found its lonely place in the *Harvard Business Review*, Gerhard Gschwandtner, a medical director in a hospital in Rye, New York, tracked down Dr. Zaleznik to talk about the article. He was working on his own article, *How to Manage Disappointment* (2010), and found the literature abundant on success. The success theme was found in twelve hundred titles, two hundred and twenty titles focused on winning. A scant sixteen titles were found on the topic of losing. He dug deeper looking for an article on disappointment. He found one, written in 1967 by Abraham Zaleznik, and then called him to have a talk about his article. Zaleznik was surprised by the visit. In the years since he wrote the article, no one had ever discussed it with him. Amazing! The most common experience of people and leaders was something no one wanted to talk about. Could it be, deep down, we all want to have some candor on this front, but we lack the place and time where we can show up and speak of our disappointments and discouragements in the gap between where we are and where we hope to be.

The messy middle contains gaps where our stress and strain tend to fester. They can tax and age our physical bodies. They may erode our emotional well-being. The gaps can also become a habit. We can fall into our gap zones multiple times per day. We can spend hours each day stuck in our gaps, ending up unhappy, resentful, regretful. If we spend extended periods of time in the gaps of the messy middle, without good middle-earth management, the compound effect of it could shorten our lifespan. Research shows that the rate at which our bodies age is modulated largely by how our genes interact with exposure to stressors (Sullivan & Hardy, 2024, p. 53). When fear and anxiety remain unnamed or unmanaged, we get discouraged, disappointed, and very weary. We also keep our heads down. We desperately need some place where such things can be named, faced, and mitigated. We have some serious invasive forces in our messy middles. It is where real emotions congregate and do their work stimulating brooding, bottling, and all kinds of behaviors that hurt more than help. We

Chapter Eight   Strengthening Our Durability

need help with learning how to wisely navigate four specific gaps. These represent our greatest threats to carrying on wisely through the messy middles of life and leadership.

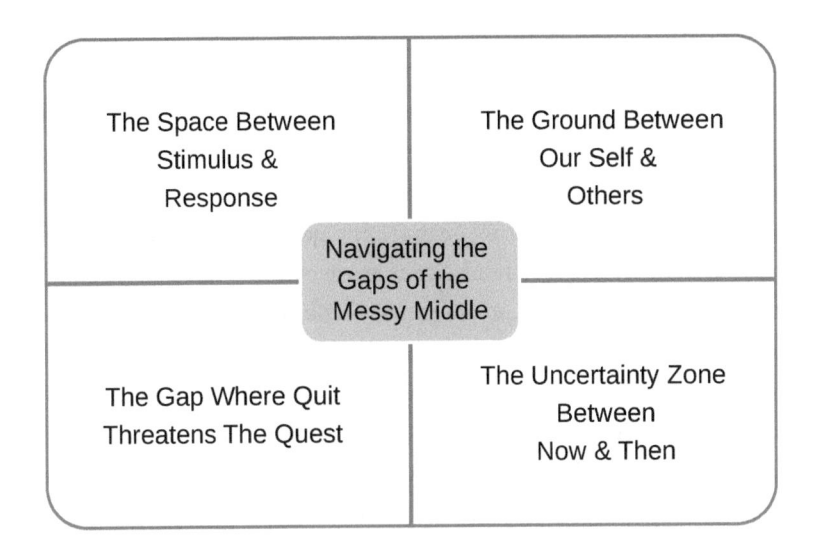

The Space Between Stimulus & Response	The Ground Between Our Self & Others
The Gap Where Quit Threatens The Quest	The Uncertainty Zone Between Now & Then

Navigating the Gaps of the Messy Middle

First, we need help navigating **the space between life's many stimuli and our responses**. Not a day goes by where we are not stimulated to act, react, move forward, or stay still. It is common knowledge that between stimulus and response there is a space, and in that space is our power to choose. This echoes the wisdom of Victor Frankl, writing about the stimuli-filled experience of imprisonment during the Holocaust. "Forces beyond our control can take away everything we possess except one thing, our freedom to choose how we will respond to the situation. We cannot control what happens to us in life, but we can control what we will feel and do about what happens to us. In our response lies our growth and our freedom" (Frankl, 1949, p. iii). The basecamp gathering can be the place of helping one another with how to choose responses to the stimuli we encounter. It is facing the messy-middle triggers in such a way that our response does not add to the mess.

Our aim should be to learn how to "struggle well" and to deal together with stressors and our response options (Kahn, 2005, p. 36). Features of functional and healthy relational systems are pivots towards one another to this end. In framing the required leadership literacies for the twenty-first century, Bob

Johansen states, "In a world of disruptive opportunity, leaders will need to learn, how to practice voluntary fear exposure. They will need safe zones to practice their leadership skills, and develop their capacities, knowledge, discipline, practices, perspective, and worldview" (Johansen, 2017, p. 40).

To struggle well with this gap is taking time to process our most recent stimulus experiences in our leadership. Things have happened, things have been said, things have gone south on us and our team, things have gotten "all dumbed up." This phrase was a favorite of my son Brad, in his younger years, as he watched movies where the plot turned in a direction he did not like. Dumb stuff happens. The processing is noting how we manage the gap between the stuff and our response. Greater and wiser durability is mastering the art of struggling well with the stimuli of life. A reminder again of Frankl's words, in our responses lie our growth and our freedom to live and lead more wisely.

We must also learn how to better tend **the ground between our self and others**. Much of life's fear has to do with encounters that produce misunderstanding, conflict, and threat. When equilibrium is disturbed, the solid ground gets muddy, the nice feeling of getting along gets replaced by a litany of get a life, get a clue, get real, or get lost. Our ability to endure and persevere can be diminished due to fear and anxiety that dwells in the gap between ourselves and others. Our choices in the gap are powering up, smoothing over, wooing in, or standing up. Powering up is using position or status to deal with divisive situations. Smoothing over is making peace however we can and often involves giving in to the discordant voice. Wooing in is using the power of personality or charisma to smooth over the rifts or the ruckus. Standing up is the willingness to clearly define our goals and desires, being non-anxious and calm, while staying in touch with the people involved. In a basecamp gathering, the prompt needed by trusted friends when relational turbulence is in play is, let's learn how to stand up (Friedman, 2007, p. 18). The options of powering up, wooing in, and smoothing over are often standard operating procedures in leadership situations, but the greatest gift we can give our leadership settings is a calm, non-anxious presence.

This is where the work of strengthening our self-differentiation becomes the most important work we can do. In my early leadership journey, a great gift was the work of Edwin Friedman and his book, *Failure of Nerve: Leadership in the Age of the Quick Fix* (2007). For the first time in my leadership experience, I

Chapter Eight   Strengthening Our Durability

found a way to think about my posture and place that brought better health to myself and a wiser stance of leadership in my context. It was Friedman's concept of self-differentiation. I have tried to think of a more accessible term, but to date none has been found. Self-differentiation is, at its heart, the learned posture of a non-anxious presence in what is often a turbulent and anxious system. It is present when a leader and/or a leadership group is clear about values and goals, taking a clear and non-reactive stance, while also staying in touch with those they serve and lead. The result, like good parents in a healthy home system, is a non-anxious presence, where the children know where both mom and dad stand. In such environments, children live and grow in the healthiest way through the gift of self-differentiated parents. The same is true in organizational life. Often, an organization or team can be anxious and seeks rescue from those who lead. Self-differentiation is the stance of humble strength that stands in the midst bringing calm. To strengthen our durability and to be more resilient in leadership, this gap between our self and others needs attending. The basecamp can be a good practice field for learning how to stand up with greater confidence and calmness. If our quest is to lead an organization, enterprise, or congregation well, self-differentiation is a vital ingredient. We won't reach our summit, whatever that summit might be, without it.

There is also the basecamp assist in minding **the uncertainty zone between now and then**, or the gap between current processing and future action. Durability and perseverance through the messy middles is never a straight line between current reality and our preferred future. In seeking clarity, we take time with current reality. We share our balcony perspectives on what is really going on, but we also take time clarifying and focusing our quest. Our aspiration for the future is somewhere distant, and our navigation with what is in front us is close at hand. Around the fire, most of our conversation is about the middle of this journey between two poles. The gap between now and then is where we must endure. It is where our talk and our walk are tested. It is one thing to talk through our current reality with basecamp members and quite another thing to fully step into the fray or cross the crevasse in our representative Everest Khumbu Icefall or K2 Bottleneck. These icefalls on Everest and K2 are where these mountains are at their most perilous (Penson, 2022, p. 2). The gap between lower elevations and our summit cannot be mended or removed, only faced, and crossed. There is danger to be encountered and facing it with others is the ultimate test of minding this gap. Absent courageous action, we can stay safe, but we can also stay miserable. I have often reminded myself that much of my unhappiness in life is due to my unwillingness to go straight at things. When locked in our anxiety or fear, we can stay frozen in place and our problem or challenge simply endures.

> *A liminal space is the time between the "what was," and the "next." It is a place of transition, waiting, and not knowing. Liminal space is, where all transformation takes place, if we learn to wait and let if form us.*

As framed in the chapter on giving and receiving the gift of clarity, it is a wise move to bring to the basecamp gathering situations where we don't know what to do next. In this gap, we often feel puzzled, scared, anxious, or wearied. The upside in minding and crossing this gap is we discover our deepest growth in messy middles. We are in over our heads, feeling lost in familiar or unfamiliar places, and emotions can run riot over our well-being. At such times, it is amazing what a secure base of true friends can bring. To clarity is added agility with a boost of durability by bringing the fear into the light and allowing fresh perspective and perseverance to be born. We find help and hope through the gap between our now and then.

A final gap to mind is **the gap between quitting and carrying on**. Strengthening durability involves coming to terms with the power and peril of quit zones. When I was a teenager, my brother-in-law, Jim Janz, spun me a piece of profound wisdom. He reminded me that between the great dream and the grand accomplishment is the vast region of grinding it out. Since then, I have discovered how one of my greatest dangers in that vast region of grinding it out was the turnback, giving up, and reaching for the towel to throw in the ring declaring "I'm out". In the words of Dan Sullivan, the gap wins, and the gain gets lost (Sullivan & Hardy, 2024, p. 53). In this gap, the grand accomplishment is abandoned, the great dream dies, and the vast region wins the day while we and the world lose. Extended periods in the effort zone can exhaust us. The sacrifice syndrome can enter where our very effectiveness contributes to a spiral. In the giving of ourselves, we give too much, leading us eventually to a point of being

Chapter Eight   Strengthening Our Durability

less effective. We under-function personally and then professionally (Boyatzis & McKee, 2005, pp. 40, 207).

It takes immense energy to face and travel the gaps covered thus far, but this final gap is perilous to our quest because it introduces the option that we can always make a U-turn. Adversity and challenge can cause us to flinch and turn for home. We can draw back or shrink away from what is difficult or unpleasant. As Julien Smith puts it, "Most of our fears are ghost stories that the flinch has taken over" (Smith, 2011, p. 5). Minding this gap is helping each other move from the flinch by discovering the wonder of a single step forward. The essential move may be making it to the next turn in the pathway. In Sullivan's work, it is getting firmly in touch with the gain. In the work of Kolditz and Pfeifer, it is facing outward and forward rather than inward. Fear by its very nature blocks the way. "Fear is incompatible with functioning" (Kolditz & Pfeifer, 2007, p. 122). There are times and places where the quit zone looms large in our thinking. We want to nail our feet to the ground or pull back. We flinch and the gap takes over. It turns out our perception of events is what almost always keep us in flinch territory. Fear-based perception makes us complicit in the creation of obstacles that appear larger than they are. The minding of this gap is finding in the presence and prompting of others, words of hope and belief that there is a way forward.

The quit impulse is a progress blocker and hijacker of breakthrough moments. There is great power in providing one another a secure base environment for reframing the fear and stress of the quest. As noted earlier, the action of bumping one another from states of rumination or negative mental loops into healthier states of reflection is a game changer. A secure base environment can be a wonderful gift when the temptation to flinch and quit threatens our quest.

The Three Rules of Mountaineering
It's always further than it looks.
It's always taller than it looks.
It's always harder than it looks.
Belden Lane, *Backpacking With The Saints*

All of us encounter turning points in the messy middle. It is called messy because no journey through the challenges of stimulus and response, through the ground between self and the other, or through the vast region between now and then; no journey like this is exempt from problems, challenges, pressures, and perils that prompt the flinch. The poet, Robert Frost, wrote of those times when our road diverges in a kind of yellow wood. Which road, should we travel? In the end, Frost notes he chose the one less traveled, and it made all the difference (Frost, 1923, *The Road Not Taken*). When it comes to the vast region of grinding it out, the road less traveled is forward. The road most traveled involves the flinch. It is easier to turn back and give up than it is to face forward and endure. The basecamp gathering is a place where fellow adventurers face the flinch factor honestly and together find a way to freshly engage the quest.

Around the Fire

We all have challenges with the gaps inherent in the messy middle of life. Which gap is most challenging for us right now? The gap between stimulus/response? Self/others? Now/then? Flinch/forward?

What have you been learning lately about yourself in how you default to certain responses or reactions with these gaps?

In our strategy of late, where have we seen our attempts at powering up, smoothing over, or wooing in to lead or influence people in our context?

What is our greatest struggle in the messy middle between our now and then?

Where are we feeling the flinch temptation right now?

The first three promises for increasing our durability, assessment of our resilience portfolio, flipping our scenarios, and minding our gaps are realized in the

Chapter Eight   Strengthening Our Durability

safe attentional space provided in a basecamp. Honest assessment of our current resilience strength is paying attention to our resilience investments to date, providing a baseline from which we can move forward into greater resilience. Honest acknowledgement of our current scenarios is granting permission to say in community, "I am struggling and quite frankly stuck right now in the following." Minding our gaps is working out with others the most challenging aspects of the messy middle. Honesty on all these fronts optimizes the basecamp potential for helping us to better endure and sets us up for the final provision for strengthening durability, refueling our courage.

Refueling Our Courage

The final provision in a basecamp setting for strengthening our durability is a refueling of our courage. Our secure base can be just what we need to endure and keep on. We can give one another the gift of greater durability by listening that wisely informs our words of encouragement. Encouragement is putting courage back into one another when our courage has lessened or has fully leaked away. A secure base is where the discouraged are encouraged; where the scared are urged with a dare to face the fear and carry on. In the early days of working on the Basecamp Manifesto, the fear factor was framed as one of the major factors to address in a secure base environment. We have chosen to wrestle with the fear dimension here as one aspect in the multi-faceted picture of overall resilience.

In my doctoral journey, I probed several dozen leaders who had been in a peer cluster for more than two years on what were the greatest gifts they received from their peer cluster and community of practice. Courage building stood out among the top three gifts. The other two were load lightening or gaining greater agility of life and soul, and sense-making or gaining clarity in the fog of leadership. In numerous interviews, these leaders spoke of discouragement as one of their greatest challenges. The struggle was how to mitigate the doldrums of discouragement and find some fresh measure of courage. Peer cluster members in one setting in South Carolina utilized a twofold process. First, they realized their fear and discouragement had to be named and faced before it could be navigated. Then, they had to do the work of living out a sacred text imperative, we must encourage one another. This involved infusing courage where fear and discouragement once dwelt (Young, 2004).

One of the peer-cluster accomplishments was lowering the discouragement level and raising the courage ceiling. As I interacted with these leaders, there were numerous stories of discouraged leaders finding renewed courage through the sheer presence and prompts of a few colleagues. They found in their basecamp of sorts, rejuvenated spirits to return to their respective front line to face the dragons that previously appeared unmanageable. One leader went so far as to state, "This group saved my life" (Young, 2004). His threat was not an ice face or a blizzard at 22,000 feet; his threat was a leadership context that had slowly taken a toll, and he had reached his quit zone. His peer-cluster partners brought enlivening presence and encouraging words at the right place and the right time. A leadership literacy for thriving in a future of extreme disruption and distributed everything will involve creating and sustaining positive leadership in concert with others. It is not optional for leaders to provide one another the zone for such renewed energy to be realized (Johansen, 2017, p. 117).

Another way to frame the refueling of courage is to think of the basecamp as an energy network and encouragement ecosystem. A grounded view of energy in social networks, according to Cross and Parker, is recognizing how energy lives in the sweet spot of conversations. Such conversations are often in the space where problem-solving is in view. These relate directly to the Manifesto questions of what is our quest and where is our basecamp? The mix is a compelling goal, the possibility of contributing, a strong sense of engagement, the hope and perception of progress, and the deep belief that our cause or quest can succeed. For those who want to inspire energy, hitting a good mid-point in these dimensions is the challenge and the key in shaping a vibrant energy network (Cross & Parker, 2004).

The reason we took time with the question of "Leader, Where Art Thou?" is the consequential nature of our current base of relationships. St. Exupery, a soldier of long ago in the barren deserts of Northern Africa, wrote about moments where "we measure ourselves against an obstacle." These moments are when we discover the essence of self-discovery, and we find a way to shape our own answerable courage (Klein & Napier, 2003; Sweet & Beck, 2020). It is a wonderful state to be in when we have others helping us do the measuring against our obstacles. Energy and encouragement networks can be positive and life-giving, but they can also be negative and debilitating. Our network or current base is either lifting us or lowering us.

Chapter Eight   Strengthening Our Durability

Around the Fire

What has been our experience of encouragement in the past few years? What has been most helpful in putting courage back in when we have been discouraged?

A way in which we as basecamp dwellers can bring a courage infusion and energy boost to one another is through some great questions. There are five factors of courage that can transform our quest in life. You can utilize the guide below to explore and hopefully expand your courage infusion work. Our courage-building tutorial can be processed via five questions, adapted from the work of Klein & Napier, in *The Courage To Act* (2003, p. 40):

- ✓ Query One – Let's have the courage to speak and hear the truth. Are we committed to brutal honesty when it comes to our current reality? CANDOR is *The Core of Courage*.

- ✓ Query Two – Let's have the courage to pursue lofty and audacious goals. Are we committed to leading our setting in picturing an inspiring preferred future? PURPOSE is a vital element of resilience and a key driver of courageous action.

- ✓ Query Three – Let's have the courage to inspire optimism, spirit, and promise. Are we committed to communicating our preferred future through leading conversations? A strong WILL fuels the daily challenge of life and leadership.

- ✓ Query Four – Let's have the courage to invent disciplines and make them stick? Are we committed to action plans which build the tangible bridge between current reality and our preferred future? Without RIGOR the quest for greater courage proves difficult if not impossible.

- ✓ Query Five – Let's have the courage to empower, trust, and step forward. Without the RISK and vulnerability of love, our courage can remain a hard-edged virtue incapable of inspiring hope and purpose in others.

Returning to the definition of a basecamp, a basecamp is to serve as a place of perspective-taking, preparation, resourcing, and doing reconnaissance for what is ahead. It is also where we and our crew check our equipment. Equipment can be both a noun and a verb. In our case, at basecamp, it is both. We check our gear, our tools, our ropes, and the things that will keep us alive. But we also check our internal equipment. Our states of mind, heart, and will must also receive assessment and adjustment if we are to better take on our respective quests. The resourcing function must be processed in basecamp because when disruption happens or the earth shakes beneath our feet, that is not the time to check to see if we have what we need. Our secure base crew are our lifeline to wiser preparation, resourcing, and reconnaissance. We grant one another the gifts of enablement and encouragement and in the mix, something is always strengthened – agency, perspective, courage, wisdom, patience, or grit. The potential is heightened by focused attention towards the matters of resilience and durability discussed in this chapter. This involves going full circle through the nine questions. Doing a checklist review of these queries. Noting the gaps, affirming the strong suits, and taking time to spur one another on regarding which dimension would be most important to take hold of in a stronger way? It also involves flipping our scenarios, minding our gaps, and then refueling one another's courage.

The Durability Advantage

- Resilient people run in the company of "a happy few." – Gordon MacDonald
- Resilient people figure out how friendship, kinship, and mutual partnering works.
- Every basecamp is a platform for assessing and improving our resilience and durability for the journey ahead.
- We must remember that resilience is a kind of ordinary magic, and we all have it, but it has a relative strength depending on our investment in strengthening our resilience dimensions.
- For our given quest, we need help flipping our scenarios, facing our fears, and renewing our courage.

Chapter Eight   Strengthening Our Durability

- o Tracking in concert with our basecamp is doing wise reconnaissance that deepens insight and focuses outsight.
- o Raised resilience is never the product of a solo endeavor. Iron is the only thing that can sharpen another piece of iron.

CHAPTER NINE

Heightening Our Generativity

*We reach the greatest heights when we attach our
bootstraps to other people's boots.
If multiple credible supporters believe in us,
it's probably time to believe them.*

Shawn Achor (2018, p. 150)

This Manifesto is based on a dance between two questions. What is our quest and where is our basecamp? As a Manifesto, it may appear that the weighting is one-sided. What matters is the finding, shaping, and nurturing of a basecamp or secure base for a more effective and healthy life. This is clearly in view, but the quest question surfaces the vital need for a focused and robust purpose in life. We best develop when we have strong bias towards a meaningful mission. We also best develop when we have developmental relationships of the quality proposed in a secure base environment. We have an ecosystem to support and spur us on towards our envisioned quest.

By ourselves, we have a micro-ecosystem of one, but with our basecamp, we magnify our opportunities for growth. In *Big Potential*, Shawn Achor (2018) wonderfully frames the idea of an "eco-system of potential" as the key to fullest development. The various "base" conditions framed earlier are matched by outcomes. Over time, each one lessens potential and generative power and love. These bases also have a direct impact on our stewardship of life. For now, our premise is this: the secure base raises our potential and momentum to their highest levels.

How do we become better at who we are and what we do? How do we get and stay in the optimum zone of purpose and contribution? In a world of distractions and derailers, how can we be generative and good stewards of life? This chapter is dedicated to the place of the secure base in fostering a generative presence in the world.

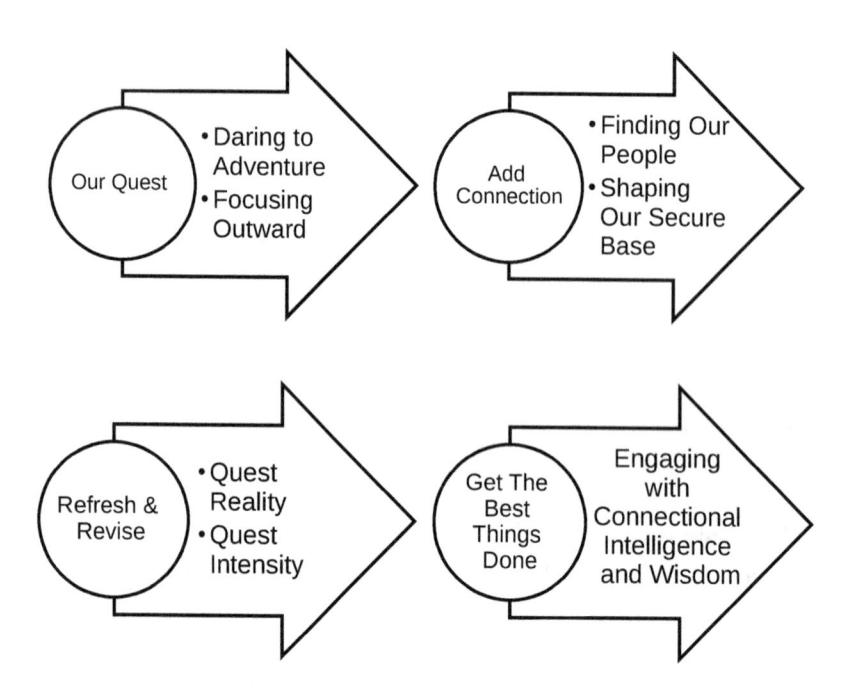

```
[Our Quest] → • Daring to Adventure  • Focusing Outward
[Add Connection] → • Finding Our People  • Shaping Our Secure Base
[Refresh & Revise] → • Quest Reality  • Quest Intensity
[Get The Best Things Done] → Engaging with Connectional Intelligence and Wisdom
```

The portrayal above is a flow of thinking on the matter of how we heighten generativity. We begin by simply acknowledging our quest. We dare to adventure. Our quest is a focus outward and forward, and to this focus, we are adding vital connection. We have committed to find our people and shape our secure base. It is in our basecamp where we have an opportunity, related to our quest, to do two things: refresh and revise. We have a safe place to honestly assess our current reality and gauge our current intensity. Intensity is never in steady state.

Chapter Nine   Heightening Our Generativity

Intensity has a way of being diminished simply by the scramble, and our aim is to encourage one another to reset when needed. Leaving basecamp, our action steps are hopefully in hand, and these steps focus on how we can get the right things done in our individual quests. The great gift in all of this is our engagement with connectional intelligence where we grant one another wisdom on how to do our best work in the world.

Remembering the stories of life's greatest quest pursuers; Einstein, Edison, and Tolkien, we find worthy quests spurred on by connectional intelligence and wisdom. Their ecosystems of potential were vibrant and filled with the vitality of human connection. They had their quests, they added connection, they constantly reviewed and revised, and in time, they got the best things done for the sake of the world.

What Is Generative Leadership?

What is at the heart of generative leadership? The word *generative*, at its root, portrays the idea of generating or creating life and well-being. For leaders who serve in organizations, congregations, or schools, the best forward focus is the desire to bring flourishing. It is the generating of work and presence that hopefully brings life. For Adam Kahane, it is the use of power and love to help a group of people to unite in service of the whole of which they are a part (Kahane, 2010, p. 138). His work gives profound insight into generativity due to its application in some of the hardest situations around the globe. Whether in post-apartheid South Africa or Northern Ireland or cartel-torn Colombia, Kahane notes when generativity has been at work, significant change has occurred. However, the vital distinction for Kahane is between generative love and power and degenerative power and love. There is far more of the latter than the former in most parts of the world. Hope and life are found, as people, groups, and countries wrestle towards using their power and their love in ways that generate life and flourishing. This is much easier said than done. It is also far deeper than visible activity. For the Manifesto, this framing gives us our line of sight on the hope of generativity.

The secure base is framed around heightening our generativity in the world. In the early stage of writing the Basecamp Manifesto, we thought of framing this final dimension of the basecamp experience as a catalyst for better productivity.

Raising our game, achieving our mission, or tackling our summit came to mind. The problem was it didn't sit well with what we were discovering in the literature and in the lives of those who had engaged in great quests. Generativity aims at the goal of fostering life, creativity, and flourishing.

For those who have taken on great endeavors in life, there was always something deeper than productivity in view. The Inklings did not gather to gauge their page counts or getting manuscripts completed in record time. Edison's Olympia Academy were not spending entire nights in conversation and debate to merely produce a solution to some equation. In the end, they did produce works and ideas, but there was something other, and we believe it was the gift of generativity. Out of their gathering's life, creativity and flourishing was generated. The concept of generativity has been chosen due to its power to take us to a deeper level beyond productivity and success.

Our hunch on the problem with the "productivity" focus was confirmed in the most recent work of Cal Newport. In his 2024 work, *Slow Productivity: The Lost Art of Accomplishment Without Burnout*, he notes an intriguing turn in our culture concerning productivity. For decades we have been immersed in a world of work where the goal of productivity has consumed our thinking, planning, and effort. It turns out we are in a time of seriously evaluating this obsession and coming to terms with the problem; we don't even have an agreed-upon definition of productivity. The one interpretation that is most common and unhelpful is that productivity is to be gauged by our visible activity (Newport, 2024, p. 21). More and more, we sense the angst with what has become pseudo-productivity. The last few decades have evidenced the rise and fall of this pseudo-productivity, and people are now looking for some better way of living and working. In the words of Tony Schwartz, *The Way We Are Working Isn't Working* (2010). The way we have been working has led many to exhausting overload. Burnout has been on the rise, and in Newport's analysis, the damage is significant. Throwing down the challenge, "Let's get more productive," is met these days with a sigh or a groan. We've tried everything we can to be more productive. We've been humanly engineered in our workplaces to be more productive. We've been encouraged to get a myriad of new tools to be more productive. However, many of us yearn for a different way. Newport's call is for a meaningful and sustainable approach to our work that involves doing fewer things; things in keeping with our true quest in life; working at a natural pace; honoring seasons and rhythms that are in keeping with how nature works; then focusing on quality; avoiding the drive for quantity or false measures of busyness (Newport, 2024, p. 41). We believe a generative lens that honors these principles can help us find our way forward.

> *When we talk about generativity ...*
> *we are talking not about outcomes but about*
> *principles, practices, and positioning a person's*
> *ability to generate positive change.*
> Andrew Lynn (2017, p. 217)

Generativity is doing the right things in the right way in the world while staying alert to forces that might seek to mitigate our cause and hinder our quest. It is persevering through the messy middle of every endeavor with two questions in mind, "Are we in our work handling our power and authority in a life-giving manner," and "Are we expressing our love for one another and those we serve in a life affirming manner?" The role of the secure base is to provide perspective, do reconnaissance, and share the resources we need for tackling our quest in this way. It is having others remind us that our intentions and the realities of our quest can be quite different. Helping one another with generativity is about honestly assessing our exercise of power and love. This is not an easy or simple conversation, as it surfaces the complex mix of the motivations and means for all we do in our leadership.

Generative leadership is for most of us a new frame for assessing the exercise of leadership. The leadership field for decades has wrestled with the best descriptor for the concept of leading and leadership. This has led to a book title contest wherein scores of adjectives in front of the word leadership have been proposed. In our website, **basecampenviro.com**, a sampling is given of the myriads of ways we currently frame the exercise of leadership. If you look at this list of book titles you may get some clarity as to why we are so confused about the nature of true leadership. As Joseph Rost points out, the thousands of leadership definitions and scores of leadership models illustrate why leadership as a social science is literally at sea. It is lost for the lack of any agreed-upon working definition or philosophy of leadership (Rost, 1993, p. 17). Many scholars agree, leadership is one of the most observed phenomena on earth, but also the least understood.

It is not our purpose to argue for a new or better framing of leadership but rather to put forward a generative frame for a basecamp to use as focus. Generative leadership is taking on our quest in life, in such a way, that it generates vitality, creativity, and flourishing in the world. The table that follows provides a way for a basecamp gathering to gauge their practice of leadership and wrestle with how to shape the generativity that brings life. We are indebted to the work of Adam Kahane (2010) for prompting this focus. In the framework below, we attempt to give a way to frame the presence of both generative and degenerative power and love.

Generative Love	Degenerative Love
* A predisposition toward helping people to flourish, to develop their full potential.	* A predisposition that believes love is possible without paying close attention.
* An approach to change and innovation that strives to co-sense, co-presence, and co-realize the best outcomes possible.	* An approach to innovation and change that desires and demands that people get on board.
* Seeks authentic connections with people engaged in the enterprise.	* Is satisfied with surface interactions or feel-good connections.
* Loves people unconditionally.	* Loves people "because of" or "so that" or "only if."
* Has an outward mindset. What do those we serve need? What are their objectives and challenges?	* Has an inward mindset rather than an outward mindset. What do or must people provide for me or us?
* Wants results that benefit those we serve first and foremost.	* Wants results that benefit the leader first and foremost.
* Models for others the virtue of self-sacrifice and is willing to go first in living out the values being upheld.	* Calls people to sacrifice but is not willing to experience sacrifice.

Chapter Nine   Heightening Our Generativity

Generative Power	Degenerative Power
* Seeks to bring a transformational leadership presence.	* Strives to maintain a transactional leadership posture.
* Accepts and practices personal agency; takes seriously the responsibility to handle authority wisely and well.	* Authority is about wielding power; wisdom in handling authority may be nice but it is not necessary.
* Acknowledges the best use of power and authority is in the service of others.	* Hungers for and seeks control over people and process.
	* Utilizes power in service to self and one's personal agenda.
* Sees title, position, and status as responsibilities to steward.	* Grasps titles, position, and status as gains to be protected.
* Seeks accountability and values a system of checks and balances.	* Shuns accountability and has disdain for process, checks, and balances.
* Welcomes feedback and input from others throughout the organization.	* Is threatened by feedback and input.
* Truly empowers people to act and accept responsibility for actions.	* Enacts pseudo-empowerment while never letting go of ultimate control.
* Ends and means must honor truth and serve people in the best sense.	* The ends justify the means. Winning isn't everything; it's the only thing.

We as leaders bring degrees of light or darkness. We can bring darkness and cast a dark shadow or provide light and refreshing direction. The mix of both generative power and love is what makes the difference. Parker Palmer, many years ago, said it best: "A leader is a person who has an unusual degree of power to project on other people his or her shadow, or his or her light. A leader is a person who has an unusual degree of power to create conditions under which other people must live and move and have their being. Conditions that can either be as illuminating as heaven or as shadowy as hell. A leader is a person who must take responsibility for what's going on inside his or herself, inside his or her consciousness, lest the act of leadership create more harm than good" (Palmer, 1990, p. 5). It is well worth our time and energy to sit around the fire and ponder the degree of power and light we are bringing to our life and leadership.

Around the Fire

Where have we seen the presence of generative power and love at work in recent days? In our own settings or elsewhere?

Where have we seen the presence of degenerative power and love at work in recent days? In our own settings or elsewhere?

If we were to heighten our generativity in the best sense, what are a few things we sense need to change to lead more generatively?

The Care / Dare Balance

It might seem strange to put forward the idea of "heightening our generativity" in a setting where peers gather to make sense of life and leadership. However, the dimension of challenge is critical to a balanced base. Support is needed and a wonderful gift, but when coupled with challenge, the full dance of development and growth can unfold.

When Robert Kegan wrote *In Over Our Heads: The Mental Demands of Modern Life* (1994), his words were apt for the last decade of the 20th century. I imagine if he wrote for our present decade, hit book could be retitled, *Way Over Our Heads: The Scrambled Demands of Post-modern Life*. Modern demands have morphed into post-modern disruptions, and in this moment in history, the unprecedented ambiguities of a globe scrambling its way through international unrest and economic

Chapter Nine Heightening Our Generativity

uncertainty puts most leaders in a perpetual state of overwhelm. Kegan's purpose, in the 1990s, was to explore the best way for people to grow and flourish when the mental and emotional demands of their environment are overwhelming. His words are apt for our proposal to all leaders to find and shape a secure base. They are also needed more than ever in today's moment of volatility and complexity. His words also honor the dance partners of caring and daring. In seeking to get at the crux of making our way through modern life, he declared, "If I were asked to stand on one leg, like Hillel (a rabbi of the 1st century), and summarize my reading of centuries of wise reflection on what is required on an environment for it to facilitate the growth of its members, I would say this: people grow best where they continuously experience an ingenious blend of support and challenge; the rest is commentary" (Kegan, 1994, p. 42).

> *A holding environment ... fosters developmental transformation, or the process by which the whole ("how I am") becomes gradually a part ("how I was") of a new whole ("how I am now").*
> Robert Kegan, In Over Out Heads, p. 43

The best dance is one of balance. If the base that I inhabit is too heavily weighted towards challenge, there is the danger of toxicity. In such settings, we feel constriction and turn defensive. But if the base I inhabit is strong on support but lacks challenge, there is the experience of boredom and devitalization over time. "The balance of support (caring) and challenge (daring) leads to vital engagement" (Kegan, 1994, p. 43). These are the dance partners in a healthy secure base. Of interest, is the way in which Robert Kegan describes our wider culture as a kind of school. His take is that we err, in the dance of development with our younger generation, on the side of "the continuous experience of challenge." We deserve high grades, he says, when it comes to providing challenge. Where we falter is the degree to which we shape environments for students in which their experience of challenge is without support, and in the end painful. "It can generate feelings of anger, helplessness, futility, or dissociation, all of which can be heard in the familiar adolescent complaint, 'Whaddya want from me?'" (Kegan, 1994, p. 43).

So, there is a conundrum with challenge and support. From our wider world, we feel the presence of incessant challenge. This is the ever-present pressure of our productivity-obsessed work world. Like adolescents in the pressure cooker of "school," we walk through our hallways sensing the siren call to perform, produce, succeed, solve, and eventually win. Why would we ever want to then sit with our secure base and be given the "gift" of more challenge. The difference is in the nature and direction of the challenge given in a life-giving secure base.

Something wonderful and distinct happens when we bring our learning from both formal and front-line settings into conversations around the campfire. In our time, these settings have been called communities of practice (Drath & Palus, 1994, p. 4). In a previous era, they were called guilds. Guilds were the training grounds for emerging craftsmen. In *The New Leadership Literacies*, Bob Johansen puts forth the idea that our 21st-century world needs a renewed connection with the old-world environment of guilds (Johansen, 2017, p. 38). Guilds were associations of craftsmen, tradesmen, or merchants, often with considerable power in their communities. Guild members had a shared purpose and a nurtured kinship for mutual benefit. Like the guilds of old, modern guilds can allow craftspeople to share their craft and learn from each other.

These encouragements give the secure base a grounded reason for existence and make the case for its necessity in a disruptive world. The guild is a skill accelerator, but it also serves as a haven for navigating challenges, fears, and dilemmas in the trade. Fellow guild members who share our trade also know when work is taking its toll. It was not uncommon for craftsmen and artisans of old to break down or burn out, and the wisdom of the guild would remind everyone of the danger of the craft entering the body. The hoped-for outcome in a guild is for all who gather to be wiser, healthier, and more effective in tackling one's work in the world.

So how does the secure base, framed as a guild, work? A guild engagement involves a commitment by members to shape a challenge culture that sits alongside a support culture. If the sacred text of the Old Testament has wisdom on this front, it comes in the words of Proverbs: "As iron sharpens iron, so one person sharpens another" (Proverbs 27:17). Sharpening cannot be done with one piece of iron. The most beneficial relationships have beneficial friction. Yet this is something we avoid. The development occurs when avoidance ends, and sharpening friction begins.

Chapter Nine Heightening Our Generativity

There are certain questions that secure base guilds learn to ask often of one another. Not only "how do you do what you do?" but "how did you discover that way of doing?" Not only, "What should I do in my situation?" but "What did you do when faced with something like this?" The questions in a guild open the learning process. It is not about more information for our moleskin journal but insight on craft and art and the softer skills of seeing and doing more skillfully and wisely.

> *There is hardly anything you can't do if you have, and you nurture, the proper support systems. Don't lower the goal, increase your support.*
> Rick Hayhurst, The Right Mountain, p. 113

Keith Ferrazzi posits the use of sparring or learning to fight with those who have our back. This is the essence of a dream team in which trusted partners get together to wrestle down, define, and refine their goals. It is engaging in free form fighting with enough rules, customs, and agreements to make injuries unlikely. The purpose of sparring is to provide an educational arena where new skills and abilities can be honed and sharpened for use in the actual ring (Ferrazzi, 2009, p. 176). For heightening generativity, daring and caring sit together. The balance is crucial for deepest development and a well-formed secure base never sacrifices one for the other. No one needs a circle that is toxic or boring. A good basecamp is neither. It is a genius blend of strong support and steady challenge; just what we need for taking on our quest.

The Dimensions of Generative Leadership

The major contribution of a guild-like basecamp is the potential to assist in the development of adaptive leadership characteristics. The profile of such leaders has been framed as those who are developing proficiency at five levels: the relational, skills, creative, big picture, and internal levels. It is assumed that such proficiencies will over time be picked up and developed or learned through the school of experience. However, most leaders never find a setting where these matters are processed and integrated in a deliberate and focused manner. In examining each dimension, a basecamp can offer some promise of development over time in a setting of caring and daring relationship.

The **relational dimension** addresses the relational strength and dexterity of a leader. In addressing "the dark side of leadership," Jay Conger points out that our relational skills in image management and communication often prove to be our Achilles' heel (Conger, 1990). When a leader is unable or unwilling to face their weak or destructive relational skills, this image blindness makes the leader vulnerable to a fall. The positive advantage of a long-term relational setting is the opportunity to work on, in a secure environment, some of the rough edges of our relational style. We can find a relational practice field for development that can foster the very skills needed for effective leadership. These skills are holistic understanding, collaboration, team orientation, listening, and the practice of advocacy and inquiry (Fletcher, 1996, p. 112). The opportunity for processing and improving these skills can be found in a relationally safe developmental setting.

The **skills dimension** focuses on the area of skills required for effectiveness in our calling. In the leadership domain of an educator, religious leader, or business leader, there are certain competencies or incompetency's that can make or break the leader. They can also shape or shatter the organization. In a development circle, part of the process is the surfacing of developmental needs and growth areas in the skills dimension. A cadre of people, each pursuing their respective quest in life, can assist one another in crafting a development plan suited to the needs of each one in a basecamp environment. A basecamp can be a setting for the question, "where is our most needed growth edge and what is our plan on this front in the months ahead?" It could be that a basecamp group prompts each member to make explicit their learning and development plan for a coming month, quarter, or year. This is a way to fold in some encouragement and accountability for starting and finishing a formal course or skill training.

The **creative dimension** addresses the need for development in perceptiveness, insight, self-awareness, and creativity. Effective and transformational leaders are people of imagination who develop the ability to see alternatives to reality as presently framed. In a sense, at the heart of all leadership dwells the vast realm of ideas. Every effective leader must become clear about their central idea, their organizational ideas, and their values ideas. These three idea areas serve to generate both the incremental and quantum changes required in excellent organizations. A basecamp, as a community of practice, can be focused as a place of dialogue, inquiry, and stretching of mind outside the box of present modes of thinking. A fun component of basecamp time can be blue-skying and posing our "what if?" inquiries.

An aspect of the imaginal dimension is the question, "Where do we go with our hunches?" What do most of us do with our idea file? If you are like me, you have a swirl of thoughts, ideas, and hunches that should see the light of day but never do. We keep our file folders, secret shelves, stovepipes, and mental echo chambers to ourselves. Sam Harrison, in his wonderful work, *Ideaspotting: How to Find Your Next Great Idea*, encourages the use of an "antibiosis file" (Harrison, 2006, p. 231). This is a file for rejected ideas and antibiosis is the term for restoring to life those things that may appear in a dead like condition. Our need is for a breakout from our conclusions and confinements to a place where we can mix, mingle, and make a mess with others. Our basecamp can be a campfire circle where we lay out our muse, our hunches, and at times our crazy ideas about how to solve some nagging problem in our lives or the wider world. Early in the Manifesto, we mentioned Edison, Tolkien, da Vinci, and others. All of them had an imaginal community that meshed the minds and muse of like-hearted people. Innovations are always tethered to a hunch, or a series of hunches and many hunches die for lack of connection or encounters with other hunches (Johnson, 2010, p. 77) The best hunches grow and bloom through the richness of connection.

The **big picture dimension** surfaces the need for leaders to strengthen their blend of perception, sensitivity, and competence to see the parts as related to the whole. This is the dimension that serves to combine one's interpersonal, instrumental, and imaginal skills, so that the leader develops "declarative knowledge." This form of knowledge contrasts with "procedural knowledge" and implies the ability to develop a set of concepts and principles that permit creative connections to be drawn between events (Conger, 1999, pp. 216, 217). The basecamp experience can foster such a knowledge because of the features of time, an iterative process, and the opportunity to experiment with a systems lens. The simple question, "What else might this be?" is the invitation to see more widely a given problem or dilemma. We all have vision, the ability to see, but most of us have lost much of our peripheral vision. The big picture dimension is all about rediscovering and improving our ability to see broadly the signs and signals often missed due to our love affair with focal vision. (Day & Shoemaker, 2006, p. 24). Every secure base should have as one of its outcomes the development of greater systems skills or in layman terms, the stronger ability to see the forest and the trees.

Finally, there is wonder and mystery of the **internal dimension**. The realm of our inner theater is where our true self resides and from which our on-stage life emerges (Kets de Vries, 2006). We might object to how this has anything to do with our generativity in the world. Like the cartoon depiction of the man talking with his therapist, we declare, "What's going on inside of me is none of my own damn business." The internal dimension is more than our own business; it becomes everyone's business because everything backstage eventually shows up on-stage. This dimension is the most sensitive area for honest and humbling exploration.

Our lives are filled with circles. We navigate in and with these circles every day. Yet, as Parker Palmer notes, not all circles honor the soul. Thus, false community abounds. Our circles are seldom those places where it is safe for the soul, our internal dimension, to show up. This calls for some honesty about our current circles. Each one is a base from which we operate or navigate. The critical question is whether our base is a help or hindrance for our journey. Parker Palmer states, "The only guidance we can get on the inner journey comes through relationships in which others help us discern our leadings" (Palmer, 2004, p. 26).

A circle of trust calls for a wonderful paradox. A willingness to avoid being invasive or evasive with another. A circle of trust is where we learn how to sit quietly "in the woods" with each other and wait for the shy soul to show up (Palmer, 2004, p. 58). The kind of base we need, a secure base, is the place where we stay present while stifling all impulse to barge in to fix one another up or to change the subject. This honoring of the soul will have deep outcomes for our work in the world because what is inside always, at some point, shows up on the outside, for good or for ill.

Chapter Nine Heightening Our Generativity

When the spine of identity is well established, it is possible to risk relating in depth to those who are different from us. When the spine of identity is weak, everything is a threat.

James Fowler

The internal work we can do with one another is like tracking our way along a mobius strip. Parker Palmer illustrates the mobius strip by, what he calls, a Quaker power point (Palmer, 2004, p. 45). No slide or projector, just a piece of paper. We take a one-inch strip from a five-and-a-half inch by eleven-inch piece of paper. On one side of the strip is written the phrase "our on-stage life," while on the other side is written "our back-stage life." For most of us, this strip is like a high wall. We show the world one side, the on-stage part of us, but keep hidden the other side, the backstage realities. On-stage is what we display and promote and market. It is our displayed brand. Backstage is what we disguise and protect and keep under wraps. It is can be our dark side. The mobius strip, however, takes the strip and twists it to join the two ends. What you end up with is a strip of paper that allows a person to pass their finger across the entire surface. It is the mobius strip made available to trusted others that is needed in a leader's life. A secure base is where our on-stage and the backstage realities can be seen and sensed by self and others. It brings what is from below and hidden into the light and where integrity begins to get real. Without this, we are walled off from the very care, wisdom, and at times confrontation we need to hunger well, journey well, and live well with stronger integrity.

What does this have to do with generativity? What are the things that take leaders down and out? Think about the things that take leaders up and further. Sometimes it is a skill deficit or a skill dedication. Sometimes it can be a decision debacle or a strategically brilliant move. The sadder and more numerous take-downs are the personal and private stumbles that suddenly flash across public screens. Think about the things that take leaders up and further. These brighter and less talked about aspects of deepening character and virtue are seldom considered newsworthy. We are drawn to burning buildings or train wrecks, not construction sites or trains showing up on time. On the one hand, we witness daily the stories of hunger games that have gradually but then suddenly ended the career, the marriage, or the ministry. On the other hand, we are hard-pressed to find stories of good hunger games that gradually but then in time make the career, the marriage, or the ministry move from good to great.

The inner theater is where life hangs in the balance. It is well worth granting our trusted and trusting basecamp members a ticket of entry into our inner world. In time we grant a right of way with others that makes the revealing of one's internal dimension a risk worth taking. This dimension is most often the breakthrough point towards the deepest and richest basecamp environment. When a small cadre of trusting friends let their secret worlds be seen and known, that is when true community begins to emerge in ways few have ever experienced. After this, it must then be respected, honored, and never betrayed.

In addressing our need to bring generative love and power to our life and leadership, and then weaving the five dimensions of well-rounded generative leadership, we are bringing to our quest the potential for optimum flourishing and effectiveness. In concert, these dimensions will be more important than ever due to the scramble of our world. We need, in the words of David Nour, "curve benders" in the face of the forces we are personally and collectively facing in our world. In his mapping of forces impacting our future, he notes multiple forces in play in four domains of life: personal, organizational, transitionary, and industry. These forces will dramatically impact the way we work, live, play and give in the next two decades (Nour, 2021, p. 41). These four echo our focus in Chapter 6 on the things we carry and our basecamp work of increasing and improving our agility. Combined these forces make our lives more complicated and, in their interaction, more volatile. All of this accelerates the relevancy of people in our life who are curve benders. "Curve benders are strategic relationships that will power our non-linear personal and professional growth in the future of our work. They have the power to reroute our growth journey" (Nour, 2021, p. 5). In our language, they are secure base relationships that excel in every way for our growth, support, and ultimate impact.

The sobering news is that secure base relationships and the presence of curve benders is rare in our world. We have far more defective and destructive bases in life than secure, life-giving bases. We have far more fender benders than curve benders. Our lives become populated with people who take us in directions other than where our quest must go. This is why we provide the challenge to

Chapter Nine   Heightening Our Generativity

think honestly about the quality of our ecosystem and to prioritize the matter of finding, shaping, and nurturing our own basecamp of secure base relationships.

The Generativity Advantage

- o   Every basecamp is quest aware and provides a profound opportunity to prepare, do reconnaissance, and be better resourced for the adventure.
- o   Having a safe place where we are regularly asked "What business are we in?" and "How is business?" can be a much-needed reset. (These are the first two questions Peter Drucker asked of most leaders and organizations he consulted with.)
- o   The need of our world is the presence and practice of people who bring generative love and power to their work in the world. A secure base can be the safe place to gauge such generativity.
- o   We must remember that there is a vast difference between wise and unwise engagement with one's quest. A basecamp gathering is a call to wisdom.
- o   A basecamp is also a call and practice field for relational, skills, creative, big picture, and internal strengthening.
- o   Our quality of work in the world will reflect the four or five people we hang out with the most. Greatness inspires greatness! Mediocrity breeds … (you know the answer).
- o   Moving one another from good to great is a communal activity and is one of the greatest gifts a vibrant community of practice can extend to its members.

Overview of the Basecamp Advantages

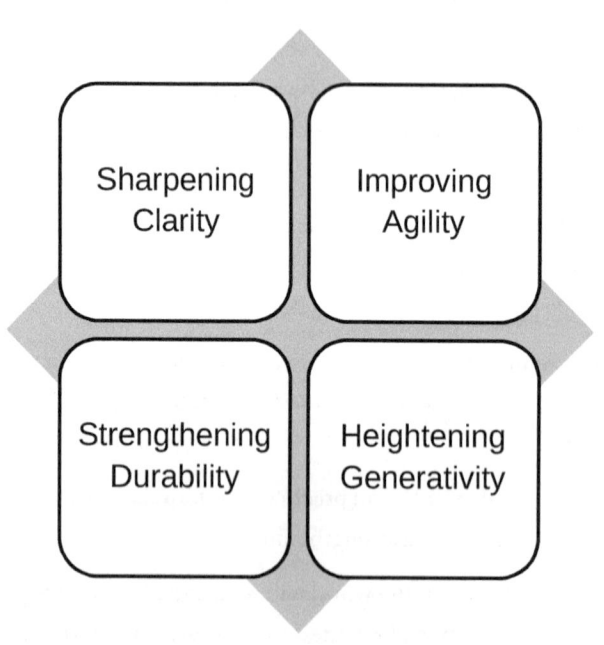

```
┌─────────────┐  ┌─────────────┐
│ Sharpening  │  │  Improving  │
│   Clarity   │  │   Agility   │
└─────────────┘  └─────────────┘
┌─────────────┐  ┌─────────────┐
│Strengthening│  │ Heightening │
│  Durability │  │ Generativity│
└─────────────┘  └─────────────┘
```

Why are we here, together, at this place and in this time in our lives?

We are here to sharpen one another's clarity.
We are here to increase and improve one another's agility.
We are here to strengthen one another's durability.
We are here to heighten one another's generativity.

We do so one conversation at a time. We rarely if ever will do all of this in a single basecamp gathering, but over time these gifts will be given and received. Collectively, these equip and embolden us for pursuing our quest.

Basecamp Excursus
Is it all-in-one or a constellation?

In building the case for "the basecamp" in the life of a leader, it is fitting to pose a question: What if I have a base of relationship right now but one or two of the basecamp provisions are not possible with my basecamp mates? This is the realistic take on secure base relationships. Most groupings of peers cannot be all things to all who inhabit that base of relationship.

The constellation is the goal. If the bringing together of gift offerings that include clarity, durability, agility, and generativity are present in our band of brothers or sisters, we have a rarer circle of relational provision. However, in more basecamps, there will be a provision of clarity, agility, and perhaps durability strengthening. For the provision of care in the internal dimensions, this may then be sought in a counselor, therapist, support/recovery group, or spiritual director. For the provision of generativity, a coach, mentor, or trainer may be in play. Or the mix for us may vary from this portrayal. You may shape and nurture a basecamp that is very effective in helping the circle of people with clarity, agility, and generativity. The missing links of durability strengthening, and integrity deepening may require links elsewhere. The most important point is being able to answer for yourself the following:

✓ Where and with whom am I sharpening my clarity these days?

✓ Where and with whom am I gaining greater agility through load management and lightening these days?

✓ Where and with whom am I strengthening my durability and resilience these days?

✓ Where and with whom am I improving my generativity in the world these days?

It may be fully in the basecamp circle we find, shape, and nurture. It may be partially in the circle we shape and nurture. The rest is the matter of finding the other aspects of our developmental constellation. The other point of qualification is the recognition that the four dimensions of the manifesto have a relative "right of way," depending on what we are leaning into at any given moment. Clarity and generativity matters have an easier right of way for honest conversation and wrestling. Durability is also an easier right of way but may be a bit more challenging since most of us shield others from seeing how non-resilient we may be at this moment in time. The common quest for greater agility may be an even more challenging right of way because of our shyness or reluctance to surface with others the deepest things that we carry in our souls. Above the water line, load is easy to talk about, but when a basecamp mate keeps asking, "What else are you carrying?" the shy soul, as Parker Palmer labels it, wants to run off and hide in the bushes.

In the early stages of basecamp development, it may be wise to frame the journey as a patient process towards a fuller right of way with one another. The shaping of true community is an organic process not a mechanical building project. In the study of great groups, there is always a journey from presence to confidence to trust, and this often takes place over time and with patience. Nothing is worse than starting with some sense that each person must sing for their supper or completely open up as soon as the tent pegs are in the ground, and you gather around the campfire for the first time. None of us like to sing for our supper. Acknowledge the shared shyness of the soul and be patient. Share your lives. Tell your story. Let one another in as you sense you are ready. Let trust grow. Be there for one another and the gifts will come. Lastly, apologize whenever you pry too quickly or too deeply when our colleague is not ready. In time, our shy souls relax in the presence of loving care and genuine challenge.

GETTING TO BASECAMP

CHAPTER TEN

From Hesitation to Embrace

The Basecamp Manifesto has been an invitation to find, shape, and nurture our secure base in life. Our hope is for a determined embrace, but we are realistic enough to know there is hesitation. There are blocks and barriers that cause a pause from forming a serious circle of trust. A more disturbing question might be, why do we tolerate the barren, shallow, pseudo, or contested bases of life, almost without thinking? An honest assessment of the resistance factors reveals an array of common excuses for putting off or setting aside the work of shaping a robust secure base for one's life. In most of life, our journey to a better day, involves facing what we are up against in terms of our hesitation to pursue deeper change. Facing the resistance is getting honest about the forces working to subvert our flourishing. In these final pages, we are confronting the forces bent on keeping us from the vital work of finding, shaping, and nurturing our secure base.

In our encouragement for leaders to form their basecamp, we have sought to keep in view the quest or our summit. The visual of the Everest basecamp is a rich and compelling picture because the goal is ever in the background, and it is no small goal. Kim Cameron, in *Practicing Positive Leadership*, calls one specific category of goals "Everest Goals" (Cameron, 2013, p. 113). This is the highest level of aspiration in the goal constellation of life. This Everest goal distinction has everything to do with urgency in finding and shaping a basecamp. You just don't *go* to Everest, and you certainly don't go it alone if you want to return home alive and well. If our goals are Everest type goals, then our resolve to find, shape, and nurture our crew is exponentially higher than if our goals are non-Everest in their focus. If I have easy goals or generic goals, then let's admit it, we're going for a walk. Why would I need a basecamp for engaging in a walk?

Our hesitation to the next steps of establishing our basecamp may simply reflect the minimal size of our goals and a common-sense dismissal of the need for shaping a laser-focused secure base to stay alive. On a walk, I can pretty much stay alive on my own. I may be choosing to go on an arduous hike and even a multi-leg trip like so many do on the Appalachian Trail. However, like so many who have taken on such challenges, we know it can be done alone if we so choose. It is just more fun and more doable with a few hiking companions. However, a secure base or a basecamp constellation doesn't rise to the level of a necessity. I may have a bigger goal than a walk in the park, but I am not thinking or dreaming of an Everest.

If our goals are ratcheted up to a seriously robust category, we cannot venture out without the support and challenge of a basecamp. With the kind of goals Mark Murphy frames as HARD goals, we must be able to name our support system. The HARD acrostic stands for goals that are Heartfelt, Animated, Required, and Difficult (Murphy, 2011, pp. 11, 12). What stands out from Murphy's call for living and leading with HARD goals is the way the book concludes. He shares the story of eight CEOs gathered in Anguilla to wrestle with the setting of their own set of HARD goals. These CEOs were a basecamp of sorts, and they gathered several times a year to think, share, brainstorm, and push each other. The joint realization was that they could not do any of their most serious goal pursuit without help. Fear was a common confession around the circle, and one member said he felt like an alcoholic who upon returning home would sink into his old ways. One of his colleagues said, "Pat, if you feel like an alcoholic, I'll be your sponsor. I'll call you for five minutes every day and check in on you. And since I have the same fears as you, you can check in on me too" (Murphy, 2011, p. 167). To Murphy's surprise, the group took a next step in their goal's work: they **all** agreed to pair up. When our chosen summit is daunting and dangerous, we had better be able to name our sponsor.

It is no small or insignificant endeavor to take time with our quest clarity, asking, "What is our summit?" "What is OUR Everest?" As we sharpen our answer, the follow-on question is "Can we do this alone? Are we going for a walk in some park by ourselves from Point A to Point B or is our aspiration of such a quality that we must be able to clearly name our ecosystem of potential, circle of trust, life-line relationships, and our consistent secure base?" This is the question we must focus on and then work to answer. This is about more than secure base creation. It is about higher and deeper life aspiration, which makes the band of brothers or sisters the vital link to our personal and world-focused aspirations. The "I can't do it alone" sense must be felt at a visceral level and acted upon at a practical level. We must move through our hesitation factors that lead us to conclude, "I don't get the need for this," to the place of embrace where we declare, "I can't go another day without this."

The Hesitation Factors

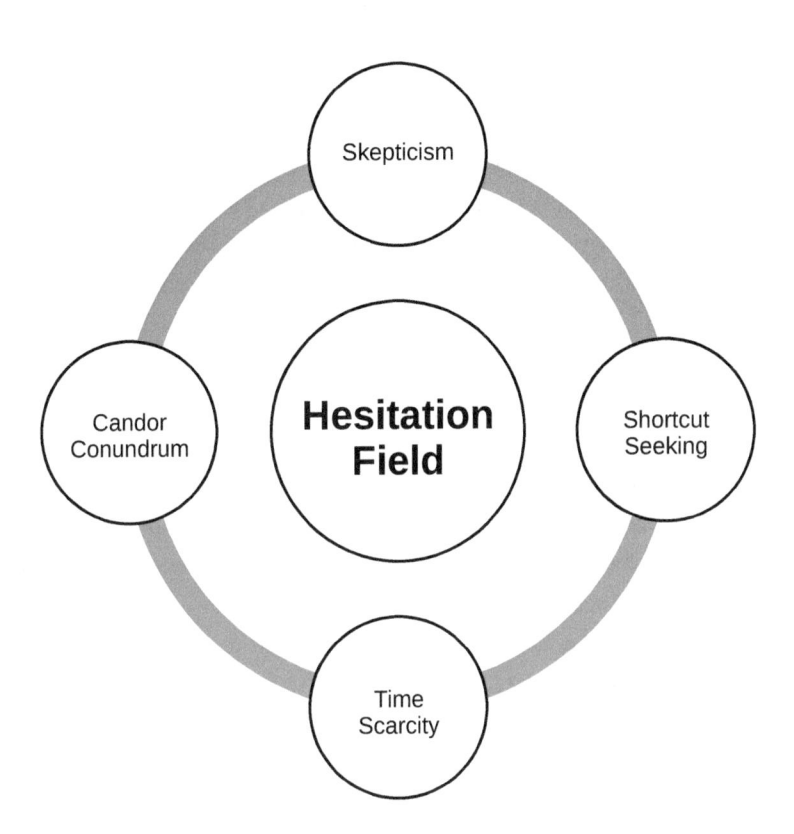

- Skepticism
- Candor Conundrum
- Hesitation Field
- Shortcut Seeking
- Time Scarcity

Starting Line Skepticism

The first hesitation factor may be our struggle with starting line skepticism. Why would we need a basecamp for our measly quest? Halfway through working on the Basecamp Manifesto, there was a point of serious wondering. What if people see little need for a basecamp because there is no reason or resolve to climb a mountain. If there is no Everest-like purpose, why would anyone construct a basecamp? It seems like a lot of work for what we have in mind right now. There is a quest-to-basecamp calculus that states, if my quest is small and easy, then the need for a robust basecamp is correspondingly small and unneeded.

There may be a wondering about wrestling with either question – what is our quest or where is our basecamp? Why start with something (shaping a basecamp) that has little bearing on my life because I am frankly on a stroll (not a quest), doing what I need to do to survive, pay the bills, and stay employed. This is fine if this is the path one chooses. There is nothing wrong with paying the bills and keeping one's job. The rigor of the basecamp framed in these pages would seem to be unnecessary or a bit much considering the course we are on. Yet, the course we are on does matter and we would put forward the challenge that we are doing much more than paying the bills. If we have a family, a circle of friends, a community, a church involvement, or a desire to plan a good future, we have a quest that matters. Don't do this alone. It is much more than a walk in a park.

The absence or presence of a firm resolve to take on a quest surfaced a quandary in the early writing of the Basecamp Manifesto. Maybe our audience shrinks to a scant few who are highly focused on an Everest-like summit. Maybe this isn't worth writing, producing, or shipping as a general appeal. Or, maybe, from a different vantage point the audience for this call is fewer than we at first imagined. This musing on our part further prompted an additional focus for the Manifesto. Our challenge to find, shape, and nurture our basecamp must come with another challenge. Are we seeing fully the nature of our life journey as we define it right now? Are we thinking, dreaming, and resolving to live into the future in Everest terms? If not, why not? Each of us must answer this to our own satisfaction. Then if we are leaning into our own challenging quest, the follow-up question, "Where is our basecamp?" makes far more sense and calls for a much more robust answer. Shouldn't everyone be able to name their crew, their four or five, who stand as their secure base in life?

Chapter Ten From Hesitation to Embrace

For anyone who dares to clarify their own summit challenge and comes to terms with what it will to take to reach that future, agnosticism should dissipate. Our need for a band of brothers or sisters to resource, facilitate, and navigationally assist us to stay alive and take on our life adventure makes great sense. We are also confronting the conventional wisdom we learn so well, "stand on our own two feet." This phrase has also entered our individualistic leadership training. All of it is ill-founded and, frankly, dangerous. No one just goes to their Everest, and no one should go alone.

Our skepticism to pursue secure base formation can also be rooted in previous experiences. Over a life course, we experience a good number of groups, relational settings, and teams. Some experiences bring back good memories, while others are experiences of which we do not want to speak. This hesitation factor is all about "bad camping experiences." Settings where someone, somewhere came crashing through the bushes trying to get us to open up or come clean or get real, like being asked for our driver's license at a check stop. Our attempts or excursions through the land of community that turned out to be less than helpful or awful can add to our skepticism. For many, the bitter memories of small groups or peer clusters of the past erect a wall of hesitancy that becomes almost too high to climb.

With bad camping experiences, like bad life experiences, the way through and over such conclusions is to turn those bad days into good data. Squeezing wisdom from our bad camping experiences, those things that fall into a "never again" list, can set us up for a better and healthier process of finding, shaping, and nurturing our own secure base. A resolve to make our future basecamp distinctive from past bad encampments is what we are seeking to help with by providing the rigor of a find–shape–nurture journey.

Our breakthrough past skepticism comes with a commitment move. Mountain climbers tell of the "commits" they must make if they are to progress. None of these "commits" are free of fear or the flinch. Our commit moves can be scary, but on the other side is gain but never without some strain or pain. Ronald Rolheiser recounts his experience of meeting with a group of priests who had moved past their hesitancy and skepticism towards deeper community. As one of the priests stated, "We started our group four years ago because we needed to do something in our lives. I was a good priest, but I wasn't a great priest, and I can name the reasons for both" (Rolheiser, 2014, p. 138). He acknowledged a life of compensations he had been making to cope with the tensions of ministry. He, with a small group of colleagues, had chosen to "commit" to a weekly gathering to practice, what they called, radical sobriety. They defined this sobriety as full transparency, and full transparency was full honesty. After this priest lost his father, he made a resolution that if he was going to be a priest, his quest would be that of becoming a great priest. No more compensations and no more mediocrity. Then, with frankness, he stated, "I had to learn what everyone who has ever overcome bad habits has to learn, namely, you cannot correct your life by willpower alone, you need grace and community" (Rolheiser, 2014, p. 139). To get there we need to make a move.

Shortcut Seeking

The second barrier may be the ease with which we can select a different path. When we look for ways through the challenges of life, we know we have options for path selection. The simple phrase, "the path of least resistance," tumbles off our lips as if we are tapping into some folk wisdom that has been around since the dawn of time. Robert Fritz popularized this phrase in his groundbreaking work on *The Path of Least Resistance* (1989). Every day is a dance between readiness and resistance as we journey through the testing ground of our values and beliefs. It turns out that our deepest values and beliefs, reinforced over time, set us up for resistance to needed change and raise the fear factor toward a different and better day. So, how do we choose? We reach for the path of least resistance. We do have a natural leaning towards paths that have less friction and resistance under foot. These paths give profound insight into the challenge of finding, shaping, and nurturing our basecamp environment.

Most of the other bases, framed in Chapter 3, offer little resistance on my part or on the part of others. I can enter and exit them with ease and on a whim, and no one balks or complains (too much). However, a genuine and deep base of relationship is a qualitatively different circle. It has purpose and intentionality towards profound life and soul work. It involves the searching out and questioning of deepest values and beliefs we would rather keep under wraps. The shy and fugitive soul we all carry resists finding out or runs from fuller exposure. We are shy and others are shy, so we push back and away from the brighter lights of vulnerability. In short, we opt for paths of lesser and least resistance and end up with relational bases that keep the shy soul still hidden and relatively unexplored. A common trait of human behavior is that we tend to make convenient decisions, not necessarily right decisions. There is no shortcut to greater clarity, agility, durability, or generativity. Such gains come to us through the gifts and presence of others. Again, with a variation on the words of Robert Frost, there are roads less travelled that can make all the difference.

Time Scarcity

The third hesitation factor is the excuse of the ages – the time crunch. On most important fronts in life, we have ready our well-worn excuse card: "We're too busy." Not having enough time has become our default answer to almost everything. Our physical shape, marital state, garage condition, friendship debacles, financial tangles, parenting puzzles, and our mental malaise; they'll have to wait because we just don't have time. We know they're important and maybe in a state of crisis, but where will we find the time to move from our unpleasant "now" to some mysterious land of a better "then"? We don't have time. We're too busy.

This is one of the most fascinating quandaries of life. The very thing we need more of is left unaddressed and untended because we are so busy doing and tending to what we need less of, and out comes our excuse card. It is a form of upside-down thinking that on the face is ludicrous. I have time to carry on in malaise and mess and misery, juggling the tasks that keep me in a chaotic current reality, when an equal investment of time and energy in a positive direction would move us meaningfully to a much better preferred future. Most of us are more comfortable with the certainty of misery than we are with the misery of uncertainty. My day-to-day realities may be miserable, but I know what I am dealing with.

The deeper issue here are hidden assumptions around the malaise and mess of life. We need the help of others to break through the deception and denial at the root of so much in the words above. We need some "other" to call a foul and say, "Wait a minute, you're telling us that your current state is to be tolerated because you think you are too busy, or you don't have time?" Let's look at your time and ask, "What is your present and full time on task and what is that getting you?" It is getting you exactly what you are getting.

"Time on Task" is a concept that my friend Jungle Jim Hunter uses to reveal the truth about how and where we are currently spending our time, minute by minute. It captures the brutal story of how time is spent or invested in a day or a week of time. His follow-up with athletes, business leaders, and parents is the portrayal of how present time-spending will never get us to where we want to be as an elite athlete or an effective business owner or a loving parent. We have all the time we will ever get. The problem is ever and always the lack of clear intention and planning crowded out with an abundance of reckless time-spending sprees. New resolve, added to new priority, added to new daily and weekly rituals is what moves us to time investments that gets us out of our malaise and mediocrity into our meaning and generativity in the world.

> *The best job security today is horizontal, not vertical. Depth and breadth of your network and your commitment, to perpetual student-hood.*
>
> Tom Peters

We also know the rules about taking time. What is the culture's answer to what we must take time for? If we put forth taking time for regular solitude or sitting with friends on a weekly basis for a few hours, this is viewed as a nicety, but the hope is that we will get on with the real work of life as soon as possible. ASAP can also stand for "always seeking a promotion." Our time orientation has been influenced for the last century to be action-oriented, production-focused, and profit-realizing. There is a vague-to-deep guilt that hovers when we stop to be still or when we disconnect to then connect with a band of friends. As time crunchers, we admit, pit stops are needed. Then we fool ourselves into thinking the only value is in the race, and our pit stop experiences, if we need them, should be modelled after Nascar – let's do it in six seconds or less. With the basecamp analogy, we acknowledge the vital need for more than the six second pit stop. We need a place of fueling and repair and resetting because we are in the race to win it. We need a place of reconnaissance to do some work before the work because we're on our mountain to climb it. Ask any member of YPO, the Young Presidents Organization, which now numbers close to 50,000 members,

Chapter Ten From Hesitation to Embrace

and they will all declare that their one day a month gathering with a small cadre of President peers, is the most valuable and impactful experience in the YPO universe. They are all busy but not too busy to spend a day a month around their fire.

This Manifesto is centered around the confluence of the two questions: What is our quest, and where is our basecamp? The first question is the stuff of legends and the promoter of time-scarcity thinking. It is the question that gets the lion's share of focus and marketing for the success motivation industry. It is the question that the leadership development industry markets to and promises to help us realize. Quest pursuit is what life is all about, and this commitment can lead to tunnelling tendencies where time is the determiner of all things. The world is full of highly dedicated people. The mission, the vision, the cause, the success; these are our drivers. They can also be blinders to deeper things that call for attention and that lie at the foundation of true and lasting success.

Our struggle with finding time for something other than engaging our front line of work is an indication of quest obsession. The first question we ask in the Manifesto, "What is our quest?' becomes the only question that matters. Think of the last time we were in a social setting. Did anyone ask, "Where is your basecamp, secure base, crew, or band of brothers or sisters?" No, we are always asked, "What do you do, how is business, are things going well at the job site?" Dr. Ed Hallowell wrestles with this conundrum with a reminder, "the vital and essential ingredient for emotional and physical health is connectedness" (1999, p. 11). Across the world, the healthiest zones are the most connected zones in terms of human relationships and friendships. Our quest obsession is justified with our declaration, "I am free to do as I please." Such personal freedom, however, exacts a great price and that price is often disconnection. As Hallowell declares, "you want freedom ... fine ... but you will have to live with the voids you create" (1999, p. 15).

Letting go of friends is like dumping money in the river.
Not only that, it can cut years off your life.
                Ed Hallowell

The time-crunch excuse added to our quest obsession requires confrontation. We do find time for a whole host of things that contribute little to nothing to our purpose and how we show up in the world. What would a few hours a month or an hour per week contribute if that time spent was in an ecosystem of potential, a circle of trust, or a robust holding environment? Confronting the time excuse is a vital step in recalibrating our choices, and every day we make choices that count for good or ill towards our future. The wisest investors of time calculate the dividends. A secure base investment yields incredible dividends for that future that will come, but that right now we cannot see. Let's take it on faith and step forward with the choice to find, shape, and nurture our secure base.

Candor Conundrum

A fourth factor is our fear of candor. This hesitation and resistance factor is a combination of how we are socialized and the fear we experience going against the grain of how we have been raised and trained.

In Western culture, we grow up with a strong value for autonomy. We must stand on our own two feet. If it's going to be, it's up to me. You can be an army of one. These "life sentences" easily become a way of being. The message is clear: help-seeking is a weakness. We are suspicious of those who admit, I truly need others, or I desperately need help, or I can't do this thing called life without leaning on others.

I remember the point in my doctoral journey in which an article was placed before us for a good read and some personal reflection. It was entitled, *The Problem of Candor in Professional Life*. At first, it looked intriguing, but then it took a turn and proved quite disturbing. I realized I was in a vocation that had a serious candor problem. I was in good company because the author noted an array of professions that suffered due to inherited rules concerning the danger of candor or simple honesty about the shape of things, particularly on the inside of life. Being honest is not simple or easy work, and thus we avoid places where the lights are turned up and the chairs are turned towards others to answer that great question of John Wesley, "How is it with our soul?" The priest's story a few pages back joins together the confrontation of thinking some easier way can be found with the need to embrace candor as the pivotal move that sets us as prisoners

Chapter Ten From Hesitation to Embrace

free. For lack of candor, we remain locked alone in our inner theater, and the story remains unrevealed, untouched, and unresolved.

The Problem of Candor article particularly raised concern with the medical profession. Typically, doctors are not very eager to display candor. They have been socialized and trained to diagnose, treat, and hopefully heal. They are also known to self-diagnose, treat, and hopefully heal themselves. To submit oneself to diagnosis, treatment, and a curative regimen is not something medical doctors are quick to do. The same can be said for pastors, professors, lead educators, and business heads. People who are answer providers for those on the front line don't readily ask questions or reveal their absolute confusion on their own front. The cost of this lack of candor is tremendous. The absence of honesty, truthfulness, and transparency diminishes the potential for our work to be the best it can be. We may be good doctors, pastors, or educators but we cannot be great, all for lack of transparency in the presence of trusted peers.

Thinking about doctors and candor, two physicians from the University of Rochester School of Medicine and Dentistry had great concern about the need for medical professionals to process the stress of their work. Mick Krasner, a primary care physician, and Ronald Epstein, a professor of family medicine, psychiatry, and oncology, teamed up to attempt a radical strategy for increasing physician sustainability in their callings (Krasner et al., 2009). The strategy: "Teach them to be more fully present, even in difficult moments. Embrace the relationship between suffering and meaning, rather than defend against it. Most importantly, create a community of fellow physicians who share and support a meaning-making mindset" (McGonigal, 2015, p. 76). The approach was weekly, two-hour gatherings of physicians who would learn the practice of mindfulness, to pay attention to thoughts, sensations, and emotions, and to begin to be open to what is fully there. This openness is scary because when we sense the suffering of others, we tend to close the door to what is there. Then, the physicians tell stories guided by a weekly question. A story about a moment of caring for someone who was dying. A story about a surprising encounter that changed how they thought about a patient. A story about mistakes, blame, and forgiveness. In the mix of each question is an exploration of "What has made you recover a sense of calling," or "How has this been a challenge to your sense of calling?"

What happens when a meaning-making mindset is supported by a real-time process that requires busy physicians and surgeons to slow down and be present and honest with others? Kelly McGonigal, in *The Upside of Stress*, captured the results. After two months of weekly gatherings, followed by ten months of monthly gatherings, these physicians reported significantly less burnout, less emotional drainage, less likelihood of waking up each morning dreading another day of rounds, less regret for going into medicine as a vocation, less isolated in their stress, and more overall satisfaction in their day-to-day calling. Before the doctors gathered, they were surveyed on levels of depression and anxiety. Among the general population, the average score for men was fifteen, and the average score for women was twenty. The physicians' score at the beginning of the process was thirty-three, and after eight weeks, the score had dropped to fifteen. A remarkable difference in well-being was noted by the end of the full year by an average score of eleven (McGonigal, 2015, p. 78). A basecamp experience, enabling and embracing candor, made a marked difference in how physicians took on their quest to bring help and healing to one another. This research confirms the insight of Robert Kegan referenced earlier in this book, we will hold our settings of life and leadership as we are held. We are best held by trusted and trusting relationships where candor is encouraged and honored.

Moving to Embrace

How do we move to an embrace of a basecamp experience? There are three signposts that point our way to an active and robust basecamp reality:

Recognition → Resolve → Responsibility

The embrace begins with an honest recognition of the choice to be made. The Manifesto has been our attempt to provide clear perspective on the options we have for navigating life and leadership. We can pick our base or bases from which to live. We can take on our quests with minimal support or robust support. We can face our mountain, do our own reconnaissance, load up our own gear, and head out. We can face our mountain in the presence of others, do co-reconnaissance, co-gear checks, and head out knowing we have a secure base to back us up. We can identify the five people we hang out with the most and find great encouragement in our choices, or we can pause and acknowledge the need to totally rethink our relational constellation. Instead of a fab five, we

Chapter Ten   From Hesitation to Embrace

may have a flawed five. The embrace move is doing our own wrestling with these choices and recognizing what is a stake depending on our choice.

A central myth we must wrestle with in our early recognition stage is "the myth of leadership as the myth of the lone warrior" (Heifetz, 1994, p. 251). As noted earlier, leaders across many domains admit to a level of loneliness and isolation that is strange given the people-rich environments most leaders inhabit. The legend of the lone warrior or the solo hero does not fade easily or without a fight. Little surprise as to why it is lonely on the point of leadership when the legacy of leadership lore has profiled and celebrated the leader as the one who makes or breaks the organization's fortunes. As noted in the introduction, our leader-centric mindset portrays a default expectation: "Those who lead take responsibility for the holding environment of the enterprise ... we are not expected to be held. We do the holding, often quite alone. We run the risk of moral regret" (Heifetz, 1994, p. 250). What is a leader to do? Honestly recognize the loneliness and isolation as a chosen path. Recognize the default settings for much of leadership as defective and dangerous to our lives and our organizations. Then take the next step.

After recognition of need, there must be initiation of resolve. We can stay our present course or resolve to find, shape, and nurture a new base for our life. To resolve is to set one's mind and actions in a desired direction. This is where finding our basecamp begins to take shape. If we resolve to journey toward our quest in life, in the company of our happy few, then we will need to do serious thinking as to who those happy few may be. Remember, we will become most like the five people we most closely journey with. Who are our people? Who would best be in our basecamp gathering? This is not an easy question and should not be taken lightly or quickly. Begin the process of thinking long and hard about those who would most represent trusted and trusting people. Who would bring the highest measure of social and professional wellness to our life? Who has some shared ground truth in terms of our quest? Who are the people who can provide wise perspective and wisdom due to their familiarity with the mountain or summit we face? We can set aside a page in our journal for our tent drawing and the scribbled names of potential basecamp partners for the journey ahead.

In moving forward our resolve, we take a few months for thinking, scouting, discerning, and sifting through our relational connections. We then make a few calls to set up a lunch or coffee and float the offer. Simply say, I am looking to find and shape a basecamp. Define the term, frame the scene, talk of the gains and the pains. Give your friend the one-page overview, *What Is a Basecamp?* available at **basecampenviro.com**. Go to our website and take in the overview video of The Basecamp Manifesto. One version is for business leaders and another version is for leaders in non-profit religious contexts. Use these as a discussion point around the potential of forming a secure base together.

If those we connect with are open to a basecamp experience, work out a brief season of gathering that gives the basecamp of two or three others the opportunity to meet, share stories, and review together our own recognition and resolve to find our own basecamp. Give everyone time to experience the gathering with the proviso of opting out if it is not working for a given member. After this trial season, move to more formal shaping and nurturing of the basecamp, and work out a rhythm for regular gathering that works best for the forming group.

It takes resolve to enrich our personal and professional wellness. We talk a lot about personal wellness. Entire industries are dedicated to laser-focused self-care, regimens and rituals for dieting, exercising, meditating, training, and succeeding. Social well-being is a far different measure and strangely receives far less promotion or product lines. Telling people to connect more deeply with a circle of trust isn't a product to sell, so why bother. Yet, a circle of vibrant connection can be a force multiplier for every personal wellness step we take, and there is no monthly membership fee other than our dedication and attention to keep our secure base alive and well.

It is vital to gauge our relational wellness, to take stock of the measure of our emotional, mental, and spiritual insurance through the presence and provision of others. For men, this insurance is often in a deficit state in contrast to women. Women tend to have greater levels of insurance and assurance via friends than men do. Men have "deal friends" but not too many "real friends." Deal friends are transactional relationships whereas real friends are telic, they have no transactional purpose. They know and care about us because they want to know us and care about us (Conley, 2022). Resolve is our determined action to go beyond recognizing our need for a secure base, and to find and begin to shape a basecamp for the future.

Chapter Ten From Hesitation to Embrace

From recognition of need to the pivot move of resolve, we must then take hold of responsibility. In a forming basecamp, everyone wrestles with this question: What is it we must personally bring to our forming and eventually formed basecamp? The approach to shaping and nurturing a secure base begins with our posturing. Our posture must be both inward and outward. The outward move is a giving posture. We pursue the creation of a secure base environment because of what we can give to others for their life, cause, and leadership. The inward move is a receiving posture. We seek such an environment because of what it will provide to our life, our cause, and our leadership. A secure base is not an either/or proposition. The greatest gain is in working well the dance of human relationship. To make "giving" our primary objective and "receiving" our secondary objective is to practice the dance of wise connective relationship. We all become better in the company of those who both give and receive the gifts of a secure base. Faithfulness in both directions balances and enhances the blessing of both givers and receivers.

The outward mindset, popularized in the work of the Arbinger Institute, is to so posture ourselves in any given situation with one question, "What are the issues, challenges, and objectives of the person or persons before us and how can we be of best service in helping them take on their world?" (Arbinger Institute, 2016, p. 32). Imagine a circle of peers where such a posture is in play. It captures the heart of "mutual benefit partnering." This kind of partnering is one of the most helpful steps in growing, what is called our "right of way." As Bob Johansen observes, "Growing our right of way will be increasingly about nurturing and amplifying our own network of trust. If we can grow our span of trust, we can widen our reciprocity right-of-way" (Johansen, 2014, p. 74). Relating to one another with an outward mindset expands our potential and opens a stronger right of way for resourcing, perspective-taking, support, and preparation for our individual explorations and adventures.

So, what are the best we can bring to our basecamp gatherings? For a circle of three or four people, our best is taking personal responsibility for bringing generosity, humility, honesty, and answerability to our basecamp environment. These are four vital gifts that nurture a basecamp into an ecosystem of relational richness.

Bring generosity. Gather with your basecamp with a focused desire to give and contribute to their clarity, agility, durability, and generativity. Make more deposits into other's accounts than withdrawals. Seek to outdo one another in going first in this department. A generous presence is the key to a vibrant and robust basecamp.

Bring humility. Humility is the crown jewel of virtue and the essential light for true community. In our basecamp, we leave our ladders and measuring devices at home and gather to humbly acknowledge we are all pieces of work in need of refinement, renewal, and sometimes thorough-going renovation. Opening the top of our backpacks and unlocking the door of our inner theater is the humblest, yet bold, move we can make. It is also the vital move that grants provision for what we need in our times of confusion, heaviness, weariness, and despair.

Bring honesty. A basecamp is not the place for small talk or tall talk. The avoidance or embellishment of reality are the common traits of unhelpful bases in life. A healthy and robust basecamp permits and promotes candor or the brutal acknowledgement of current reality. Plenty of time will be spent gauging clarity, agility, durability, and generativity. When we are at our best, we will be urging one another to get to the truth. How are we, really? We let honesty open the way to the love, mercy, patience, and wisdom that is around our fire.

Bring answerability. We commonly refer to accountability as a key to wise and sustainable life and leadership. We are changing it up with the idea of answerability. This is the virtue of bringing to our relational setting a positive stance of assurance that we will answer the call to be a trusted and trusting peer, dedicated to the health, growth, and success of those we have committed to around our circle. Accountability comes off as a bothersome check on one another's life. Answerability is a bold step towards one another's life to love, serve, and protect. For these things, we will be answerable.

So, there we have it. **Recognize** our need for a secure base. **Resolve** to move steadily towards finding, shaping, and nurturing such a base for our life and leadership. **Responsibly** embrace an outward mindset and the action of mutual benefit partnering, by bringing our best through generosity, humility, honesty, and answerability.

Chapter Ten   From Hesitation to Embrace

Make the embrace, stay at it, see what happens. Our secure base may just save our life and leadership in the scrambled world we now inhabit. It is our desire to help leaders with this embrace of secure base living. To this end we are providing an array of resources on our website, **basecampenviro.com**. The core webinar, resources and micro presentations are designed to bring inspiration, encouragement, and skill training for your forming or formed basecamp. Our hope and prayer are that many more will know how to answer well the question, "Where is your basecamp?"

CHAPTER ELEVEN

Bring on the Scramble

We began the Basecamp Manifesto with a word of welcome to the scramble. This welcome was our reminder that we now inhabit a world where the scramble is on. Previous depictions of volatility, uncertainty, complexity, and ambiguity are now wrapped together in a scrambled world where disinformation, misinformation, distrust, and disruption abound. Adding to this picture are updated prognostications that we haven't seen anything yet. By itself this picture causes many to conclude that flight would be a sane response if flight were possible.

The scramble is real, but it need not be a kind of depressing reality to be endured. It is simply a way of honestly acknowledging our current reality. It is a way of defining and declaring what we are up against. Our quest, whatever it may be is situated in conditions we are thrown into and much of it is beyond our control. What is in our control is how we situate ourselves in our world. Teresa of Avila, a Carmelite nun of the early 1500s, wisely stated, "We must always remember, there is more than one way to be in a place."

We can be in the scramble and be fully at the mercy of the winds and waves. We can also choose to be in the scramble in a different way. We can be situated and secured in a base of relationship that serves as our place of preparation, guidance, resourcing, and support. This is the potential in a basecamp where we, in concert with others, can safely address our vital needs for clarity, agility, durability, and generativity in the middle of the scramble.

Our focus in a basecamp is mostly on how we are currently functioning and navigating in our life and leadership. As much as the world whirls around us, the quiet and slower ambience of a basecamp gathering, and our nearby fire circle allows us to tend honestly to our greatest challenge. Our quest in the world is a challenge, but our greater challenge is dealing first with ourselves. In the deepest sense, the mountain is us. Our inner quest for increasing clarity, improving agility, strengthening durability, and heightening generativity is the mountain we must conquer before we can best conquer the mountain of our life and leadership quest.

The basecamp, as an encampment for preparation, reconnaissance, and resourcing, serves as a mindset transformer. Almost all our struggles with seeing clearly, traveling lightly, enduring faithfully, and serving wisely come down to attitudes and thinking. The work before the work is internal and personal. A basecamp provides the place and space for mindset facing and altering. Such a place is rare in the lives of most leaders these days. The scramble can fill our field of vision, or we can be learning to see the scramble from a place of strengthening from which we declare, bring it on.

Shutterstock – 2424420079 – Enhanced License Permission

A good question to ask is, "Are we in a place where we can confidently declare, bring on the scramble?" Our own hesitation in answering with a confident "yes" reveals a great deal. Many leaders admit to a nagging sense of frustration, weariness, and wondering. The wondering is often about how long we think we can keep on for the long path ahead. For many, the idea of a new or renewed quest is met with a sigh. The last thing we need is another mountain to climb. Surviving has displaced thriving. Floundering has replaced flourishing. The scramble is bringing many people down emotionally, physically, and spiritually. Yet, the world desperately needs men and women who can say with confidence, bring it on. This confidence does not mysteriously or magically appear. It is the fruit of robust human community. A basecamp can be such a community.

Our hope is that this work has been a catalyst for our own thinking and evaluation of where we are based these days. We trust you hear our hope for you that your base will be a secure base. A regular setting where you have the experience of both caring and daring towards a life of clarity, agility, durability, and generativity.

> *In everyone's life, at some time,*
> *our inner fire goes out.*
> *It is then burst into flame by an*
> *encounter with another human being.*
> *We should all be thankful*
> *for those people who*
> *rekindle the inner spirit.*
> Albert Schweitzer

The Basecamp Advantage

- Leader sustainability and health cannot be left to chance. A basecamp removes sporadic development and support with intentional and deliberate focus.

- Leaders are vital to the health and vitality of any organization or cause. The leader's health and vitality cascades to that of a team and wider organization. A basecamp environment strengthens the leader but also the settings they influence.

- Leaders are often "lonely at the point." The pursuit and provision of a secure base mitigates the lonely and isolated leader.

- The secure base, holding environment dimension, will become more important than ever in a fractured and chaotic world. We all need to ask, "Where is our anchor or still point in a scrambled world?"

- This basecamp prompt has enduring quality for the years to come. It will become more essential as the intensity increases.

- The secure base need is applicable across multiple domains – education, business, entrepreneurship, service, ministry, students, politics, and health care.

- The neglect and deficit side of this pursuit is disturbing. Leaders alone on the point are left with the ongoing struggle with ambiguity, heaviness, lowered resilience, and weakened momentum and generativity.

- The investment side of this pursuit is profound. The granting of the gifts of increased clarity, agility, durability, and generativity are game changers for leaders in today's scrambled world.

- An elegantly simple guide on how to find, shape, and nurture a secure base is needed in all domains. To this end, The Basecamp Manifesto has been written.

References

127 Hours [Film]. (2010). Pathé, Everest Entertainment, Film4 Productions, HandMade Films, & Cloud Eight Films.

Achor, S. (2018). *Big potential: How transforming the pursuit of success raises our achievement, happiness, and well-being.* New York, NY: Currency Books.

Ainsworth, M. (1967). *Infancy in Uganda: Infant care and the growth of attachment.* Baltimore, MD: John Hopkins Press.

Alighieri, D. (2001). *The divine comedy* (H. F. Cary, Trans.). Bartleby. https://www.bartleby.com/20/ (Original work published 1909)

Allender, D. (2006). *Leading with a limp: Turning your struggles into strengths.* Colorado Springs, CO: Waterbrook Press.

Arbinger Institute. (2016). *The outward mindset: Seeing beyond ourselves.* San Francisco, CA: Berrett-Koehler Publishing, Inc.

Bailey, C. (2018). *Hyperfocus: How to be more productive in a world of distractions.* Toronto, ON: Penguin.

Barna Research. (2022, April 27). *Pastors share top reasons they've considered quitting ministry in the past year.* Retrieved January 10, 2023, from Barna Research Group, barna.com

Barrentine, P. (1995). *When the canary stops singing: Women's perspectives on transforming business.* Oakland, CA: Berrett-Koehler Publishers, Inc.

Baumeister, R. F., & Leary, M. R. (1995). The need to belong: Desire for interpersonal attachments as a fundamental human motivation. *Psychological Bulletin, 117*(3), 497–529.

Becoming Warren Buffett [Film]. (2017). [Motion Picture]. George Kunhardt & Teddy Kunhardt.

Bender, T. (1982). *Community and social change in America.* Baltimore, MD: John Hopkins University Press.

Bennis, W. & Biederman, P. W. (1997). *Organizing genius: The secrets of creative collaboration.* Reading, MA: Addison-Wesley.

Berger, W. (2014). *A more beautiful question: The power of inquiry to spark breakthrough ideas.* New York, NY: Bloomsbury.

Bolsinger, T. (2020). *Tempered resilience: How leaders are formed in the crucible of change.* Lisle, IL: InterVarsity Press.

Bowlby, J. (1977). *The making and breaking of affectional bonds.* British Journal of Psychiatry, 130, pp. 201-210. New York, NY: Tavistock.

Bowlby, J. (1988). *A secure base: Parent-child attachment and healthy human development.* New York, NY: HarperCollins.

Box, G. E. P. (1979). *Robustness in the strategy of scientific model building.* In Launer, R. L., & Wilkinson, G. N. (Eds.), Robustness in Statistics, Cambridge, MA: Academic Press, pp. 201-236.

Boyatzis, R., & McKee, A. (2005). *Resonant leadership: Renewing yourself and connecting with others through mindfulness, hope, and compassion.* Boston, MA: Harvard Business School Press.

Brazeman, M. (2013). *The power of noticing: What the best leaders see.* New York, NY: Simon & Schuster.

Brooks, A. C. (2022). *From strength to strength: Finding success, happiness, and deep purpose in the second half of life.* New York, NY: Penguin.

Bryant, A. (2011). *The corner office: Indispensable and unexpected lessons from CEOs on how to lead and succeed.* New York, NY: Times Books.

Bushe, G. (2001). *Clear leadership: How outstanding leaders make themselves understood, cut through the mush, and help everyone get real at work.* Palo Alto, CA: Davies-Black Publishing.

Cabane, O., & Pollack, J. (2017). *The net and the butterfly: The art and practice of breakthrough thinking.* New York, NY: Penguin.

Cameron, K. (2013). *Practicing positive leadership: Tools and techniques that create extraordinary results.* San Francisco, CA: Berrett-Koehler Publishers.

Carr, N. (2010). *The shallows: What the Internet is doing to our brains.* New York, NY: W. W. Norton & Company.

Chariots of Fire [Film]. (1981). Allied Stars Ltd & Enigma Productions.

Churchill, W. (1948). *The second world war.* Vol 1.

References

Cloud, H. (2016). *The power of the others*. New York, NY: HarperCollins.

Coffey, M. (2003). *Where the mountain casts its shadow*. New York, NY: St. Martin's Press.

Cohen, D., & Prusak, L. (2001). *In good company: How social capital makes organizations work*. Boston, MA: Harvard Business School Press.

Coleman, K. (2019). *The proximity principle: The proven strategy that will lead to the career you love*. Franklin, TN: Ramsey Press.

Collins, J. (2001). *Good to great: Why Some companies make the leap and others don't*. New York, NY: Harper Collins Publishers Inc.

Conger, J. (1990). The dark side of leadership. *Organizational Dynamics, 19*(2), 44–55.

Conger, J. (1999). *Building leaders: How successful companies develop the next generation*. San Francisco, CA: Jossey-Bass Publishers.

Conley, C. (2018). *Wisdom at work: The making of a modern elder*. New York, NY: Currency.

Conley, C. (2022, February 12). Social wellness and men. *Modern Elder Academy podcast*. MEA.

Conner, D. (1992). *Managing at the speed of change*. New York, NY: Villard Books.

Cross, R. L., & Parker, C. (2004). *The hidden power of social networks: Understanding how work really gets done in organizations*. Cambridge, MA: Harvard Business Review Press.

David, S. (2016). *Emotional agility: Get unstuck, embrace change, and thrive in work and life*. New York, NY: Avery.

Day, G. & Schoemaker, P. (2006). *Peripheral vision: Detecting weak signals that will make or break your company*. Boston, MA: Harvard Business School Press.

DePree, M. (1989). *Leadership is an art*. New York, NY: Dell Publishing Group.

Desmet, M. (2023, June 14). Digital depression and lonely masses [Blog post]. *MattiasDesmetSubstack*. https://words.mattiasdesmet.org/p/digital-depression-and-lonely-masses.

Dhawan, E., & Joni, S.-N. (2015). *Get big things done: The power of connectional intelligence*. New York, NY: Palgrave MacMillan.

Drath, W. H. & Palus, C. J. (1994). *Making common sense: Leadership as meaning making in a community of practice*. Greensboro, NC: Center for Creative Leadership.

Dweck, C. S. (2006). *Mindset: The new psychology of success.* New York, NY: Ballantine Books.

Edmondson, A. (2019). *The fearless organization.* Hoboken, NJ: John Wiley & Sons Ltd.

Epstein, D. (2019). *Range: Why generalists triumph in a specialized world.* New York, NY: Riverhead Books.

Feiler, B. (2020). *Life is in the transitions: Mastering change at any age.* New York, NY: Penguin Press.

Ferrazzi, K. (2009). *Who's got your back: The breakthrough program to build deep, trusting relationships that create success - and won't let you fail.* New York, NY: Broadway Books.

Ferrazzi, K. (2022). *Competing in the new world of work.* Boston, MA: Harvard Business Review Press.

Flourishing in Ministry Project. (2013). *Flourishing in ministry: Emerging research insights on the well-being of pastors.* Notre Dame, IN: Mendoza College of Business.

Frankl, V. (1959). *Man's search for meaning.* Boston, MA: Beacon Press.

Friedman, E. H. (2007). *A failure of nerve: Leadership in the age of the quick fix.* New York, NY: Church Publishing, Inc.

Fritz, R. (1989). *The path of least resistance.* New York, NY: Ballantine Books.

Frost, Robert. (1923). Selected Poems. Public Domain.

Gallo, C. (2018). *Five stars: The Communication secrets to get from good to great.* New York, NY: St. Martin's Press.

Glyer, D. P. (2016). *Bandersnatch: C. S. Lewis, J. R. R. Tolkien and the creative collaboration of the Inklings.* Kent, OH: Black Squirrel Books.

Gschwandtner, G. (2010). How to manage disappointment [Blog post]. *PersonalSellingPower.*https://www.sellingpower.com/2010/02/02/4250/how-to-manage-disappointment-2

Hallowell, E. (1999). *Connect: Twelve vital ties that open your heart, lengthen your life, and deepen your soul.* New York, NY: Pantheon Books.

Hallowell, E. (2006). *Crazy busy: Overstretched, overbooked, and about to snap.* New York, NY: Ballantine Books.

Hari, J. (2018). *Lost connections: Uncovering the real causes of depression—and the unexpected solutions.* New York, NY: Bloomsbury.

References

Hari, J. (2022). *Stolen focus: Why you can't pay attention - and how to think deeply again*. New York, NY: Crown.

Hayhurst, J. (1996). *The right mountain: Lessons from Everest on the real meaning of success*. New York, NY: John Wiley & Sons.

Heard, D. (1982). Family systems and the attachment dynamic. *Journal of Family Therapy, 4*(2), 99–116.

Heath, D. (2020). *Upstream: The quest to solve problems before they happen*. New York: NY: Avid Reader Press.

Heffernan, M. (2015). *Beyond measure: The big impact of small changes*. New York, NY: TED Books Simon & Schuster.

Heifetz, R. (1994). *Leadership without easy answers*. Cambridge, MA: The Belknap Press of Harvard University.

Heifetz, R., & Linsky, M. (2017). *Leadership on the line: Staying alive through the dangers of leading*. Boston, MA: Harvard Business Review Press.

Herman, T. (2019). *The alter ego effect: The power of secret identities to transform your life*. New York, NY: HarperCollins.

Hitler, A. (2024). *Mein kampf*. Infinity Spectrum Books

Hodgetts, J. (1996). Finding sanctuary in post-modern life. In D. T. Hall, *The career is dead - long live the career*. San Francisco, CA: Jossey-Bass.

Johansen, B. (2009). *Leaders make the future: Ten new leadership skills for an uncertain world*. San Francisco, CA: Berrett-Koehler Publishers, Inc.

Johansen, B. (2014). *The reciprocity advantage: A new way to partner for innovation and growth*. San Francisco, CA: Berrett-Koehler Publishers, Inc.

Johansen, B. (2017). *The new leadership literacies*. Oakland, CA: Berrett-Koehler Publishers, Inc.

Johansen, B. (2020). *Full spectrum thinking: How to escape boxes in a post-categorical future*. Oakland, CA: Berrett-Koehler Publishers, Inc.

Johnson. (2010). *Where good ideas come from: The natural history of innovation*. New York, NY: Riverhead Books.

Johnson, P. (1988). *Intellectuals*. London, ENG: Weidenfeld & Nicolson.

Kahane, A. (2010). *Power and love: A theory and practice of social change*. San Francisco, CA: Berrett-Koehler Publishers, Inc.

Kahn, W. (1990). Psychological conditions for personal engagement and disengagement at work. *Academy of Management Journal, 33*(4), 692–724.

Kahn, W. (1993). Caring for the caregivers: Patterns of organizational care giving. *Administrative Science Quarterly, 38*(4), 539–563.

Kahn, W. (1996). Secure base relationships at work. In D. T. Hall, *The career is dead - long live the career.* San Francisco: CA: Jossey-Bass.

Kahn, W. (1998). Relational systems at work. In B. M. Staw, *Research in organizational behavior.* Greenwich, CT: JAI Press.

Kahn, W. (2001). Holding environments at work. *Journal of Applied Behavioral Science, 37*(3), 260–279.

Kahn, W. (2005). *Holding fast: The struggle to create resilient caregiving organizations.* New York, NY: Brunner-Routledge.

Kanter, R. M. (2020). *Think outside the building.* New York, NY: Hachette Book Group.

Kay, J., & King, M. (2020). *Radical uncertainty: Decision making beyond the numbers.* New York, NY: W. W. Norton and Company.

Kegan, R. (1982). *The evolving self: Problem and process in human development.* Cambridge, MA: Harvard University Press.

Kegan, R. (1994). *In over our heads: The mental demands of modern life.* Cambridge, MA: Harvard University Press.

Kegan, R., & Lahey, L. L. (2016). *An everyone culture: Becoming a deliberately developmental organization.* Boston, MA: Harvard Business Review Press.

Kethledge, R. M. (2017). *Lead yourself first: Inspiring leadership through solitude.* New York: NY: Bloomsbury.

Kets de Vries, M. (2006). *The leader on the couch: A clinical approach to changing people and organizations.* San Francisco, CA: Jossey-Bass.

Keysers, C. & Gazzola, V. (2014). *Hebbian learning and predictive mirror neurons for actions, sensations, and emotions.* London, ENG: Philosophical Transactions, June 5; 369 (1644).

Klein, M., & Napier, R. (2003). *The courage to act: Five factors of courage to transform business.* Palo Alto, CA: Davies-Black Publishing.

Klemperer, V. (2006). *The language of the third reich.* London, England: Continuum International Publishing Group.

Kleon, A. (2019). *Keep going: Ten ways to stay creative in good times and bad.* New York: NY: Workman Publishing.

References

Kohlrieser, G., Goldsworthy, S., & Coombe, D. (2012). *Care to dare: Unleashing astonishing potential through secure base leadership.* San Francisco, CA: Jossey-Bass.

Kolditz, T. A., & Pfeifer, J. W. (2007). *In extremis leadership: Leading as if your life depended on it.* San Francisco, CA: Jossey-Bass.

Krasner, M. S., Epstein, R. M., Beckman, H., Suchman, A. L., Chapman, B., Mooney, C. J., & Quill, T. E. (2009). Association of an educational program in mindful communication with burnout, empathy, and attitudes among primary care physicians. *Journal of the American Medical Association, 302*(12), 1284–1293.

Klein, N. (2020). *Screen new deal.* The Intercept, May 8, 2020.

Lanier, J. (2018). *Ten arguments for deleting your social media accounts right now.* New York, NY: Random House.

Lewis, C. S. (1960). *The four loves.* London, UK: Geoffrey Bles.

London, H. B., & Wiseman, N. (2003). *Pastors at greater risk.* Grand Rapids, MI: Baker Books.

The Lord of the Rings: The Fellowship of the Ring [Film]. (2001). New Line Cinema & WingNut Films.

Louis, M. (1996). Creating safe havens at work. In D. T. Hall, *The career is dead - long live the career.* San Francisco, CA: Jossey-Bass.

Lowney, C. (2003). *Heroic leadership: Best practices from a 45-year-old company that changed the world.* Chicago, IL: Loyola Press.

Lynn, Andrew. (2017). *Generativity: The Art and Science of Exceptional Achievement.* New Dehli, IN: Howgill House Books.

Lynn, C. D. (2014). Health and campfire influences on arterial blood pressure: Defraying the costs of the social brain through fireside relaxation. *Evolutionary Psychology, 12*(5), 983–1003.

MacDonald, G. (1986). *Restoring your spiritual passion.* Nashville, TN: Oliver Nelson.

MacDonald, G. (2004). *A resilient life.* Nashville, TN: Thomas Nelson.

Madsbjerg, C. (2017). *Sense making: The power of the humanities in the age of the algorithm.* New York, NY: Hatchette Books.

Mandela, Nelson. (1998). *Long walk to freedom.* New York, NY. Little, Brown, and Company.

Marquardt, M. (2005). *Leading with questions: How leaders find the right solutions by knowing what to ask.* San Francisco, CA: Jossey-Bass.

Marten, S., Picard, J., & Young, T. (2020). *Leadership certificate: Foundations of leadership and the principalship.* Ambrose University (Grant 2018-0252).

Martin, K. (2018). *Clarity first: How smart leaders and organizations achieve outstanding performance.* New York, NY: McGraw Hill Education.

Masten, A. (2001). Ordinary magic: Resilience processes in development. *American Psychologist, 56*(3), 227–238.

Mate, G. (2014). *The body keeps the score.* New York, NY: Penguin Books.

Mau, B. (2020). *Mau MC 24.* New York, NY: Phaidon Press Ltd.

McChrystal, S. (2015). *Team of teams: New rules for engagement for a complex world.* New York, NY: Penguin Random House.

McGonigal, K. (2015). *The upside of stress: Why stress is good for you, and how to get good at it.* New York, NY: Avery Press.

McIntosh, G. L. (1998). *It only hurts on Monday: Why pastors quit and what you can do about it.* Bloomington, MN: ChurchSmart Resources.

McKenna, D. (2005). *Never blink in a thunderstorm.*

McKeown, G. (2014). *Essentialism: The disciplined pursuit of less.* New York, NY: Crown Business.

Miller, D. (2017). *Building a story brand: Clarify your message so your customers will listen.* New York, NY: Harper Collins.

Miller, S., & Moore, J. C. (2023). *The summit mindset: Winning the battle of you versus you.* Austin, TX: Greenleaf Book Group Press.

Murphy, M. (2011). *Hard goals: The science of extraordinary achievement.* New York, NY: McGraw Hill Publishers.

Newport, C. (2024). *Slow productivity: The lost art of accomplishment without burnout.* New York, NY: Penguin.

Nicholls, D. (1989). *The testing of hearts: A pilgrim's journal.* Toronto, ON: Harper Collins.

Noer, D. (1997). *Breaking free: A prescription for personal and organizational change.* San Francisco: CA: Jossey-Bass.

Nour, D. (2021). *Curve benders: How strategic relationships can power your nonlinear growth in the future of work.* Hoboken, NJ: John Wiley & Sons, Inc.

O'Brien, T. (2009). *The things they carried.* Boston, MA: Mariner Books.

References

Office of the Surgeon General (OSG). (2023). *Our epidemic of loneliness and isolation: The U.S. Surgeon General's advisory on the healing effects of social connection and community.* US Department of Health and Human Services.

Palmer, P. (1990). *Leading from within.* Indianapolis, IN: Campus Ministries.

Palmer, P. (2004). *A hidden wholeness: The Journey toward an undivided life.* San Francisco: CA: Jossey-Bass.

Penson, B. (2022, February 23). *Comparing Everest's Khumbu Icefall and K2's Bottleneck.* Retrieved March 8, 2024, from expedreview.com

Pfeffer, J. (2018). *Dying for a paycheck: How modern management harms employee healthy and company performance.* New York, NY: HarperCollins.

Pinker, S. (2009). *How the mind works.* New York, NY: W. W. Norton.

Rabin, R. (2014). *Blended Learning for Leadership: The CCL Approach.* Greensboro, NC: Center for Creative Leadership.

Rempel, L. (2003). *Still in one peace.* Calgary, AB: Linda Rempel Art Studio.

Rifkin, J. (1980). *Entropy: A new world view.* New York, NY: Bantam.

Robbins, T. (2024). *Time to rise 2024.* Web Event

Roger, D., & Petrie, N. (2017). *Work without stress: Building a resilient mindset for lasting success.* New York, NY: McGraw Hill Education.

Rolheiser, R. (2014). *Sacred fire: A vision for a deeper human and christian maturity.* New York, NY: Crown Publishing Group.

Rost, J. (1993). *Leadership for the twenty-first century.* Westport, CT: Praeger Publishers.

Rowland, D. (2017). *Still moving: How to lead mindful change.* Oxford, England: John Wiley & Sons, Inc.

Sanders, T. (2002). *Love is the killer app: How to win business and influence friends.* New York, NY: Three Rivers Press.

Schnall, H. S. (2008). Group influence. 04(011).

Schwartz, T. (2010). *The way we're working isn't working.* New York, NY: Free Press.

Secretan, L. (2004). *Inspire: What great leaders do.* Hoboken, NJ: John Wiley & Sons Ltd.

Shapiro, E. R., & Carr, A. W. (1991). *Lost in familiar places: Creating new connections between the individual and society.* New Haven, CT: Yale University Press.

Shenk, J. W. (2014). *The power of two.* Boston, MA: Houghton Mifflin Harcourt.

Smedes, L. (1998). *Standing on the promises: Keeping hope alive for a tomorrow we cannot control.* Nashville, TN: Tho mas Nelson Inc.

Smith, J. (2011). *The flinch.* Do You Zoom Inc.

Southwick, S. M., & Charney, D. S. (2018). *Resilience: The science of mastering life's greatest challenges.* New York, NY: Cambridge University Press.

Sullivan, D., & Hardy, B. (2024). *The gap and the gain: The high achievers' guide to happiness, confidence, and success.* Carlsbad, CA: Hay House.

Sullivan, G. R., & Harper, M. V. (1996). *Hope is not a method: What business leaders can learn from America's army.* New York, NY: Random House.

Sweet, L., & Beck, M. A. (2020). *Contextual intelligence: Unlocking the ancient secret to mission on the front lines.* Orlando, FL: Higher Life Development Services, Inc.

Swenson, R. (1992). *Margin: Restoring emotional, physical, financial, and time reserves to overloaded lives.* Colorado Springs, CO: NavPress Publishing Group.

Thompson, C. (2015). *The soul of shame: Retelling the stories we believe about ourselves.* Downers Grove, IL: IVP.

Travis, R. (2004). Running Blind [Song]. On *Passing Through.* Genius.

Tyson, J. H. (2008). *Hitler's mentor: Dietrich Eckart, his life, times and milieu.* Bloomington, IN: iUniverse, Inc.

Vaillant, G. (2002). *Aging well: Surprising guideposts to a happier life from the landmark Harvard study of adult development.* New York, NY: Little, Brown.

Van Buskirk, W., & McGrath, D. (1999). Organizational culture as holding environments: A psycho-dynamic look at organizational symbolism. *Human Relations, 52*(6), 805–832.

Viorst, J. (1972). *Alexander and the terrible, horrible, no good, very bad day.* New York, NY: Atheneum Books for Young Readers.

Volf, M. (2019). *For the life of the world: Theology that makes a difference.* Grand Rapid, MI: *Brazos* Press.

Volf, M. (2006). *The end of memory: Remembering rightly in a violent world.* Grand Rapids, MI: Wm. B. Eerdmans Publishing Company.

Waitely, D. (1986). *The psychology of winning.* New York, NY: Berkley.

Waldinger, R. (2015, November). *What makes a good life? Lessons from the longest study on happiness* [Video]. TED Conferences. https://www.ted.

com/talks/robert_waldinger_what_makes_a_good_life_lessons_from_the_longest_study_on_happiness?language=en

Warner, C. S. (2009). *High altitude leadership: What the world's most forbidding peaks teach us about success.* San Francisco, CA: Jossey-Bass.

Washington, B. T. (1901). *Up from slavery: An autobiography.* Bolton, ON: Amazon.ca

Weick, K. (2001a). Leadership as the legitimization of doubt. In W. S. Bennis, *The future of leadership.* San Francisco, CA: Jossey-Bass.

Weick, K. (2001b). *Making sense of the organization.* Malden, MA: Blackwell Publishing.

Wenger, E. M. (2002). *Cultivating communities of practice.* Boston, MA: Harvard Business School Press.

Whitaker, A. (2016). *Art thinking.* New York, NY: HarperCollins.

Wick, R. (2014). *Perspective: The calm within the storm.* New York, NY: Oxford University Press.

Willink, J., & Babin, L. (2018). *The dichotomy of leadership.* New York, NY: St. Martin's Press.

Winnicott, D. W. (1965). *Maturational processes and the facilitating environment.* New York, NY: International Universities Press.

Young, T. (2004). *A multi-case study on the holding environment in peer clusters.* Spokane, WA: Gonzaga University.

Zaffron, S. (2009). The *three laws of performance: Rewriting the future of your organization and your life.* San Francisco, CA: Jossey-Bass Publishers.

Zaleznik, A. (1967). The management of disappointment. *Harvard Business Review*, Nov/Dec, 59–70.

Printed in Canada